Tempo
A Scarecrow Press Music Series on
Rock, Pop, and Culture

Series Editor: Scott Calhoun

Tempo: A Scarecrow Press Music Series of Rock, Pop, and Culture offers titles that explore rock and popular music through the lens of social and cultural history, revealing the dynamic relationship between musicians, music, and their milieu. Like other major art forms, rock and pop music comment on their cultural, political, and even economic situation, reflecting the technological advances, psychological concerns, religious feelings, and artistic trends of their times. Contributions to the Tempo series are the ideal introduction to major pop and rock artists and genres.

Bon Jovi: America's Ultimate Band, by Margaret Olson, 2013.

Ska: The Rhythm of Liberation, by Heather Augustyn, 2013.

Bruce Springsteen: American Poet and Prophet, by Donald L. Deardorff II, 2014.

BRUCE SPRINGSTEEN

American Poet and Prophet

Donald L. Deardorff II

THE SCARECROW PRESS, INC.
Lanham • Toronto • Plymouth, UK
2014

Published by Scarecrow Press, Inc.
A wholly owned subsidiary of Rowman & Littlefield
4501 Forbes Boulevard, Suite 200, Lanham, Maryland 20706
http://www.scarecrowpress.com

Estover Road, Plymouth PL6 7PY, United Kingdom

British Library Cataloguing in Publication Information Available

Library of Congress Cataloging-in-Publication Data

Deardorff, Donald L.
Bruce Springsteen : American poet and prophet / Donald Deardorff. pages ; cm. – (Tempo : a Scarecrow Press music series on rock, pop, and culture)
Includes bibliographical references and index.
ISBN 978-0-8108-8426-7 (cloth : alk. paper) – ISBN 978-0-8108-8427-4 (ebook)
1. Springsteen, Bruce–Criticism and interpretation. 2. Springsteen, Bruce–Influence. I. Title.
ML420.S77D43 2014
782.42166092–dc23 2013030573

♾ The paper used in this publication meets the minimum requirements of American National Standard for Information Sciences Permanence of Paper for Printed Library Materials, ANSI/NISO Z39.48-1992.

Printed in the United States of America

CONTENTS

FOREWORD

In the music of Bruce Springsteen, I hear what I like to think the United States of America's founding documents would sound like if plugged in some two hundred years later. Like power chord arguments. Like electrified anthems. Like the passionate promises that friends and lovers make to stick with each other while making a more perfect union. Imagine the Declaration of Independence, with all its protest and defiance, and the U.S. Constitution, with all its grandeur and aspirations, as twentieth-century pop songs. The documents provide the words and feelings. Rock 'n' roll provides a library of sounds from all the American moods present in our folk songs, our rhythm and blues, our gospel, and in the pomp of our festival and marching bands. All it would take is someone willing to study it all, learn the truths, respect the forms, and then be desperate enough to work to make it original for himself, so that it might become real and give his own life a much-needed meaning and purpose. That student was Bruce Springsteen, and that is what his music sounds like to me.

Springsteen—now a master at writing the American rock song and performing the ideas of America in his rock 'n' roll shows—reminds us that now, as then in the late eighteen hundreds, after a century of progress by the first European pilgrims, America's potential is too great and too precious—not to mention, its people too sacred—to be managed by distant authorities and impersonal institutions. Just as the poetry in those early documents inspires as it argues for liberty, equality, and unity and as the rhythm of history was empowering the colonists to take matters into their own hands, Springsteen's songs are an expression of those same dreams and that same energy for many Americans in the late twentieth century and into the early twenty-first century. For him to write and sing the songs gives him hope, and for us to hear the songs encourages us to press through the setbacks and despair that come from living in a land not yet fully realized.

As this book presents, many a Springsteen song takes us to the musical equivalent of a promised land, especially when backed by the E Street Band's joyfully thunderous noise, but we meet in them a reoccurring character who feels far from Eden. He is trapped, weak, lost, or overwhelmed by the moral ambiguity of the context of his postadolescent life. Most Springsteen lyrics are from a man's point of view, and many of the dilemmas that the songs' men face are brought about by coming-of-age in American culture after the societal revolutions of the 1960s. What, now, is the man's role at home? at work? in society? What is the measure of success for the American male now? What are the examples and role models for a man of the baby boom generation? What even makes a man a man? Springsteen's songs tell first-person accounts of walls closing in, horizons shrinking, and dreams evaporating. The young adults, brothers, veterans, husbands (and, occasionally, mothers) are not so strong anymore or so sure of what the right thing to do is, and they are not so holy as to not break a law while looking for an answer or even contemplate death as their only escape. These characters are just the ones whom Springsteen's songs are written for, and their real-life counterparts—his fans—often speak of finding solace in the songs and encountering a community of hope and healing at his concert.

Springsteen often takes the point of view of the poor in spirit, directing his anger at the injustice of a government serving the interests of only the wealthy, the powerful, or the white and at the damage done by an economy of greed that eventually robs whole sections of America of their chance to have the American dream through the dignity of work. Because he does so, Springsteen is often compared with John Steinbeck, Pete Seeger, and Bob Dylan—and rightly so. His should be the fourth face on a Mount Rushmore of twentieth-century American protest writers. But as Springsteen's medium is rock 'n' roll and as his stagecraft is influenced more by the likes of James Brown and Roy Orbison, both of whom he cites as idols, than by the Greenwich Village singer–songwriters, there is noticeably more energy and hunger in him to play to the biggest crowds and feel their adoration, even as he seeks to sway the opinions of protesters and voters. Whether working on a solo project, playing a benefit concert, supporting a presidential campaign, or just being The Boss of the E Street Band, the total effect of Bruce Springsteen's songbook is a louder, nosier music that does more than the work of social critique—it breaks apart the despair of the moment and brings healing on the spot. As the American spirit has always been willing, quite often many of our bodies are too weak. Springsteen is a believer, in the end, of the power of hope and in music as the vessel for delivering it.

Scott Calhoun
Tempo Series Editor

TIMELINE

World Events	Bruce Springsteen Career
January 1949: RCA introduces the 45-rpm record.	
June 1949: Vietnam is formed as a nation.	
September 1949: The Soviet Union explodes its first atomic bomb.	*September 23, 1949*: Bruce Frederick Joseph Springsteen born in Long Branch, New Jersey, to Adele and Douglas Springsteen. He will live in Freehold, New Jersey, for most of his first eighteen years.
June 1950–July 1953: Korean War.	
February 1950–December 1954: Senator Joseph McCarthy hearings.	
October 1954: Dow Jones Industrial Average closes at an all-time high, a sign of the economic prosperity of the 1950s.	

September 1956: Elvis Presley appears on the *Ed Sullivan Show*.

August 1957: *American Bandstand* premiers on ABC-TV.

October 1957: USSR launches *Sputnik*, escalating the "space race" and the Cold War.

February 1960: Civil Rights Act of 1960.

June 1961: Escalation of Vietnam War.

December 1962: Acquires first guitar, a Christmas present.

February 1963: Betty Friedan publishes *The Feminine Mystique*.

August 1963: Martin Luther King Jr.'s "I Have a Dream" speech.

February 1964: The Beatles appear on the *Ed Sullivan Show*, marking the start of the "British invasion."

July 1964: Civil Rights Act of 1964.

October 1965: Immigration Act of 1965 signals new immigration patterns in the United States.

December 1965–August 1968: Guitarist for his first band, *The Castiles*.

May–September 1967: Summer of love.

June 1968: Stonewall riots in New York City signal the onset of the gay rights movement.

September 1968: Student at Ocean County Community College; does not last the semester.

January 1968: Moves to Asbury Park, New Jersey, a once-thriving coastal vacation destination, now a thriving music scene.

May 1969: Forms a new band, Child, but changes the name to Steel Mill when he discovers there is already a local band named Child. The band includes future E Street Band members Danny Federici, Steven Van Zandt, and Vini "Mad Dog" Lopez.

August 1969: Woodstock Music Festival.

January 1970: Increasingly popular in New Jersey, especially at Asbury Park's Upstage Club, Steel Mill ventures to California, winning critical acclaim for its shows in San Francisco.

March 1970: First Earth Day, signaling the ascendance of the environmental movement.

May 1970: Kent State shootings over Vietnam War protests.

January 1971: Disbands Steel Mill and begins to experiment with several combinations of musicians. Groups will include Bruce Springsteen Jam, Dr. Zoom and the Sonic Boom, and The Bruce Springsteen Band.

April 1972: Disbands The Bruce Springsteen Band and begins a solo career, playing small venues in and around New York City.

May 1972: Signs with manager Mike Appel.

May 1972: Famous audition for CBS Records and the legendary John Hammond, who discovered Bob Dylan. Signs a contract with Columbia shortly thereafter and begins to assemble the E Street Band.

June 1972: Title IX enacted into law, providing women and girls equal opportunity in athletics.

January 1973: *Greetings from Asbury Park, NJ* released by Columbia to modest sales but significant critical acclaim. E Street Band members include Springsteen, Garry Tallent, Vini Lopez, Clarence Clemons, and David Sancious.

September 1973: *The Wild, the Innocent, and the E Street Shuffle* released with Danny Federici joining the original band members. Like *Greetings*, the album sales are slow, but it is well received by many critics, and the band continues to build a large Eastern seaboard audience on the strength of its live shows.

October 1973: Oil embargo of 1973 reflects OPEC's ability to

harm the U.S. economy by
regulating oil.

February 1974: Drummer Vini
Lopez replaced by Ernest "Boom"
Carter.

May 1974: Influential music critic
and future Springsteen manager
Jon Landau writes his famous line:
"I saw rock 'n' roll's future and its
name is Bruce Springsteen."

August 1974: President Richard
Nixon resigns amid Watergate
scandal.

September 1974–1980: American
undergoes its worst economic
recession in forty years.

April 1975: Fall of Saigon, end of
Vietnam War.

July 1975: Van McCoy's "The
Hustle" marks the rise of disco.

August 1975: After several
complications, *Born to Run* is
released, garnering high praise
from critics and fans. Max
Weinberg and Roy Bittan join the
E Street Band, replacing Ernest
Carter and David Sancious.
Steven Van Zandt also joins the
band. The record is a commercial
success and establishes
Springsteen as a true international
rock star. He and the E Street
band make their first appearance
in London in the fall of 1975.

October 1975: Springsteen appears on the cover of both *Time* and *Newsweek.*

July 1976: The energy crisis. Long gas lines and shortages greet the nation's bicentennial.

July 1976: Sues his manager Mike Appel for fraud. Appel countersues. The litigation will prevent any studio work on a fourth album until the summer of 1977.

August 1976: A total of 119 women enter the U.S. Military Academy; women will gradually move into combat roles in the 1990s.

April 1977: Studio 54 opens, becoming the center of hedonism representative of the "me decade."

May 1977: Reaches a settlement with Appel and returns to work in the studio.

June 1978: *Darkness on the Edge of Town* is released. Jon Landau becomes Springsteen's manager in July, and the singer appears on the cover of *Rolling Stone* for the first time in August.

March 1979: Nuclear accident at Three Mile Island.

September 1979: Chrysler files for bankruptcy, symbolic of the decline of America's most powerful industry in the face of European and Asian competition.

September 1979: Joins Bonnie Raitt, Jackson Browne, Tom Petty, and other artists at the famous No Nukes Concerts (MUSE) at Madison Square Garden. The shows are a sign of things to come in terms of Springsteen's commitment to social and political activism.

November 1979–January 1981: Iran hostage crisis.

December 1979: Inflation reaches nearly 14 percent and combines with a weak economy and high unemployment rates to produce "stagflation."

August 1980: United States boycotts the summer Olympics in Moscow.

October 1980: *The River*, a double album, debuts at number one on *Billboard*'s chart. "Hungry Heart" becomes Springsteen's first top-ten hit.

June 1981: Public identification of the AIDS virus in the United States.

August 1981: Birth of MTV.

August 20, 1981: Benefit show for Vietnam veterans in Los Angeles, another sign of Springsteen's emerging political consciousness. It is also one of Steve Van Zandt's last shows with the band until 1999.

September 1981: Sandra Day O'Connor becomes the first female Supreme Court justice.

December 1981: U.S. divorce rate nears 50 percent; it will remain above 40 percent through 2011.

October 1982: *Nebraska* is released. Springsteen's sixth

album is musically stark and
lyrically dark and is not as well
received by fans. Critics love it.

November 1982: Largest
unemployment rate since 1940, at
10.2 percent.

December 1982: "Atlantic City"
becomes Springsteen's first music
video to appear on MTV.

March 1983: Compact discs and
players released in the United
States.

March 1983: President Ronald
Reagan unveils "Star Wars"
defense system.

June 1983–1985: Famine in
Ethiopia reaches epidemic
proportions, complicated by U.S.
policies.

May 1984–November 1989:
Savings and loan scandal ends in
multi-billion-dollar bailout.

June 1984: Born in the USA is
released and becomes
Springsteen's most commercially
successful album to date. Nils
Lofgren replaces Van Zandt. Patti
Scialfa joins the band as a backup
singer.

September 1984: Criticizes
President Ronald Reagan, who
had tried to identify himself with
Springsteen for political purposes,
and begins supporting local food
banks and other organizations

dedicated to helping the homeless; he will continue this service for his entire career.

January 1985: "Dancing in the Dark" wins Springsteen his first Grammy.

September 1985: Marries actress Julianne Phillips.

August 1985: Bruce sings on Van Zandt's "Sun City," a protest song against South African apartheid.

April 1986: Chernobyl nuclear disaster.

May 1986: Five million South African blacks strike to protest apartheid.

October 1986: The Anti-Drug Abuse Act of 1986 becomes an important component on the "war on drugs."

November 1986: Iran–contra scandal.

November 1986: Bruce Springsteen & the E Street Band Live: 1975–1985 is released.

March 1987: Jim Bakker sex scandal. He will eventually be sentenced to forty-five years in prison for embezzlement, one of many televangelists to be disgraced.

October 1987: "Black Monday" sees a 22 percent drop in the Dow Jones index.

October 1987: Tunnel of Love is released and immediately goes double platinum.

June 1988: Performs live on television for the first time in France at an antiracism rally.

July 1988: Announces that he and the band will join Amnesty International's "Human Rights Now!" tour.

August 1988: *Chimes of Freedom*, a short four-song album, is released in support of Amnesty International.

October 1988: Final show with the E Street Band until 1999.

March 1989: Finalizes divorce with Julianne Phillips.

June 1989: Tiananmen Square massacre in Beijing.

October 1989: The E Street Band officially breaks up.

November 1989: The fall of the Berlin Wall symbolically ends the Cold War.

July 1990: Son Evan James is born to Springsteen and Patti Scialfa.

August 1990: Iraq invades Kuwait, drawing the United States into the Gulf War.

June 1991: Marries Patti Scialfa.

September 1991: Anita Hill accuses Supreme Court justice candidate Clarence Thomas of sexual harassment. The issue will continue to be prominent on the American landscape.

December 1991: Daughter Jessica Rae is born.

March 1992: *Human Touch* and *Lucky Town* are released on the same day. Roy Bittan is the only E Street Band holdover to work on the new albums.

April 1992: Race riots in Los Angeles reveal the underlying racial tension in the country.

April 1992: Assembles a new touring band. Musicians include Bittan, Shane Fontayne, Tommy Sims, Zachary Alford, Bobby King, Crystal Taliefero, Carol Dennis, Angel Rogers, Cleo Kennedy, Gia Ciambotti, and Patti Scialfa.

August 1992: The Mall of America, the country's largest shopping venue and an extravagant homage to American consumerism, opens in Minnesota.

November 1992: *MTV Plugged* airs.

February 1993: Islamic terrorists bomb the World Trade Center.

May 1993: Women make up 50.4 percent of law school students in the United States.

June 1993: Plays "The Concert to Fight Hunger."

January 1994: Son Sam Ryan is born.

February 1994: Releases "Streets of Philadelphia" for Jonathan Demme's film *Philadelphia*. The song becomes one of his most popular and influential compositions, winning Golden Globe, Oscar, and Grammy awards and raising consciousness regarding the AIDS virus.

April 1994: Rwandan genocide begins. Over 800,000 Tutsis are murdered by Hutu extremists. The world watches and does nothing.

June 1994: Jean Baudrillard's *Simulacra and Simulation*, a foundational postmodern work, appears in English in the United States for the first time.

September 1994: Women make up 56 percent of Yale's incoming medical school class, the first time in history that women have outnumbered men at the school.

February 1995: *Greatest Hits* is released and debuts number one on *Billboard*'s chart.

April 19, 1995: Domestic terrorists Timothy McVeigh and Terry Nichols explode a bomb outside the Murrah Federal Building in Oklahoma City.

November 1995: *The Ghost of Tom Joad*, a solo acoustic album, is released.

March 1996: *Blood Brothers*, the film chronicling the *Greatest Hits* recording session, is released.

July 1996: Dolly, a sheep, becomes the first animal to be

cloned, prompting a debate on
genetic engineering for humans.

November 1996: Plays several
benefit concerts, several of which
support his hometown of
Freehold, New Jersey, and the
surrounding area.

May 1997: Receives the Polar
Music Prize, an award considered
by musicians to be on par with the
Nobel Prize.

May 1997: Performs in Prague for
the first time and meets with
Czech President Havel. Such
meetings in which the singer
advocates for human rights will
continue to characterize his
career.

July 1997: Four New York City
police officers assault Haitian
immigrant Abner Louima while in
custody.

January 1998: Monica Lewinsky
sex scandal brings more attention
to sexual harassment and gender
issues in the workplace. President
Clinton will later be charged with
perjury.

April 1998: Douglas Springsteen
dies.

May 1998: Measured in terms of
high school and undergraduate
degrees, the educational
attainment levels of women aged
twenty-five to twenty-nine

exceeded those of men in the same age group.

August 1998: United States destroys a pharmaceutical plant in Sudan, claiming that it was a weapons factory. The factory was actually producing medicine. Many Sudanese die as the result of the explosion and the lack of necessary medications.

August 1998: Terrorist attacks on two U.S. embassies in Africa are linked to Osama Bin Laden and his al-Qaeda organization.

November 1998: *Tracks*, a four-CD set of previously unreleased outtakes, is released.

December 1998: Performs at Amnesty International's concert commemorating the fiftieth anniversary of the Declaration of Human Rights.

February 1999: Amadou Diallo, an unarmed immigrant from Guinea, is shot and killed by four New York City police officers. They are acquitted, and Springsteen writes "American Skin" in response.

March 1999: *The Matrix* is released. Highly influenced by poststructuralist theory and Jean Baudrillard, it begs the question of what is real in a world characterized by hypertechnology and simulation.

March 1999: Inducted into the Rock and Roll Hall of Fame.

April 1999: Columbine High School massacre.

April 1999: Begins a long-awaited reunion tour with the E Street Band.

June 2000: Releases "American Skin" and "Code of Silence," songs that protest the mistreatment of immigrants by the police.

April 2001: *Live in New York City*, a product of an immensely successful reunion tour, is released. It is accompanied by a television special on MTV.

September 2001: Islamic terrorists attack the World Trade Center and the Pentagon.

September 2001: Performs in several benefit concerts for the victims of the terrorist attacks of September 11.

October 2001: United States invades Afghanistan, declaring war on terror.

July 2002: *The Rising*, Springsteen's artistic answer regarding the events of September 11, is released.

March 2003: United States invades Iraq, one of seven countries named as being part of an axis of evil. These also include Sudan, Syria, Iran, Libya, North Korea, and Cuba.

October 4, 2003: *The Rising* tour, which grosses over $120 million, ends at Shea Stadium in New York. The tour is marked by an increasingly political Springsteen, who repeatedly urges his audience to question the leaders who perpetrated recent American wars in Iraq and Afghanistan.

November 2003: *The Essential Bruce Springsteen* is released.

February 2004: The Central Intelligence Agency admits that Iraq did not have weapons of mass destruction before the United States declared war in 2003.

February 2004: John Jay report reveals 10,667 instances of sexual abuse by 4,392 Catholic priests between 1950 and 2000.

October 2004: Participates in the "Vote for Change" tour, working on behalf of Democratic candidate John Kerry.

December 2004: Participates in "Flood Aid '04" to help those affected by floods in Pennsylvania.

April 2005: Records an episode for *VH1 Storytellers*.

April 2005: *Devils & Dust* released.

August 2005: Hurricane Katrina strikes the Gulf Coast, one of the worst natural disasters.

November 2005: *Born to Run 30th Anniversary Edition* is released, containing a complete show on DVD from London in 1975.

November 2005: Sirius Satellite Radio launches *E Street Radio*, a 24/7 all-Springsteen station.

February 2006: The one billionth song is downloaded on Apple iTunes, signifying the power of the digital medium.

April 2006: *The Seeger Sessions*, a tribute to Pete Seeger featuring the artist's older folk songs, is released.

October 2007: *Magic*, a critical response to the policies of George W. Bush, is released.

December 2007: The Mitchell report is released detailing the use of steroids in Major League Baseball. Over ninety players are named, including prominent sluggers Barry Bonds and Mark McGwire.

April 2008: Danny Federici succumbs to melanoma, the first member of the E Street Band to pass away.

October 2008: Congress passes a $700-billion bailout, the Emergency Economic Stabilization Act, to rescue failing Wall Street businesses due to the housing, banking, and subprime mortgage crises caused by excessive greed and speculation among several firms.

October 2008: Performs at several political rallies for Democratic candidate Barack Obama.

November 2008: Barack Obama becomes the first African American president of the United States.

January 2009: "The Wrestler," written as the theme song for Mickey Rourke's movie of the same name, wins Springsteen his second Golden Globe.

January 2009: A second *Greatest Hits* album is released exclusively through Wal-Mart, whose questionable business practices garner Springsteen considerable criticism. Springsteen, whose career has stood for defending the poor and voiceless, apologizes.

January 2009: *Working on a Dream* is released, just days after Springsteen plays in a tribute concert for Barack Obama's inauguration.

April 2009: The rise of the Tea Party reveals the deep political and cultural tension in the United States.

September 2009: Kaiser Foundation reports that since 1989 the cost of heath care for the average family has risen 131 percent.

October 2009: The nearly decade-long economic recession continues to plague Americans, with the unemployment rate surging over 10 percent.

April 2010: A British Petroleum oil rig explodes in the Gulf of Mexico; it is the largest oil spill in the history of the United States and proves disastrous for the environment and economy of the states near the gulf.

June 2010: The *London Calling: Live in Hyde Park* DVD is released.

November 2010: *The Promise: The "Darkness on the Edge of Town" Story* DVD is released.

June 2011: Clarence "Big Man" Clemons dies as the result of a stroke, the second E Street Band member to pass away.

March 2012: *Wrecking Ball* is released.

INTRODUCTION

The Land of Hope and Dreams

STORIES AND NUMBERS

Just after Thanksgiving in 1999, filmmaker Michael Sodano released *Greetings from the Parking Lot: The Springsteen Fanomenon*, an in-depth look at the tailgating rituals of Springsteen fans of all ages. While colorful and, at times, amusing, the documentary is noteworthy for the number of personal testimonies by fans regarding what Springsteen's music has meant to them. One by one, men and women relate emotional, often moving stories about where they were when they heard their first Springsteen song, when they attended their first concert, or when they actually met the man himself. However, the common thread linking all the tales is how Springsteen's art has sustained them in some way at various times in their lives. When I watched the video again in preparation for this project, it struck me how many ways a book like this could be constructed. After all, a project whose goal is to explain the cultural influence of a singer whose career has spanned nearly fifty years is no small task. There is so much material. So many songs played out over so much history and so many countries. Does one move chronologically from album to album on a march through the decades? Perhaps the best way to capture Springsteen's importance is to concentrate on the dominant themes of his considerable body of work. Or, like Sodano, one might simply document his influence by telling the stories of his fans. After all, what better way to show the power of a storyteller such as Springsteen than to relay heartfelt anecdotes that are passionately rendered by millions of his fans?

One advantage to this approach is that one would never run out of stories. There is at least one meaningful vignette for every fan. Unfortunately, there is hardly space in this volume to do more than illustrate the importance of such tales by relating a representative example. One that caught my eye was from journalist and American cultural critic Chuck Bauerlein, whose long career included an early stint as a reporter in New Orleans. He first saw Springsteen in September 1975 at the beginning of the *Born to Run* tour, writing a glowing review of the concert and the album, preceding the legendary articles in *Time* and *Newsweek* that would famously bring Springsteen to the national scene in late October of that year. He caught up with the young singer in a local tavern after the show, but Springsteen would not grant him an interview; Bauerlein was disappointed, thinking that this might be his only chance to talk with a rising star whose music and live show had touched him so profoundly. Fortunately, Bauerlein was still working in the Crescent City when Springsteen returned the following year and, as part of a promotional campaign, asked the journalist to organize a softball game that would pit Bruce and the E Street Band against local media celebrities. When *Sports Illustrated* asked a decade later for Bauerlein to write about his most cherished journalistic moment, he chose to tell the story of the softball game. Apparently, things got off to a bit of a rocky start when Bauerlein, sporting a "wide-brimmed plantation hat," jokingly asked Springsteen if he would like to place a friendly bet on the game, wagering "his trademark Our Gang hat" against Baeurlein's Southern topper. Springsteen "seemed slightly uncomfortable," and the wager "didn't make him any more forthcoming." Nevertheless, the game was a raucous, high-scoring affair in which everyone had a good time. The locals appeared to have won 10–9 until late word from the official scorer determined that the contest was actually deadlocked at 9–9. As Bauerlein tells it, his band of journalists scattered quickly, and by the time that he fully understood the situation, he only had three players left to face the E Streeters in extra innings. There was nothing left for Bauerlein to do but appeal to Springsteen's sense of fair play, which he did by offering to play a doubleheader the next time the band was in town if the Springsteen camp would be willing to declare this game a tie. Springsteen agreed but, perhaps sensing that any future games might not come to pass, shook Bauerlein's hand and said, "Why don't we just trade hats?" The game and the trade remained a high point for Bauerlein, who ten years later wrote that his only regret was that there was no photo of the exchange because his friend who took the picture of the swap forgot to the load his camera. To this day, two highlights of his stellar career are Springsteen's hat and the story to which it is attached. Such is the power of Springsteen and his music (Bauerlein).

This anecdotal approach to understanding Springsteen is now finding venues for popular expression, as two recent publications make clear. Those who would like to hear more testimonial stories might want to access Lawrence Kirsch's *For You: Original Stories and Photographs by Bruce Springsteen's Legendary Fans* (2012), or the 2013 film *Springsteen and I,* directed by Ridley Scott, which is entirely composed of fans' most intimate stories of why Springsteen is so important to them. Still, this method of understanding Springsteen's influence has its limitations. For example, while the anecdotes reveal the power of the music on individual lives, they do not necessarily point to the deeper nature of that power.

Closely related to these fan stories are the legends and myths that make up a sizable body of Springsteen lore. Most fans are familiar with these tales, many of which are true, which function as important markers of Springsteen's cultural significance. For instance, Springsteen's upbringing as a poor outcast situates him squarely within the great American tradition of the rags-to-riches story, the Horatio Alger motif in which a seemingly unwanted exile rises from the mean streets on the strength of his nearly supernatural talent. Fans are also familiar with Springsteen's stormy home life, especially his tumultuous relationship with his father. As Springsteen would famously say in concert raps that were standard fare at his shows for his first fifteen years onstage, "there were two things that were unpopular in my house. One was me and the other was my guitar." Thus, Springsteen played the role of the rebel at a time in American history when being out of step with parents and mainstream society was a cool thing. This role especially worked for Springsteen because he was not a destructive rebel. Indeed, his work ethic and dedication to craft, as well as his drug-free lifestyle, became part of his legend. This was the kind of poetic genius that one could get behind. Great songs. Marched to the beat of his own drummer. Rebellious but constructive. Dissatisfied but romantically inclined. Beaten down but hopeful. This is the Springsteen mystique that so many fans latched onto in the 1970s and 1980s.

This sort of paradoxical mythology has continued to evolve over the course of his career. Most longtime fans know the story of Springsteen feigning mental instability when he had to take his army physical during the Vietnam War. He reportedly even told the recruiters that he was gay, a bold step for the times. In addition, he has continued to be critical of American institutions, even taking aim at the police in a song such as "American Skin" (1999). Yet, his love of country is just as legendary, and most of his fans see him as a protector of a newly constructed, more inclusive American Dream. He has called the American justice system on the carpet for racism, but no one has performed in more benefits for the families of fallen officers. With songs such as "Your Own Worst Enemy" (2007) and "Wrecking Ball" (2012), Springsteen has been brutally critical of American government and industry, yet he is so revered as a defender of American values that in the weeks after terrorists attacked the United States in September 2001, a fan yelled to Springsteen across a parking lot in New Jersey to make sure that The Boss knew that "we need to hear from you." Many people, especially in the New York area, looked to Springsteen in their hour of need. Such is the power of his reputation as a larger-than-life legend who has always seemingly had the kind of spiritual insight needed in confusing times.

Still, for all the lore, including the four-hour shows, the purchase of his famous rhyming dictionary in preparation for his first album, and the legendary stories surrounding the formation of the E Street Band, including the nearly surreal entrance of Clarence Clemons in a club called the Student Prince in 1971, the myth of Springsteen goes only so far in helping one explain his overall cultural significance. That runs deeper than the stories so loved by fans, even though those stories do contribute to an overall mythic persona that has been psychologically attractive to millions of people for many decades.

Yet another way of measuring his cultural impact is the impressive list of numerical figures and accolades that define Springsteen's professional life. As mentioned, there is the career that spans nearly fifty years dating from 1965, a remarkable achievement considering the short shelf life of many musicians. Then there are the seventeen studio albums and forty-two albums overall, as well as the fact that he has sold over 65 million records in the United States and over 120 million records world-wide as of 2013. He has completed twenty major world tours, perform-ing over five thousand concerts. He has been the recipient of twenty Grammy Awards from 1984 to 2009, and he has earned four American Music Awards, two Golden Globe Awards, two MTV Video Music Awards, as well as each of the following: an Academy Award, an ASCAP Film and Television Music Award, a Brit Award, a Broadcast Film Critics Association Award, a Critic's Choice Award, a John Steinbeck Award, a Juno Award, a Kennedy Center Honor, a Meteor Ireland Music Award, a MusiCare Person of the Year Award, a Polar Music Prize, and a Rammy Award. Finally, he is a member of three halls of fame, including the Rock and Roll Hall of Fame, the Songwriters Hall of Fame, and the New Jersey Hall of Fame. In recent years, he has been the subject of two traveling exhibits, three major academic confer-ences, and a multitude of academic and popular books. He has even performed at halftime of the Super Bowl, a mark of cultural poignancy in America if there ever was one. Yet, all these numbers and awards merely underscore the enormous scope of his popularity and influence; they do not explain it.

A POET FOR THE TIMES

The fan stories and the lore and the accolades reveal the powerful effect that he has had, but they do not explain exactly why this man became such a pervasive, resonant voice in his culture. Springsteen is a poet for his times, whose personal background and music met the changing psychological needs for so many people over five decades. His themes that resonated in the 1970s still resonate today. While his popularity on the national scene has ebbed and flowed, none of his influence is rele-gated to a particular time. He did not, for instance, have a tremendous influence on working-class youth in only the seventies but not the nine-ties or in 2013. Yes, there are fans who are his age that have literally grown up with him, but he has many young fans today as well. The point is that while he has played with different musicians, used many musical styles, and changed his views as he has lived and learned, the compelling thematic components of his work, as well as the psychological and spiritual effects that they have on his audience, have remained consistent. That is why I chose to construct the book thematically as opposed to chronologically, focusing on the dominant ideas that have attracted people to Springsteen for so long.

Chapter 1 is entitled "Adam Raised a Cain: Biographical and Musical Influences," and it focuses on the events of Springsteen's life and the musical influences that have shaped and reshaped his artistic vision over the course of his long and illustrious career. It seemed important to begin with an analysis of his life because so much of his appeal revolves around his status as a person who, by all rights, should not have achieved success but who rode his poetic genius and raw determination to not only fame and fortune but a useful life filled with meaning. For nearly three generations, young people have found inspiration in Springsteen's story. What is not to like? A sensitive young boy with a sad family history and stifling home life becomes a social outcast who fails at nearly everything he does. A college dropout, he clings to the one thing that he knows and that gives him any joy: his music. He endures years of poverty, all the while playing his guitar as if he were playing for his very life. Finally, his vivid, soulful songs find an audience, and the former exile has a place. People want to listen to him. He has a function. As he says, "I was into writing music that was going to thread its way into people's lives. I was interested in becoming part of people's lives. And having some usefulness—that would be the word. I would imagine that a lot of people who end up going into the arts or film or music were at some point told by somebody that they were useless" (Strauss). With so many Americans of his and subsequent generations struggling to make ends meet and with so many young people feeling unsure about their prospects for success in a volatile world, it is no wonder that Springsteen's life and the songs that reflect that life have fascinated his audiences. This chapter explores the multiple influences that helped Springsteen transform from a kid with seemingly no future to a prophetic artist with legions of fans.

The second chapter, "Those Romantic Young Boys: Reviving the Quest in the 1970s," springs from the fact that much of Springsteen's music in the 1970s features young, often desperate characters trying to escape their circumstances in a quest for fulfillment. Typified by his epic *Born to Run* (1975) and anchored in his troubled upbringing and the bleak cultural landscape of the decade, this mythos remains an important part of his music today. For Springsteen, "The importance of . . . bands all across America is that they nourish and inspire the community," helping struggling people believe that happiness "could exist" (Duncan). This deep longing for fulfillment, though rooted in different personal and historical circumstances in each decade of his career, is for Springsteen the basic human condition of the contemporary age. Perhaps this is why so many people have identified with him and his music. When they listen to the songs, they hear their own stories, complete with the dark foreboding and undefined emptiness that they have felt and with the stubborn hope and sustaining vision in which they want to believe.

Chapter 3, "Streets of Fire: Working-Class Heroes," focuses on the fact that one of the main reasons why Springsteen's characters are so unhappy is that they occupy the economic underside of the American class system. This is especially true of his music in the late 1970s (*Darkness on the Edge of Town*) and early 1980s (*The River, Nebraska*). However, his concern for those left behind never diminishes. Through the recessions of the seventies and early twenty-first century and the heady pockets of prosperity of the eighties and nineties, Springsteen's songs have remained haunted by ravaged characters who remind those at the bottom of the ladder that they are not alone. Springsteen said as recently as 2010 that his music addresses the fact that "the economy has shifted in such a way that it's benefitting a small percentage of Americans at the top, squeezing the middle and ignoring the bottom. That's got to be altered. . . . There have been people who have been in a recession or a depression for thirty years." While "their concerns have been fundamentally ignored" by those who wield the power, Springsteen has given voice to their pain in each of his twenty-first-century albums, especially *Magic* (2009), *Working on a Dream* (2007), and *Wrecking Ball* (2012) (*Charlie Rose Show*).

The next chapter is "Boys Try to Look So Hard: Reinventing Masculinity." Springsteen and his audience either grew up with or inherited the feminist movement of the 1960s and 1970s, the shocking technological changes of the last half century, and a jarring transition from a volatile industrial economy to an uncertain information-driven economy, which have all contributed to the tense nature of gender relations over the last fifty years. This major cultural rift is the primary topic of the album *Tunnel of Love* (1987), but Springsteen never abandons his exploration of what a man should be or how men and women might make their way together in a brave new world. His men are fraught with human problems that reflect the various decades in which they are situated. Because his career has lasted so long, both Springsteen and his male characters cover a great deal of ground, including teenage angst, philosophic uncertainty, sexuality, marriage, divorce, raising children, coping with joblessness and dehumanizing working conditions, war, and the haunting specter of failure and emasculation. They are terribly flawed yet likable and sympathetic, and they inspire empathy and pity. Thus, like his working-class heroes, they carry the ability to sustain men and women in an age of divorce and broken relationships.

No Springsteen analysis would be complete without a discussion of government corruption and its effects on everyday people. This is the subject of chapter 5, "I Had a Brother at Khe Sahn: Redefining Patriotism in an Age of War." The Korean Conflict, the Vietnam War, and the wars in Iraq and Afghanistan underscore a powerful concern among generations of Americans. Can we trust our government, and what do our government's policies do to the average American? Springsteen relentlessly explores these questions in albums, from *Born in the USA* (1985) and *Lucky Town* (1992) to *Devils & Dust* (2005) and *Magic* (2007). Springsteen's popularity is partly due to his remarkable ability to be the critical conscience of a people tired of war and ineffective government while still being a man who clearly loves America and what he believes it can achieve.

Springsteen's vision for America is largely based on his desire to remedy social inequalities that those who hold power would largely ignore. Chapter 6, "It Ain't No Sin to Be Glad You're Alive: Social Justice," addresses the fact that Springsteen has dedicated a significant portion of his career to making sure that we cannot ignore those who are suffering because the United States is not living up to its promises. In an America characterized by economic desperation, broken relationships, and institutional distrust, how do we proceed to fight racial and ethnic discrimination, homophobia, poverty, homelessness, and child welfare issues such as malnutrition, abuse, and inaccessible health care? Springsteen champions the cause of social justice, a theme that runs through much of his career but that most powerfully resonates in his works of the last two decades, many of which draw attention to the downtrodden and advocate for financial and political help for those most in need. Many of the songs on *Tracks* (1998), *The Ghost of Tom Joad* (1995), and *We Shall Overcome: The Seeger Sessions* (2006) are driven by a call for us to do what it takes to make life more just, more bearable for others. Nowhere is this more apparent than in his landmark song "Philadelphia" (1993), which was one of the first popular tunes to confront the American public regarding the mistreatment of gays and lesbians. The song, the title track to Jonathan Demme's famous film of the same name, galvanized the gay rights movement in the 1990s, long before it was fashionable for mainstream artists to take such a stance. As Springsteen said, he did it because "you've got to move the world in the right direction so that there is acceptance and tolerance, so that the laws protect everybody's civil rights" (Wieder). This spirit of inclusion, fought not with angry words but with beautiful, humanizing songs, is part of Springsteen's magic.

Chapter 7, "Deliver Me from Nowhere: Redemptive Myth," is an attempt to account for the idea that the entire Springsteen canon plays out against a postmodern landscape in which many Americans have lost faith in traditional narratives. Even in his first albums, *Greetings from Asbury Park, NJ* (1973) and *The Wild, the Innocent, and the E Street Shuffle* (1973), Springsteen's characters are searching for redemption. Loss of faith in traditional religion, government, marriage, and even the American Dream only intensifies the search over the next two decades. So many of Springsteen's songs are replete with the Catholic imagery on which he was raised, and while his goal is clearly not to evangelize in any Christian fashion, he does redefine a spiritual vision that is attractive for a jaded, weary populace. *The Rising* (2002) and *Working on a Dream* (2009) reveal his most complete redefinition of a spiritual American Dream, the culmination of his lifelong attempt to rescue his audience with a larger narrative that can be trusted to nurture and redeem. When considered against the landscape of discarded philosophies of the late twentieth and early twenty-first centuries, is it any wonder that Springsteen stands as a nearly prophetic figure for so many people?

Finally, chapter 8, "The Ministry of Rock 'n' Roll," explores the musical and cultural influence of Springsteen on American culture. Springsteen's musical legacy is considerable. In this chapter, I discuss bands such as the Gaslight Anthem, the National, Arcade Fire, the Hold Steady, and The Killers, among others, and the musical debt they owe to The Boss. Also noteworthy is his growing influence in folk and country music, especially on artists such as Badly Drawn Boy, Josh Ritter, Steve Earle, Jesse Malin, Kenny Chesney, Rodney Atkins, and Eric Church. And that is not to mention luminaries such as Lady Gaga, U2, Patti Smith, Kenny Rogers, and Johnny Cash. Equally interesting is the extent to which Springsteen and his songs are now casually referenced in the American lexicon. An analysis of film is a good way of illustrating this, and I touch on works by John Sayles, Paul Schrader, Sean Penn, Tim Robbins, Cameron Crowe, and others to illustrate Springsteen's artistic reach. This chapter also attempts to explain the curious phenomenon of Springsteen's incredible surge in popularity in Europe, where he now routinely sells out stadiums and sells more records than he does in America.

FINAL WORD

As I was writing this book, Springsteen accepted an invitation to give the keynote address at the Southwest Music Festival in Austin, Texas. His speech was, as usual, timely, comedic, and thoughtful. Near the end of his talk, he gave some advice to younger musicians trying to make their way in the entertainment industry: "Don't take yourself too seriously, and take yourself as seriously as death itself. Don't worry. Worry your ass off. Have ironclad confidence, but doubt—it keeps your heart awake and alert. Believe you are the baddest ass in town, and . . . you suck!" His advice to "keep two completely contradictory ideas alive and well inside your heart and head at all times" seems like good advice for artists but also for scholars, since most of us have a tendency to take ourselves too seriously. One should remember that while cultural analysis is important, in the end Springsteen's popularity is partly due to the fact that his songs are just really good. They feature provocative lyrics, memorable characters, powerful arrangements, and great instrumentation from some of the best musicians in the world. Plus, you can dance to them. I remember hearing "Born to Run" for the first time when I was thirteen and thinking, *Wow, who is that?* All Springsteen fans have had this moment. You then listen to the rest of the songs, and they cry out to you, but you do not quite know why. You know you like the beat, the music, his voice, the power, and the beauty. You know that you cannot forget the characters, but you do not know why. This book is about appreciating the beauty of Springsteen's art and critically appraising its importance. It is about answering that question *why?* and knowing that when it comes to great art, it can never fully be answered.

I

ADAM RAISED A CAIN

Biographical and Musical Influences

THE POWER OF PLACE

Bruce Frederick Joseph Springsteen was born on September 23, 1949, in Long Branch, New Jersey, the first child and only son of Adele and Douglas Springsteen. It would hardly be an understatement to say that he and his sisters, Virginia and Pamela, had an inauspicious beginning. The family settled in Freehold, a working-class town about a half hour from the fading tourist retreat of Asbury Park, whose reputation Springsteen would later establish as part of rock 'n' roll's geographic lore. But that would come much later. In the fifties and sixties, Springsteen was trapped on the wrong side of the tracks in Freehold, "the kind of place where the inferiority complex comes built in" (Marsh 234).

It wasn't that there weren't nice areas of Freehold occupied by middle- and upper-middle-class families enjoying the upside of the postwar American Dream. It's just that the Springsteens were stuck in the gritty, depressed underside of that dream. Bruce deeply felt the economic and spiritual poverty that enveloped his house on South Street next to Ducky Slattery's gas station. Douglas Springsteen was often out of work; when he was employed as a bus driver, jail guard, or laborer in a local rug mill, the jobs featured low pay and long hours, leaving him unfulfilled, angry, and isolated.

If his home life was characterized by silence and desperation, it wasn't much worse than school. Springsteen attended public and parochial schools, but at both St. Rose of Lima Catholic School and Freehold Regional High School, he was largely invisible, a poor to average student who "didn't even make it to class clown" (Alterman 16). He was certainly intelligent, but there seemed to be no institutional avenue for him to apply his ability. He tried sports, football and baseball, but nothing seemed to give him any sense of belonging or purpose. At St. Rose, he constantly ran afoul of the nuns. In third grade, a nun stuffed him into a trashcan, telling him that is where he belonged. A few years later, one of the sisters disciplined him for "acting up," by sending him to the first-grade classroom and having one of the young boys slap him in the face. Springsteen would later say, "I was there eight years . . . but I don't remember anything nice about it" (Marsh 23). High school wasn't any better. Springsteen's long hair, ragged dress, and unusual personal style upset his classmates, causing him to be derided as a freak. One teacher even suggested to the other students that Springsteen not be allowed to participate in the graduation ceremony, to preserve the solemnity and importance of the occasion. At best, it "was like I didn't exist. It was the wall, and then me" (Alterman 16).

Not surprising, Springsteen's early music reflects the bleak nature of his upbringing and, in particular, his fear of never making it out of the cycle of poverty and drudgery that he watched his father and friends live out. For instance, his first album, *Greetings from Asbury Park, NJ*, features the lonely, "ragamuffin gunner" of "Lost in the Flood." The protagonist is "like a hungry runaway" who has no roots; he wanders from town to town as if he is in search of some great dream that always eludes him. Resigned to his fate, he tries to carve out a place to stand, by racing "Sundays in Jersey in a Chevy stock car super eight." His car is painted red, white, and blue and bears the words "bound for glory," but it becomes clear that although he is brave and even heroic, his longing will remain undefined and unrewarded. Like the bravest of soldiers, he rides "into the hurricane," but he cannot overcome the confusing array of societal forces set against him, forces embodied in the word *flood*. The kids may have romanticized him as "Jimmy the Saint," but in the end, "there is nothing left" of his body; his blood stains the road, and the wreckage of his car is strewn on the horizon. The song's landscape, populated by "wolfman fairies dressed in drag for homicide," disintegrates into a surreal riot, the police fighting gangs of kids. Lives are snuffed out in "five, quick shots," a hail of bullets ripping through the town. A church towers over the scene, but religion can't help any of the characters. Bald pregnant nuns are "pleading immaculate conception," and all the characters are "wrecked on Main Street from drinking that holy blood." There is no meaning, no solace, no reason why. There is only desperation, pain, and death. The young men may be heroic in their insistence on trying to find a purpose in life, but none of them make it out of the flood. As Springsteen concludes, "those cats are sure messed up," and as a kid who grew up watching dreams die in Freehold, he knew what he was writing about.

Other early songs focus on his father, clearly the most influential family member on Springsteen's initial view of the world as a hostile place that can leave you lonely and numb if you aren't careful. Springsteen's raps about the tension between him and his father were standard concert fare in the 1970s, as if the stage became a therapeutic platform on which he could exorcise the demons of his childhood. Sometimes the stories were comedic. He frequently joked with his audience, "When I was growing up, there were two things that were unpopular in my house; one was me, the other was my guitar" (Marsh 11). Usually, however, the tales lamented the volatility of the relationship between a man who felt like a failure and a son whose desire not to end up like his father was so strong that he frequently ran away. When his mother inevitably retrieved him, the story was always the same: "We'd always end up screamin' at each other. My mother she'd end up runnin' in from the front room, cryin' and tryin' to pull him off me" (Marsh 26).

This raw emotion is most palpable on *Darkness on the Edge of Town*. In "Factory," Springsteen revealed that he understood his father's plight. The father in the song rises early to plod to his dead-end job that "takes his hearing"; he trudges "through the mansions of fear" and "pain." The singer can see his "daddy walking through them factory gates." The job is brutal; it takes everything from the men who work at the factory, and by the end of the day, they have "death in their eyes." Still, they will have to be back the next day and every other day to make ends meet. Their frustration and anger will build until it spills outside the factory and into their homes where "somebody's gonna get hurt tonight."

Even after he had released *Born to Run* in 1975, an album that established him as a bona fide rock star, Springsteen felt the pain of his father's legacy and wrote about it in "Adam Raised a Cain." Released on *Darkness on the Edge of Town*, the song opens with the protagonist being baptized as his "father held him to his side." Though it has been many years, the speaker can still remember, "how on that day I cried." He acknowledges that, even then, he and his father were like Adam and Cain, "prisoners in love, a love in chains." The second stanza reflects his fear that no matter what he does, he will never be able to outrun his father's legacy, which is "never over" and "relentless as the rain." When the album came out in 1978, Springsteen had just won a lengthy lawsuit against his first manager, Mike Appel. The legal victory freed Springsteen to sign with new manager, Jon Landau, and produce his first new album since *Born to Run*. He was a star; he had more control over his art and career than ever; and his concerts sold out in minutes from coast to coast. Yet, as the song indicates, his fear of not being able to outrun his father's fate was so powerful that it still defined him; he still worried that he wouldn't be able to escape "paying for the sins of somebody else's past." He knows that his "daddy worked his whole life for nothing but the pain." This image is permanently ingrained in the mind of the son who, no matter how much he succeeds, must still "inherit the sins" and try to battle to free himself from "the dark heart of a dream."

Springsteen's father isn't the only family member whose difficulties influenced him. In 1980, Springsteen released *The River*, a double album whose title track tells the story of his older sister, Virginia, who had married young, had children, and in the late seventies was trying with her husband to hold her family together through perilous economic times. The words spring from a young disillusioned husband who loves his wife but feels beleaguered by life's events. The young man is from a small town where "you were brought up to do like your daddy done." Like Springsteen and Virginia's husband, he clearly dreams of a better life, and he and his girlfriend would often "ride out of that valley down to where the fields were green." He fondly remembers diving into the river with his beautiful Mary, and the listener is struck by the images of renewal, almost as if they were being born again into a better life. However, the sense of hope is soon extinguished. He "got Mary pregnant," and after a joyless wedding, he is presented with "a union card" and gets a job working construction. Soon, he is laid off, and all of their dreams "just vanish right into the air." The couple grows distant, with him acting like "I don't remember" and Mary acting like "she don't care." The memories of his hopes haunt him "like a curse," sending him and Mary back to the river in search of what seemingly has been lost forever.

Yet, Springsteen himself did not fall prey to the darkness. He felt it deeply for himself, and he would always feel it for others, but he also transcended it. His mother, who loved music, particularly Elvis Presley, was a major reason why. When he was nine years old, he and his mom watched Elvis play on the *Ed Sullivan Show*, a pivotal event in his life. "I was nine years old when I saw Elvis on *Ed Sullivan*, and I had to get a guitar the next day. I stood in front of my mirror with that guitar on . . . and I knew that that's what I was missing" (Alterman 17). His mother encouraged him to pursue music, protected him from his father's anger, and eventually took out a sixty-dollar loan to buy him his first professional guitar. It was a substantial amount of money, and Springsteen never forgot it, later remarking that his mother "was just like superman" (13). He would later write "The Wish," released on *Tracks* in 1998, as an homage to his mother who, though she could not keep him from looking through his father's eyes to "a world so deadly and true," did prevent him "from crawling through."

Instead, Springsteen found hope in music. Onstage, he had a purpose, even a home. He joined his first band, the Castiles, in 1965 thanks to Tex and Marion Vinyard, a Freehold couple that sponsored local bands. He played with the group through high school, when most of the other band members moved on to nonmusical pursuits. After dropping out of Ocean County Community College, he formed several bands on the Jersey shore in the late sixties and early seventies, including Earth, Child, Steel Mill, Dr. Zoom and the Sonic Boom, and the Bruce Springsteen Band. He was doggedly dedicated to music as a way of finding a place, so much so that, unlike other musicians, he refused to work other, nonmusic jobs and even faked a mental illness to evade the draft. For Springsteen, music literally was life. Music "gave me a sense of purpose. What I wanted to do. Who I wanted to be. The way that I wanted to do it. What I thought I could accomplish through singing songs" (*60 Minutes*, 2008). Perhaps this is why many of his early songs are infused with hope. *Greetings* may have featured "Lost in the Flood," but it also featured "Growin' Up," a rollicking song of youthful exuberance in which Springsteen "combed my hair till it was just right and commanded the night brigade." He is unafraid, confident, and ready to stand up when everyone tells him to "sit down." In the end, he "lost everything I ever loved or feared" and boasts that he "found the key to the universe in the engine of an old parked car." *The Wild and Innocent* includes "Rosalita," a powerful, upbeat rocker in which a young musician believes that he will make it big, and he exhorts his girlfriend to tell her father that "this is his last chance to get his daughter in a fine romance" before the "record company" gives him a "big advance." *Born to Run* boasts "Thunder Road," in which the speaker tries to sweep the girl he loves off her feet, beckoning her to leave their "town full of losers" and pull "out of here to win." In *Darkness*, Springsteen testifies to his belief in a better life in "The Promised Land," a song in which the seemingly hopeless speaker rallies and insists that he will "blow away the lies that leave you nothing but lost and brokenhearted." Even on *The River*, home to several songs of bleak desperation, there are hopeful tunes, such as "Two Hearts" and "I Wanna Marry You," in which the protagonists insist on the possibility of love and meaning, and "I'm a Rocker," in which a feisty, fiery musician tells a girl that he is better than "James Bond" or any another "secret agent man." He is a "rocker, every day." He'll never quit, and he will rescue her, just as he was rescued by his guitar and his music.

This was Springsteen. Redeemed by his guitar, he needed only a band as dedicated to rock 'n' roll as himself. He found the musicians that he needed in and around Asbury Park in the early seventies. By the fall of 1972, Springsteen had formed the initial cast of the E Street Band, including Clarence "Big Man" Clemons on saxophone, drummer Vini "Mad Dog" Lopez, keyboard player David Sancious, and Gary Tallent on bass. Before the *Born to Run* album in 1975, Springsteen replaced Lopez with the now legendary Max Weinberg. Sancious left the group and was replaced by Roy Bittan. Danny Federici was added to play the organ and accordion, and Springsteen's long-time friend Steven Van Zandt joined the band as a producer and guitar player. With the E Street Band at his back, Springsteen's career took flight. After receiving critical praise but disappointing sales for his first two albums, Springsteen became a star—and a profitable one at that—with *Born to Run*, an album that would eventually sell over six million copies. After a three-year absence from the studio due to a contentious lawsuit,

Springsteen returned in 1978 with the relentless *Darkness on the Edge of Town*, another critical and commercial success. He then delivered *The River* in 1980. The double album sold over 1.5 million copies in the first few months. By the end of *The River* tour in late 1981, Bruce Springsteen was an international star. The poor kid from Freehold, with little hope and a stormy past, had made it.

A sure sign that Springsteen had reached superstardom was what he did on his next album, *Nebraska*. Released in 1982, Springsteen recorded most of the works in his house in New Jersey with his guitar and a four-track cassette recorder. Surrounded by all the trappings of success, Springsteen might have reveled in his money and status. Instead, he turned his attention to those who, like his father, were disenchanted and discouraged with life in the 1980s. With fans and record company executives expecting the powerful, perhaps even joyful rock sound of the E Street Band, Springsteen instead manifested his growing sense of autonomy by issuing eleven stark, austere solo songs that reflected the dark side of American life. Springsteen may have transcended the hopelessness of his childhood and his father's rage, but the pain of others was not lost on him. In fact, his commitment to serving others by exposing their plight seemed to emerge most forcefully in *Nebraska*, where songs force the listener to stand in the shoes of those less fortunate—songs such as "Reason to Believe," in which the speaker struggles with the incomprehensibility of life and the difficulty of maintaining faith; "Highway Patrolman," which tells the tale of a good man caught between duty to his wayward brother and his job; "Used Cars," which underscores the humiliation of a working-class family trying to scrape up enough money to buy a cheap car; and "Johnny 99," in which a man on death row explains the desperation that led to his crime.

Springsteen's songs clearly still had a dark, sobering quality to them. He was still looking into the darkness, but it wasn't simply his own darkness; it was the pain and frustration of others about which he was writing on the *Nebraska* album. This transference of subject matter from his own life to the lives of others marked a significant transition period for Springsteen. As he recognized by the end of *The River* tour, "I drew a lot of my earlier material from my experience growing up, my father's experience, the experience of my immediate family and town. But there was a point in the mid-eighties when I felt like I'd said pretty much all I knew how to say about all that. I couldn't continue writing about those same things without either becoming a stereotype of myself or by twisting those themes around too much. So I spent the next ten years or so writing about men and women—their intimate personal lives" (Percy). On his next album, *Born in the USA*, Springsteen would continue to develop his identity as a writer for the people, especially for the invisible members of the downtrodden masses whose voices would never otherwise be heard. Unlike the stark, lonely sound of a single guitar often heard on *Nebraska, Born in the USA* exploded in the ears of listeners in true rock fashion. The album spoke for millions who were struggling, with songs such as "Downbound Train" and "Glory Days," but it also insisted that there would be a light at the end of the tunnel. Numbers such as "Cover Me," "Dancing in the Dark," and "No Surrender" featured characters with problems and imperfect lives who still saw possibilities for joy and triumph amid their difficulties. The title song, "Born in the USA," is an angry work in which Springsteen takes up the cause of forgotten Vietnam veterans, but the story's protagonist is still a "cool rocking Daddy" who will never give up. The album's most personal song, "My Hometown," is replete with images of "troubled times," including racial tension, violence, and economic deprivation, but there is still a sense that the speaker and his wife will not give up on the place. Darkness but also light. Pain but also possibility. The record became a commercial bonanza. Seven of the ten songs reached the top ten on the singles charts; the album itself went to number one on *Billboard Magazine's* chart, and it eventually sold over fifteen million copies in the United States alone. Tickets for the *Born in the USA* tour sold out in minutes, even for the larger, football-sized venues, such as London's Wembley Stadium or the Cotton Bowl in Dallas. The tour grossed over $80 million. Springsteen followed up with a long-awaited live album, *Bruce Springsteen & the E Street Band Live: 1975–1985*, which was just as successful. The world experienced Brucemania, and Springsteen became one of the most famous and richest musicians in the world.

On top of the world, Springsteen married actress Julianne Phillips in May 1985. However, the working-class New Jersey rocker and the upper-class Los Angeles model proved to be incompatible, and the gradual dissolution of the marriage exacted an emotional toll on Springsteen. The marriage ended in March 1989, just after Springsteen released what some might argue is his most biographical record, *Tunnel of*

Love. While the album clearly resonates with anyone who has gone through a divorce or rough times in a relationship, it remains a powerful expression of Springsteen's personal emotions. In "Brilliant Disguise," a man is "struggling to do everything right." He wants to love his wife, but he is plagued by doubt and insecurity. He hears someone calling her name from "underneath our window," and he watches her hide something "in shame underneath your pillow." He "walks this world in wealth," just like Springsteen, but he is tormented. Is she cheating? Does she love him? Does he love her? "Is that you, baby, or just a brilliant disguise?" In the end, "his bed is cold," and he is "lost in the darkness of our love." All he can do is utter a weak prayer for God to "have mercy on the man who's not sure what he's sure of." Likewise, "Tunnel of Love" underscores the frightening, destabilizing nature of a marriage gone wrong. A young couple at an amusement park embarks on what should be a fun, romantic ride; however, "when the lights go out," they find themselves "in a room of shadows." They see only in mirrors, in distorted "5-D" vision, and they come face-to-face in the dark with "all that stuff we're so scared of." This isn't a funhouse; it's a chamber of horrors where "it's easy for two people to lose each other." Love should be "easy" and "simple enough," but "the house is haunted and the ride is rough." In the end, all you can do is hold on and "learn to live with what you can't rise above."

Tunnel of Love took on an additional layer of meaning when Springsteen went through another breakup after his 1988 tour. Early in 1989, Springsteen parted ways with the E Street Band. In some ways, perhaps the separation was necessary. Springsteen needed time to move beyond being "The Boss," a rock idol, a superstar, or any of the other highly pressurized roles that an international megastar must reluctantly accept as part of his fame and fortune. He needed time to figure out who he was and how to live with being, as he would write in "Better Days" in 1992, "a rich man in a poor man's shirt." He played with several artists, experimented musically, and, most important, fell in love with a woman with whom he could form a lasting bond. In June 1991, Springsteen married Patti Scialfa, whom he had known since the early days of his career on the Jersey shore and with whom he had an affair in the mideighties. Scialfa was a Jersey girl who grew up in the same area as Springsteen. She was a musician. They shared a common language and a common history. Between 1990 and 1994, the couple had three children: Evan, Jessica, and Sam. With his wife and children, Springsteen seemed to develop a greater sense of self, an identity that was more than just being a singer. It also brought him a deeper sense of joy: "My relationship with Patti and the children brought an enormous amount of faith and hope. There's little babies! You can't afford despair, you gotta find faith someplace" (Sweeting).

In 1992, Springsteen released *Human Touch* and *Lucky Town*, neither of which earned the same type of critical acclaim or exuberant fan reaction as his earlier albums. However, several of the songs revealed his growing feeling of contentment. In "Better Days," Springsteen acknowledges that he has been through some hard times, but he affirms that "these are better days with a girl like you." He confesses that he was a sad sight, a man who was "livin' in his own skin and can't stand the company." Yet, by the end of the song, he's "half way to heaven and just a mile outta hell." He proclaims that "better days are shining through." In "Living Proof," he reveals the hope that he found in the birth of his son. He admits that "he had crawled deep into some kind of darkness." He had done "some sad and hurtful things." Yet, he had not stopped "searching for a little of God's mercy," and in his son, he had "found livin' proof." He understands that life is still "a house of cards" and that the world is "so fouled and confused," but it does not dampen his joy. The song ends with the warm image of husband and wife cuddling in their bed with their infant son as a storm rages outside. He repeats that he has experienced "God's mercy" and will be content with what he has received from "the treasures of the Lord." *Lucky Town* also includes "Leap of Faith," in which the speaker delights in being "born again" as the result of falling in love, and "If I Should Fall Behind," a touching song in which the speaker and his lover vow to wait for each other no matter what evils await them.

If Springsteen was less productive in the 1990s in terms of total album output and concerts played, perhaps it was that he had settled into a more contented role of husband and father. Yet, he was still making great art, music that showed that he had found and accepted his place as a spokesman for those who had missed out on their "beautiful reward." In 1993, he played "The Concert to Fight Hunger." A few months later, he wrote the soundtrack for Jonathan Demme's landmark film *Philadelphia*, the story of a man who suffers the pain of discrimination and ridicule as he slowly dies from AIDS. "Streets of Philadelphia" would win Springsteen a Grammy Award as well as an Oscar and, more important, create empathy for AIDS victims and increased acceptance for gays and lesbians. In 1995, Springsteen released *The Ghost of Tom Joad*, an acoustic album in the spirit of John Steinbeck's *Grapes of Wrath*. Every performance on the *Joad* tour was a reminder to the most prosperous nation on Earth that it had an obligation to protect its poorest citizens, which seemed to be growing in number even as the economy soared in the mid- to late nineties. Springsteen also turned his attention to the plight of immigrants, legal or illegal, on the album, writing "Sinaloa Cowboys," "Galveston Bay," "Across the Border," and "The Line," all of which made his listeners question whether America was living up to its reputation as a place that welcomed the starving masses yearning to breathe free.

By the midnineties, Springsteen had moved his family home to New Jersey, leaving Los Angeles, where he had lived since 1990. He had found his place as a family man, as a humanitarian musician in the tradition of Woody Guthrie and Pete Seeger, and as a man deeply rooted in the life and culture of the Jersey shore. As such, he spent the rest of the decade playing benefits for many worthy causes, many of which were centered in Freehold and Asbury Park. In 1997, he received the Polar Music Prize, essentially the music world's answer to the Nobel Peace Prize, for his humanitarian work in the United States and around the world. In 1999, he was inducted into the Rock and Roll Hall of Fame. As the clock ticked away on the twentieth century, Bruce Springsteen had it all: a healthy family, wealth, a firm sense of professional and personal place, and all the accolades a man could ever want. Yet, one thing was missing—a reunion with the band that had helped make him great. Early in 1999, Springsteen once again joined ranks with the E Street Band, and they spent over a year barnstorming the United States and Europe, much to the delight of legions of fans. In 2000, he released *Live in New York City*, a collection of songs from the tour's final stand in Madison Square Garden. The work was also released as a DVD, a production that won two Emmy Awards.

Unlike most reunion tours, which often end with farewell performances and reveal a band that just is not what it used to be, Springsteen and the E Street Band were better than ever and getting ready to embark on a remarkably productive and creative decade. Sadly, the renaissance was jump-started by the terrorist attacks of September 11,

2001. Much of the destruction was in New York City, just across the river from Springsteen's home in Rumson, New Jersey. Americans, particularly New Yorkers, were hurting. Springsteen responded with *The Rising*, to this date one of the only records to seriously address the terrorist attacks. With numbers such as "Empty Sky" and "You're Missing," the album allowed fans to cry and mourn the losses from the tragedy. In particular, "My City in Ruins" struck a chord with millions of listeners. Indeed, the song became a kind of rallying cry for many people who, inspired by Springsteen's love for New York, were moved to renew their love for their town. People mourned the ruins, but they also felt the hope that is infused in the song and throughout the record. In "The Rising," Springsteen invites his audience to "come on up for the rising," to "come on up" and "lay your hands in mine." It is a call for healing through community and solidarity, and it partners nicely with "Lonesome Day," in which Springsteen unites with his fellow Americans to accept the pain of the events and to encourage one another to look into the face of evil and defy it. The song is loud and powerful, and Springsteen is in full voice as he shouts, "Let Kingdom Come I'm gonna find my way through this lonesome day." The song's chorus is even more inspiring and is designed to be repeated by both singer and audience as a communal mantra of resistance: "It's alright, it's alright, it's alright!"

The first decade of the twenty-first century revealed an increasingly political Springsteen, a man who had accepted his place as an artist whose duty it is to question authority for the good of the people and to use his art to ameliorate human suffering. Released in 2005, *Devils & Dust* revisits many of the subjects and themes of the Springsteen canon. Lonely boxers, desperate lovers, world-weary cowboys, and several other long-suffering characters appear on the record, but the most notable song is "Devils & Dust," in which Springsteen takes the administration of President George W. Bush to task for waging fruitless wars in Iraq and Afghanistan. Specifically, Springsteen warns those in power not to make decisions based on fear, since those decisions often lead to wars fought by young people such as the song's protagonist, a young man who might kill or be killed at any time. Springsteen seemed to be looking American leaders squarely in the eye when he sang that "fear's a powerful thing" that can "take your God filled soul" and "fill it with devils and dust." In 2006, Springsteen unveiled *We Shall Overcome:*

The Seeger Sessions, in which he remade several of Pete Seeger's songs as a tribute to the great American folksinger. The tone, of course, was different from that of the songs on *Devils & Dust*, but the message was in keeping with Springsteen's newfound political voice that insisted on reminding Americans what is great about their country. The songs thus champion hard work, faith, hope, and humor as a way of overcoming evil and fear.

In 2007, *Magic* arrived in time for the presidential election season. The album includes "Last to Die," in which Springsteen asks his government who "will be the last to die for a mistake?" "Long Walk Home" features a father professing his love for his town, a place that proudly flies the American flag as a symbol for "things that are set in stone." It is representative of "who we are, what we'll do, and what we won't." Springsteen clearly wonders what has happened to those promises in an age where a government fights wars based on lies and commits atrocities in the name of freedom. Something has gone terribly wrong, he cautions his audience, and it is "going to be a long walk home" as we try to reinvent the best of America. Springsteen pulled several of the songs out of his bag at various political rallies, a first for him, as he championed Barack Obama's presidential campaign.

In the end, Obama won the election, but Springsteen did not stop working to promote his own version of an American Dream. In *Working on a Dream*, Springsteen reissued his call for tolerance, inclusion, love, family, and sacrifice. In the title track, the speaker is a kind of everyman, whose "nights are long and days are lonely." The rain is "pourin' down" and "trouble can feel like it's here to stay," but he vows to "straighten my back" and keep "working on a dream." His enduring hope is that "our love will make it real someday." As the album moves on, the listener gets a sense that, for Springsteen, that day has arrived. He will never stop speaking for the poor or for those who are hurting because, one gets the feeling, he knows and loves his place as an artist, a husband, a father, a friend, and a community leader. In "My Lucky Day," the speaker has seen some hard times, but "the grace of your smile" reminds him how lucky he is. Similarly, the speaker in "What Love Can Do" bears the mark of Cain but insists that "we'll let the light shine through" and that he'll "show you what love can do." In "Kingdom of Days," he counts "his blessings that you're mine for always" as they "laugh beneath the covers and count the wrinkles and the grays." Finally, there is "This Life," in which the singer declares, "With you I have been blessed, what more can you expect?" As he fingers the hem of her dress and considers the meaning of "this life and then the next," he concludes that "my universe is at rest." The kid from Freehold whom no one liked, who was stuffed in a trashcan by his teacher, had come a long way—and yet, he was only a few towns away from where he grew up.

THE POWER OF ART

As an artist, Bruce Springsteen is the definition of eclectic. He is a student of human nature, of books, films, newspapers, and journals. Of course, his earliest and most powerful influence is music. Yet, it is difficult to determine exactly who influenced Springsteen and how those influences play out in his music. Certainly, it is impossible to say that any one artist had a disproportionate influence on him. As he said in a 2010 interview, he did not mimic or copy other musicians for any of his songs. Yet, his music was generally informed by many performers: "That's studying. And whether you're drawn to gospel music or church music or honky-tonk music, it informs your character and it informs your talent" (National Public Radio, New York). As biographer Dave Marsh says of *The River*,

> [it] courses through a dozen styles: the rockabilly nuances of "Cadillac Ranch," the Stones-like raunch of "Crush on You," the British Invasion beat of "The Ties That Bind," the folk rock of "The River," the white soul of "I Wanna Marry You," the Duane Eddy twang of "Ramrod," the frat-party noise of "Sherry Darling," the plain-spoken country western voice of "Wreck on the Highway," and the ballads that are a mutant form, derived from Dylan and Van Morrison, but now recognizable Springsteen's: "Stolen Car," "Point Blank," "The Price You Pay," "Independence Day." They are part of a genre all their own. (230)

To this day, Springsteen listens to hundreds of bands a year. His influences are hard to pin down, but one can piece together certain patterns.

Springsteen himself has said several times that his earliest influence was Elvis Presley. The cover of *Born to Run* features Springsteen wearing an Elvis button. In 1976, Springsteen, emboldened by his recent success, jumped the fence at Graceland and tried to meet his boyhood idol. Elvis was not home, and Springsteen was escorted off the grounds. It's difficult to find a song where one can say the lyrics or music come straight from Elvis, but Springsteen thought enough of the King to record a cover of "Viva Las Vegas," which appeared on *The Essential Bruce Springsteen* in 2003, and he wrote a powerful tribute song, "Johnny Bye Bye," to lament Presley's death. The song appeared on the 1998 release *Tracks*.

Another prominent influence on Springsteen's early works was Bob Dylan. Springsteen was signed at CBS Records by John Hammond, the same executive who signed Dylan. Hammond saw in Springsteen the "new Dylan" for whom everyone had been searching. Initially, CBS wanted Springsteen to perform as a solo artist in the manner of Dylan, and despite his use of the E Street Band, several songs on *Greetings* have a solo feel. In addition, the free flowing, raucous wordplay is reminiscent of Dylan. The album's first song, "Blinded by the Light," opens with "Madman bummers drummers and Indians in the summer with a teenage diplomat" and continues with "In the dumps with the mumps as the adolescent pumps his way into his hat." This is clearly reminiscent of Dylan's "Subterranean Homesick Blues." Springsteen also covered several Dylan songs, including "Chimes of Freedom," which he remade and released in 1988 as part of the Amnesty International human rights tour. Indeed, the commitment to political reform and civil rights is perhaps how Springsteen most resembles Dylan. As Springsteen says, "I used to say when I heard 'Highway 61,' I was hearing the first true picture of how I felt and how my country felt. And that was exhilarating." Dylan had "tremendous courage to go places where people hadn't gone previously. So when I heard that, I knew I liked that" (National Public Radio, Toronto).

Two folk artists, Woody Guthrie and Pete Seeger, continue to be important influences on Springsteen, who has clearly picked up the torch as spokesman for the oppressed. Guthrie earned the moniker "the Dust Bowl troubadour," and Springsteen covered his famous "This Land Is Your Land" on his 1985 live album. Still, Guthrie's biggest influence is felt on *The Ghost of Tom Joad*, a record dedicated to forcing middle- and upper-class America to notice those who are most vulnerable, those whom they do not want to see. Songs such as "Just across the Border" even sound like Guthrie's songs. Seeger, a friend of Guthrie and fellow socialist, was so influential on Springsteen that he dedicated an entire album, *We Shall Overcome: The Seeger Sessions*, to ensure his legacy. As Springsteen said in 2010, "there's a part of the singer going way back in American history that is of course the canary in the coalmine. When it gets dark, you're supposed to be singing. It's dark right now. And so I went back to Woody Guthrie and Dylan and the people who said, 'Take Pete Seeger, who doesn't want to know how this song sounds, he wants to know what's it for'" (*60 Minutes*, 2009).

Country artists who affected Springsteen's work include Hank Williams, Johnny Cash, and Roy Orbison. The latter is featured in Springsteen's classic "Thunder Road," in which the singer identifies himself as "Roy Orbison singing for the lonely." Orbison's theatrical influence is felt on Springsteen's early records in songs such as "Incident on 57th Street." Orbison and Springsteen collaborated on several songs, and Springsteen inducted him into the Rock and Roll Hall of Fame in 1987. Springsteen viewed Cash as the ultimate blue-collar man who, like his characters, lived life heroically in the face of certain devastation. The entire *Nebraska* album is, in its own way, a tribute to Cash, thematically and stylistically. Cash himself was so taken with "Johnny 99" that he covered it later in his career. Springsteen returned the favor by signing "Give My Love to Rose" as a tribute to the Man in Black. In the late seventies, Springsteen started listening to Hank Williams, whose "Long Gone Lonesome Blues" inspired the lyrics to the song "The River."

Of course, one can never outrun one's youth, and Springsteen certainly absorbed and ingrained the rhythms and ideas of his early rock 'n' roll heroes. Springsteen loved Buddy Holly's innocence and respect for his characters, on display in "Peggy Sue" and "Oh, Boy," and those same feelings are felt in the songs "Little Girl I Wanna Marry You" and "Thunder Road." Springsteen remade Holly's "Not Fade Away" on *The River*. As Springsteen remarked in the late seventies, "I play Buddy Holly every night before I go on. That keeps me honest" (Leftfield). Another staple of midcentury radio that had an impact on Springsteen was Chuck Berry, whose good-time vibes that define "Maybelline" and "Johnny B. Goode" can be heard in the songs "Ramrod" and "Cadillac Ranch," which, using cars as their centerpiece, harken back to a more carefree age. Springsteen also admired the passion of Gary U.S. Bonds.

For years, Bonds's "Quarter to Three" was a staple in Springsteen's shows, and his joy and sense that rock music is supposed to be fun and liberating are seen in songs such as "Two Hearts" and "Crush on You."

Other influences from his formative years as a musician include Mitch Ryder, Van Morrison, Duane Eddy, the Animals, and Phil Spector. Springsteen covered Ryder's "Devil with a Blue Dress On" and "Jenny Take a Ride" for years onstage, and his intense, loud rock sound is most powerfully felt in *Born in the USA*. Springsteen admired Morrison's poetic storytelling that made "Moon Dance" and "Brown Eyed Girl" so riveting, and one can feel Morrison's influence in many Springsteen songs. "Jungleland" and "Drive All Night" are two of the best. Eddy's "Rebel Rouser" and the Animals' "It's My Life" were also early concert fixtures whose raw rock power is evident in so many Springsteen songs. Spector, the famous producer, founded "the wall of sound" techniques that provided the big sound that Springsteen was looking for on *Born to Run*. The album made Springsteen a star, especially the title track, whose deep, powerful sound became his most lasting anthem.

Springsteen's musical influences are simply too numerous to catalogue, but the films and books that moved his art are varied as well. He told Will Percy, "I go through periods where I read, and I get a lot out of what I read, and that reading has affected my work since the late seventies. Films and novels and books, more so than music, are what have really been driving me since then." A poignant example of this is *Nebraska*, which in part sprang from several literary influences, including Henry Steele Commager and Allan Nevins's *History of the United States*, the fiction of Flannery O'Connor and Bobbi Ann Mason, and Robert Franks's photo essay *The Americans*. Springsteen was particularly moved by O'Connor's *Wise Blood*, with its grotesque, desperate characters struggling to survive and make meaning in a brutal world. As he later said, "right prior to the record *Nebraska*, I was deep into O'Connor," and he clearly understood what she offered:

> There was something in those stories of hers that I felt captured a certain part of the American character that I was interested in writing about. They were a big, big revelation. She got to the heart of some part of meanness that she never spelled out, because if she spelled it out you wouldn't be getting it. It was always at the core of every one of her stories-the way that she'd left that hole there, that hole that's inside of everybody. There was some dark thing-a compo-

nent of spirituality-that I sensed in her stories, and that set me off
exploring characters of my own. (Percy)

Certainly, *Nebraska* allows the reader to feel the meanness of the human soul, especially when that soul is ravaged by poverty, loneliness,
and hopelessness.

Born in the USA, the album that followed *Nebraska* in 1984, was
inspired by Ron Kovic's *Born on the Fourth of July*, a powerful memoir
of the Vietnam War. Kovic told the tale of being a kid growing up in the
fifties and being taught to revere war heroes and to believe in his country's leaders and causes. His unquestioning patriotism brought him to
Vietnam, where he lost both of his legs. Paralyzed, Kovic was ignored
and mistreated once he returned home, just like so many veterans of a
war that many did not believe in and that we could not hope to win.
Springsteen used "Born in the USA" to make sure that people could not
forget about the veterans who were strewn across the American landscape and that no other generation of boys would be brainwashed into
blindly trusting a government that would so carelessly lead them into
war. As he wrote in the song, too many veterans had "nowhere to run"
and "nowhere to go." Springsteen has remained steadfastly determined
to do everything that he can through his music to ensure that this does
not happen again.

Other notable literary influences on Springsteen include John Steinbeck, Walker Percy, and Philip Roth. Springsteen was impressed with
Steinbeck's willingness to risk himself as a writer to help others, and he
was especially taken with John Ford's film interpretation of *The Grapes
of Wrath*. In 1995, Springsteen wrote *The Ghost of Tom Joad*, which
functions in part as an homage to Steinbeck and Ford in its dedication
to exposing the difficulties faced by present-day immigrants. The essays
of Walker Percy were important to several of Springsteen's songs in the
early nineties: "I think about the part in the essay 'The Man on the
Train' where [Percy] talks about alienation. He says the truly alienated
man isn't the guy who's despairing and trying to find his place in the
world. It's the guy who just finished his twentieth Earl Stanley Gardner
Perry Mason novel. That is the lonely man! That is the alienated man!
So you could say, similarly, the guy who just saw the fifth Batman
picture, he's the alienated man" (Percy). One can hear this most vividly
in "57 Channels" on the 1992 *Human Touch* album. In the song, a man

shoots his television and is arrested for disturbing the peace. When the judge asks for a defense, the man just says, "Fifty-seven channels and nothing on." The judge responds, "I can see by your eyes friend you're just about gone." Finally, there is Roth, whose *American Pastoral, I Married a Communist*, and *The Human Stain* "just knocked me on my ass. To be [in his 60s] making work that strong and so full of revelations about love and emotional pain—man, that's the way to live your artistic life: Sustain, sustain, sustain" (Tucker). This is exactly what Springsteen continued to do in the first decade of the twenty-first century. In 2012, at the age of sixty-three, he released *Wrecking Ball* with its powerful track "We Take Care of Our Own," in which the speaker has "been knocking on the door that holds the throne." Getting no satisfaction, he decides that "wherever this flag is flown, we take care of our own." No doubt, Springsteen will continue reading and performing in an attempt to take care of those who will listen.

THE POWER OF SOCIAL AND POLITICAL EVENTS

By the mideighties, Springsteen had moved from being a deeply introspective writer to an artist dedicated to "being introspective but not autobiographical." He recognized that "it wasn't until I felt like I had a stable life in that area that I was driven to write more outwardly—about social issues" (Percy). By the early nineties, Springsteen enjoyed that stability and has dedicated the last two decades to making his career a study in the type of social and political activism that he had begun to practice as early as 1979, when he participated in the Musicians United for Safe Energy concert at Madison Square Garden. Springsteen has continued to use his music to battle nuclear energy over the years. On September 20, 1981, Springsteen played the first of what would be many benefit shows for Vietnam veterans in Los Angeles. By 1984, Springsteen had adopted the cause of the homeless; starting with the *Born in the USA* tour, he began dedicating proceeds and fan contributions from each concert to food banks in the city in which he was playing. The practice continues to this day. In 1984, he participated in Michael Jackson's "We Are the World" project, as well as Bob Geldof's "Do They Know It's Christmas" recording to help fight hunger in Ethiopia. In 1985, he helped Steven Van Zandt with his hit song "Sun City" and supported the boycott of Sun City, a resort town in South Africa whose profitability continued to make apartheid possible.

Throughout the nineties, Springsteen continued to perform several benefit concerts every year to raise awareness for underrepresented groups or individuals at risk. For instance, in 1998 he arranged a Come Together benefit for Sgt. Patrick King and his family (a police officer killed in the line of duty). This type of practice has only increased in the new century. There are too many concerts to mention, but a few examples illustrate his commitment to serving those in need. In 2000, he performed at the first Light of Day concert to fight Parkinson's disease. He has performed at all twelve of the Light of Day Foundation's fundraisers. In 2004, he volunteered his services for the flood victims of Hurricane Ivan. In 2008, Springsteen went to bat to save the Count Basie Theater in Red Bank, New Jersey, one of many concerts that he has played in the last fifteen years to help save or restore local landmarks. In recent years, Springsteen has focused on helping children's causes. In 2009, for instance, he played the Concert for Autism as well as the Bridge School Benefit to help special-needs children, another event in which he now participates annually.

Springsteen's commitment to social justice has informed his studio efforts since *Darkness on the Edge of Town* told the story in 1978 of people who, despite their hard work and dedication, never achieved the American Dream. Certainly, he had people from his hometown whom he knew and loved in mind when he wrote *The River* and *Nebraska*: "I went back to where I was from, and I looked into that world and those lives, which I understood was only tangentially going to be my life from there on in. But if I was dedicated to it, and if I thought hard enough about it, and if I put in my time, I could tell those stories well. And that's what I did" (DeCurtis). He did it not only to give them a voice but to encourage Americans to demand that their leaders address racism, class inequality, and unfair economic policies that held back so many people. The same can be said of *Born in the USA* and his three-decade quest to make sure that Vietnam veterans are treated with dignity. In "Streets of Philadelphia" (1994), Springsteen drew awareness to the ugliness of the discrimination against gays and lesbians in a way that powerfully affected many of his listeners. As mentioned, *The Ghost of Tom Joad* (1995), released in a time of growing anti-immigrant sentiment, is dedicated to reminding Americans that we are all descended from immigrants and that current immigrants deserve respect and humane treatment.

In *The Rising* (2002), Springsteen confronted terrorism in a way that gave courage and hope to the victims without demonizing the perpetrators. The album remains one of a handful of artistic voices of reason that stood in marked contrast to less measured, emotional responses by government officials. Of course, the worst of those responses were the wars in Iraq and Afghanistan, which inspired Springsteen to write some of the songs on *Devils & Dust* (2005) and *Magic* (2007). As he confirmed in a 2009 interview, "we've lived through a nightmare . . . in the past eight years here. We had a historically blind administration who didn't take consideration of the past; thousands and thousands of people died, lives were ruined and terrible, terrible things occurred because, there was no sense of history, no sense that the past is living and real" (Hagan). Songs such as "Devils & Dust," "Gypsy Biker," "Devil's Arcade," and "Livin' in the Future" were all written to make sure that such historical amnesia never happens again. Indeed, it was his deep desire that no Americans die in unjust, illogical wars and that all Americans have a reasonable chance to partake of the promises of the American Dream that prompted Springsteen to use his music to campaign for Barack Obama in 2008. As he said from the stage at an Obama rally, "I spent most of my life as a musician measuring the distance between the American dream and American reality. For many . . . the distance between that dream and their reality has never been greater or more painful. I believe Senator Obama has taken the measure of that distance in his own life and work. I believe he understands in his heart the cost of that distance in blood and suffering in the lives of everyday Americans. I believe as president he would work to bring that dream back to life" (Hagan). In *Working on a Dream* (2009), *The Promise* (2010), and *Wrecking Ball* (2012), Springsteen continued to use his art to keep his version of the American promise alive for future generations. As he said in 2008, "I don't know about you, but I want my country back, I want my dream back. Now is the time to . . . roll up our sleeves and come on up for the rising" (Hagan).

2

THOSE ROMANTIC YOUNG BOYS

Reviving the Quest in the 1970s

The quest for fulfillment is central to the great American myth. The idea that it is our inalienable right to pursue—and ostensibly obtain—life, liberty, and happiness is the central premise of one of our most sacred documents. It is a sentiment that followed naturally from the theology and spirit of the Europeans who came to America in the seventeenth century. The Puritan belief that God had given them the task of establishing the new world as a city on a hill combined nicely with the Protestant work ethic that promised divine blessing in exchange for keeping one's shoulder to the wheel. Manifest destiny, the rags-to-riches tales of Horatio Alger, and the idea that it is each new generation's right to exceed the material wealth and station of its parents are all manifestations of this notion that we have a right to be fulfilled, a notion that is so well known throughout the world that it has motived wave after wave of immigrants for over two centuries.

Yet, by the 1970s, this part of America's mythic foundation seemed to be crumbling, and it is therefore not surprising that so much of Bruce Springsteen's music in the first half of the decade features young, often desperate characters trying to escape their circumstances in the quest for fulfillment. Typified by his epic *Born to Run* (1975) and originally anchored in his troubled upbringing and the bleak cultural landscape of the decade, this mythos remains an important part of his music today. This deep longing for fulfillment, though rooted in different personal

and historical circumstances in each decade of his career, is for Springsteen the basic human condition of the contemporary age. Perhaps this
is why so many people have identified with him and his music.

In truth, one might argue that Springsteen's popularity in the 1970s
was due in part to his uncanny ability to resurrect faith in the possibility
of fulfillment during a decade in which the quest for the American
Dream seemed all but lost for many young people. The seventies were
characterized by social implosion, political corruption, a loss of national
prestige, and, perhaps most important, deep economic recession and
inflation that made the economic booms of the fifties and sixties a
distant memory. As Bruce Schulman writes, "by 1970 the great
American ride had stalled" (9). Things only got worse. Adreas Killen
confirms, "By any standard, 1973 marked a genuine low point in U.S.
history" (4). As unemployment soared, "people's faith in their political
and professional leaders waned," spreading "disillusionment about the
competence of the dominant institutions of society" (Berkowitz 6). Influential critic Christopher Lasch claimed in his landmark work *The
Culture of Narcissism* that "American confidence has fallen to a low
ebb," driven ever lower by "defeat in Vietnam, economic stagnation,
and the impending exhaustion of natural resources" (xiii). The bountiful
years of the two decades that followed World War II were over. Stephanie A. Slocum-Schaffer writes, "By the time of the early 1970s, the
suspicion was already growing that the golden era was ending, and there
was a pervasive sense that something was deeply and terribly wrong"
(203). Even the musical landscape seemed atrophied, with the joyous
early rock 'n' roll of the Elvis era and the powerful folk singers of the
sixties having been replaced by punk, new wave, generic corporate rock,
and the intellectually and spiritually barren world of disco. It was
against this uncertain background that Bruce Springsteen made his
mark in the 1970s as an artist who, for some, rescued rock 'n' roll and
breathed life into the fading mythos of the American quest.

THE GHOST OF HOLDEN CAULFIELD

Bruce Springsteen grew up in the halcyon days of the 1950s, what some
Americans tend to remember nostalgically as the "golden age" of the
twentieth century. There is some reason to think of the fifties this way.

Parents buying one of Bill Levitt's mass-produced houses or eating out at a new restaurant chain called McDonald's did so in the context of some terrible memories. The collapse of the stock market in October 1929 marked the beginning of two decades of suffering. The fiscal downturn of the Great Depression was exacerbated by the Dust Bowl (1934–1936), one of the worst ecological disasters in American history. With the country already reeling from the full brunt of the financial collapse, the Japanese bombed Pearl Harbor in 1941, pulling the United States into World War II. By the conflict's end in 1945, over 400,000 Americans had been killed. Even the families who did not lose a loved one in battle felt the pain of wartime shortages and rationing, whose sting was all the harsher on the heels of the depression.

Americans in the 1950s, then, were psychologically ready for good things to happen. In many ways, good things did. The war, for all its hardships, jump-started the sluggish economy. The country's industries revved up during and after the war while the infrastructure of Europe was in ruins. With the United States' chief competitor on the sideline, America found itself the world's dominant power. The automobile and aviation industries soared. Fueled by low mortgage rates for returning soldiers and new low-cost, prefab homes, the housing market exploded. That meant a windfall for the construction business. Of course, all the small businesses that supported these larger industries also benefited, and the increased power of unions ensured that American workers enjoyed wages and benefits that would place many of them in the growing ranks of the middle class. The unemployment rate dipped to record lows. The nation's gross national product rose from near $200 billion in 1940 to over $300 billion in 1950 and over $500 billion in 1960 (Dunar 167). Eventually, the Marshall Act of 1948 supplied aid to rebuild Europe, resulting in healthy markets for U.S. goods by the mid-1950s. Truly, the hardships of the depression seemed a world away.

Not only did more Americans feel financially secure, but they also had more consumer choices on which to spend their money. This was largely the result of advances in technology, and, without a doubt, the two most important investments for most people were houses and cars. For people displaced from their homes and land by the events of the thirties, home ownership was a top priority. Low-cost homes grouped in new areas called "suburbs" made many Americans first-time homeowners. Mass production combined with technological innovation to give families plenty of domestic appliances with which to fill their homes. In particular, the television made its presence felt, and families gathered in living rooms to watch upbeat shows such as *Lassie, Father Knows Best*, and *The Adventures of Ozzie and Harriet*, programs that radiated images of health, wealth, and happiness, everything that Americans coming out of a war and a depression wanted. A growing number of housewives, allegedly as happy as June Cleaver from *Leave It to Beaver*, benefited from microwaves, Tupperware, Teflon pans, and newly re-modeled and affordable refrigerators, ovens, dishwashers, and vacuum cleaners. Kids enjoyed portable record players to use in their rooms, and record sales boomed. As David Halberstam writes, "Shopping and buying were to become major American pastimes as the ripple effect of the new affluence started to be felt throughout the economy" (144).

The automobile, suddenly affordable for the average family, dramat-ically changed American life as well. Fast-food restaurants, shopping malls, motels and hotels, rest stops, and drive-in theaters were only a few of the new businesses that sprung to life as the result of this new-found mobility. The automobile industry dominated American life, en-suring that millions of American workers could enter the middle class, and the Federal-Aid Highway Act of 1954 put thousands of people to work building a transportation network that would allow car owners access to the open road. Andrew J. Dunar writes, "The automobile permeated the daily lives of Americans in ways few could have antici-pated, enabling people to shop, eat, and even worship from their auto-mobiles" (170). The car represented the freedom and sense of possibil-ity in which so many Americans reveled as they glided through a decade in which "the automobile represented far more than transportation. It signified power, sex, freedom, and technology" (Salamone 54). The American quest for fulfillment was alive and well.

Yet, as much as this happiness was psychologically soothing, it was, to some extent, a veneer that masked several problems with which a generation beaten up by the depression and World War II was not ready to grapple. First, the economic renaissance didn't positively affect everyone. Families such as the Springsteens struggled to get by, often just barely making enough to pay the bills. In many ways, the Spring-steens of the world suffered even more because they had to watch so many of their contemporaries reaping the benefits of an American Dream that always seemed to be just out of their reach. In addition, women and minorities were either ignored or assigned lesser cultural roles. African Americans, for instance, remained second-class citizens, a condition very difficult to accept in the wake of the promise of the Harlem Renaissance and a war fought to end racially motivated genocide. Television news coverage of the violence that met Rosa Parks's effort to integrate the busing industry in Alabama, the 1955 trial of young Emmett Till's murderers in Mississippi, and Elizabeth Eckford's attempt to walk to a formerly all-white school in Little Rock, Arkansas, in 1957 reminded the nation that all was not well. Some white Americans tried to ignore the signs, but two hundred years of racial discrimination were about to catch up to a country whose fundamental creed is that we are all created equal.

Not only was the civil rights movement just around the corner, but the women's movement and the second wave of feminism were coming with it. So many of the television shows and advertisements of the era featured women who were supposedly fulfilled as wives and mothers who cooked, cleaned, and took care of their families with a sense of joy usually connoted with Dickensian heroines. Yet, many women were not happy being relegated to these roles, especially those who had been a critical part of the workforce during the war. A growing number of women wanted to pursue their education and career goals; in short, they wanted to be equal partners in the American quest. Many men were surprised and confused by this, but the powerful sales figures and cultural impact of Betty Friedan's *The Feminine Mystique* in 1963 made the burgeoning gender tension hard to ignore. Interesting is the fact that Friedan's groundbreaking work was preceded by Sloan Wilson's *The Man in the Gray Flannel Suit* (1955), a best-selling novel whose popularity revealed that even middle- to upper-class white men felt a discontentment with a lifestyle that, though filled with privilege, was also materialistic, conformist, and spiritually barren.

In truth, the pleasant television images and frenzied buying were covering not only a great deal of dissatisfaction but also a significant amount of fear that made the possibility of fulfillment seem less tangible. In 1945, the United States ended World War II by dropping atomic bombs on Japan. By the end of the decade, American forces were stuck in another war, this time in Korea with the forces of communism. The Cold War, as it would come to be known, pitted the United States and its democratic, capitalist allies against the USSR and its communist and socialist partners. Senator Joseph McCarthy of Wisconsin ignited the "red scare" in 1950 when he insisted that communists had infiltrated every walk of American life, including the government. Though his accusations were found to be baseless, the good citizens of the fifties were alarmed by his crusade. When the United States pulled out of Korea without winning, the tension worsened. Then, in 1957, the Soviets launched *Sputnik*, the first satellite to orbit Earth. When the United States tried and failed to emulate the Russian experiment, fears escalated that America was losing the space race. The dangerous communists had the capability of carrying missiles into American airspace, and the United States could not respond. People feared atomic attack, and the bomb shelter industry thrived. Certainly, hiding beneath the ground in one's backyard must have seemed antithetical to the quest for fulfillment to some Americans.

The red scare and rigid gender and racial norms deepened the already suffocating conformity that defined the decade. Underneath the "perfect"-looking families and full church pews brimmed a considerable amount of closeted behaviors trying to find expression. For instance, in an age of unquestioning patriotism, the military draw in Korea, as well as the unclear reasons why the "police action" was fought in the first place, caused more Americans to question the role and power of their military. In addition, the war caused some Americans to lose faith in their government—that, plus the Salem-like mentality of the McCarthy purges and several scandals, such as that of the United Fruit Company (1953), in which a company, whose investors included several prominent government officials, overthrew a democratic government in Guatemala in favor of a military dictatorship to fend off competition (Halberstam 374). Socially, the fifties were supposedly a moral time characterized by sexual purity, but the Kinsey reports (1948 and 1953) made it clear that sexual experimentation, including masturbation, premarital sex, adultery, and even homosexuality, were far more common than what would first appear (272–281). Likewise, family values ruled the public sphere, but male readers, many of them "family men," made Hugh Hefner a millionaire by buying his pornographic magazine *Playboy*, which started showing up at homes and offices in plain brown wrapping in 1955. Appearances belied reality at every turn. In the *Saturday Evening Post*, America was populated by small towns with a pure, Rockwellian feel; yet, Grace Metalious's *Peyton Place*, a novel about the unseemly happenings in a small New Hampshire village, revealed what most small town residents already knew: the public images of the fifties, replete with perfect, happy families, were very different from the private realities of sexual experimentation, immorality, gambling, alcoholism, unhappy marriages, and angry, sometimes spoiled children (576–80).

The American Dream of the fifties, then, was a material dream borne out of the desperation of the depression and the war years and made possible by the postwar economic boom. It was a conformist dream, made so by fears of communism, possible racial and gender changes, and not measuring up to public societal ideals. And it was a dream bolstered by religion: church attendance soared, and houses of worship became centers for promoting patriotism, democracy, and capitalism. However, Americans would find out that there is a cost for using Christianity to bolster a secular dream whose tenets violate the foundations of that religion. In the end, the dream was stifling, discriminatory, and spiritually vacuous. Not surprising, young people were the ones to express their dissatisfaction with the dominant fifties culture. Not simply content to enjoy newfound prosperity like their parents— who had been so scarred by the events of the thirties and forties that they were willing to accept the shaky foundations of the fifties dream in exchange for financial security—some of the country's youth began to demand justification for why things were the way they were. Why did women have to be housewives? Why were blacks still being denied access to jobs? Why did we go to war in Korea? Why was it immoral to listen to Elvis Presley? If things are so good, why are my friends and I so unhappy?

When there seemed to be no reasonable answers, discontentment began to move toward revolt. Hollywood captured some of this anger with a slew of films about juvenile delinquents and angst-ridden youths, the most famous of which is *Rebel without a Cause* (1955), which features James Dean as a privileged yet alienated high school student who cannot find a place in a society that he sees as being counterfeit. Perhaps the most famous rebel of the age is Holden Caulfield, the troubled antihero of J. D. Salinger's *Catcher in the Rye* (1951), whose disillusionment with what he sees as a phony society pushes him toward a mental breakdown. What was truly disturbing for parents of the fifties was how many of their kids identified with Holden. If Holden represented high school angst, the beat poets were his college and postcollege counter-parts. Gregory Corso, William Burroughs, Gary Snyder, and Lawrence Ferlinghetti denounced the dreams of their parents and revived the romantic poetic quest for spiritual insight through verse. Allen Gins-berg spoke for many in his 1955 poem *Howl*, in which he wrote, "I saw the best minds of my generation destroyed by madness, starving hyster-ical naked, dragging themselves through the negro streets at dawn look-ing for an angry fix" (9). In 1957, Jack Kerouac produced the "bible of the beat generation," *On the Road*, in which Sal Paradise eschews the hollow American Dream to search for the great "IT," the spiritual "fix" that Ginsberg had referred to two years before. Thousands of young Americans hit the road, looking for an alternative to their parents' ver-sion of the American Dream.

In the end, discrimination, forced conformity, fear, insincerity, and a lack of spiritual foundation made the fifties zeitgeist unsustainable. Women and minorities would demand their place at the table of power; Americans would question their government and demand accountabil-ity from their institutions; and young people would demand authenticity and philosophic justification for social mores and political decisions. Holden Caulfield wasn't going to go away. The 1960s were on the way.

A GENERATION WITHOUT THE WORDS

That there were plenty of Caulfields, Ginsbergs, Steinems, and Eck-fords became evident in the sixties. If the 1950s saw a growing restless-ness with the American Dream and the institutions that sustained it, the 1960s brought a spirit of revolution to the proceedings. The 1950s gave America Patti Paige with her 1953 number-one song "How Much Is That Doggie in the Window?" The immaculate blond appeared on tele-vision beautifully coiffed, in pearls, a mink stole, and a fancy suit to sing her hit song about wanting a cuddly puppy to give to a well-dressed cute little boy. Only three years later, Paige was supplanted by Elvis, who shook his hips to the strains of "You Ain't Nothing but a Hound Dog" on the *Ed Sullivan Show*. Elvis was in a suit and sported a clean-cut look, but his thrusting pelvis and loud guitar were clear signals that change was brewing. Still, if the early Elvis marked a desire to break free of fifties conformity, only ten years later several artists revealed a

Ginsberg-like desire to smash all conventions and forge a new narrative: The year 1966 saw the Beatles' "Nowhere Man," the Rolling Stones' "Paint It Black," Bob Dylan's "Rainy Day Woman," the Troggs' "Wild Thing," and the Who's "My Generation." Long, disheveled hair, scraggly beards, earrings, faded jeans, ripped shirts, flamboyant hats, and dirty boots had replaced the clean, scrubbed look of the previous decade. The lyrics were now political, angry, and foreboding. By the following year, a raspy-voiced, free-spirited singer from Texas named Janis Joplin made Patti Paige look like a relic from a bygone era. When Joplin covered "Ball 'n' Chain" at the Monterey Pop Festival in June 1967, it was clear that something dramatic had occurred in American culture. The festival was a seminal event, attracting over 100,000 people, many of whom were taking drugs, drinking, protesting, and having open, casual sex. With her wildly unkempt hair falling in her ruddy face, Joplin's voice strained while her sweaty, shaking body convulsed to the lyrics: "I don't understand why half the world is crying, man, when the other half of the world is still crying, too." When she forlornly screeched, "I can't get it together," lamenting that life in America descends on you like "a ball, oh daddy, and a chain," she spoke for many of her generation who wanted to search for a new way of living, apart from the suffocating narrative of their parents.

Indeed, the young people who set out on a quest to blaze new trails in the sixties were remarkably successful in many ways. The social and political upheaval resulted in important positive changes. The feminist movement, for example, produced increased gender equality in almost every facet of American life. Even before Betty Friedan published *The Feminine Mystique* in 1963, legalization of the birth control pill in 1961 gave women unprecedented control of their reproductive rights. Two years later, Helen Gurley Brown released *Sex and the Single Girl*. A decade after that, the feminist movement had enough political muscle to influence *Roe v. Wade*, a landmark Supreme Court decision that resulted in legalized abortion. Sexual independence symbolized women's gains in other areas. By the early seventies, women had made significant advances in the workforce, integrated every Ivy League school, ensured access to athletic opportunity via Title IX legislation, flexed their political muscle with the establishment of agencies such as the Equal Employment Opportunity Commission (1964), challenged religious orthodoxy, and changed divorce laws to allow greater freedom from domestic constraints.

In truth, equality in general was the defining quest of the sixties, and it was powerfully manifested in the civil rights movement. Parks, Till, and Eckford were three of many individuals whose sacrifices paved the way for the Civil Rights Act of 1964, a landmark piece of legislation that effectively removed all legal and de facto measures intended to prevent African Americans and other minorities from voting. The act also out-lawed all discrimination based on race, ethnicity, or religion in busi-nesses engaged in any interstate commerce, in public facilities, or in places of employment. It encouraged desegregation of public schools and prevented any agency that received federal funds from engaging in discriminatory practice. Finally, the act gave the federal government and its acting agencies the power to enforce all civil rights legislation, including making sure that all defendants would be granted a fair trial regardless of race, an important feature that empowered civil rights workers, whose actions often landed them in front of biased judges and juries. It is hard to overestimate the influence of the civil rights move-ment. It hardly eliminated racism, but it established the institutional infrastructure that would gradually lead toward increased racial equal-ity.

This emphasis on equality and reform benefited many other groups as well. Gays and lesbians made significant advances and by 1970 were able to hold the first LGBT Pride Parade in New York City. The Archi-tectural Barriers Act (1968) was one of several pieces of legislation that advanced the rights of the disabled, in this case making sure that no new building could be erected using federal funding that did not fully guarantee handicapped access. President Johnson declared a "war on poverty" and introduced the Social Security Act of 1965, which enacted Medicare and Medicaid programs to help the elderly and welfare recip-ients gain access to health care. Congress increased the minimum wage to help the poor and created Head Start to help low-income and "at risk" children compete in school. The Immigration and Nationality Ser-vices Act of 1965 ended quotas based on nationality, allowing thousands of impoverished people to pursue greener pastures in the United States. Finally, several pieces of legislation were passed to protect the environment, ensuring that national lands and historic places would be protected and that industries would have to observe stricter standards regarding pollution and the disposal of hazardous waste.

All these advances were made possible, in part, because of an economy that continued to roar. The construction industry boomed as the demand for houses soared. Automobile companies, buoyed by high demand and low oil prices, made annual record profits. A sign of things to come, the computer industry began to flex its muscles as integrated circuits and easier programming languages paved the way for the rise of the computer. Real wages grew steadily, and unemployment rates fell as quickly as the gross national product rose. Inflation was a concern, but rising prices were overshadowed by the fact that by the end of the decade, the average American wage had increased by 50 percent (Fischer and Hout 117). Thus, while the social constrictions, complacency, philosophic banality, and homogeneity of the 1950s American Dream were attacked in the sixties, people continued to enjoy material prosperity. Life seemed promising in the United States.

Yet, if life was so good, why was some of the most popular music of the sixties so angry and confrontational? Why was Bob Dylan singing "Blowin' in the Wind" (1963), and why were so many young people responding? Why did the Beatles move from being four clean-cut boys in suits playing "Love Me Do" to being discontent, long-haired Eastern mystics playing "Revolution" and "Nowhere Man"? Why did so many privileged young Americans attend the countercultural festivals in Monterey and Woodstock, embracing the drug culture of psychedelic rock and the free-love philosophy of hippies grooving to the sounds of the Grateful Dead?

Perhaps the reason lies in the uncertainty and tumultuous nature of the changes that characterized the decade, as much as it does in the dissatisfaction of young people with the conformist, exclusionary nature of their parents' vision for the country. For example, while from an objective twenty-first-century perspective, the sixties offered tremendous advancements toward racial equality, those gains were frightening for many white Americans living in the middle of the decade's tense action. Southern whites watched their region embarrassed time and again on national television via news coverage of vitriolic reactions to a variety of local protests, such as the Greensboro sit-ins in 1960, to several prominent attempts to desegregate schools, such as James Meredith's matriculation at the University of Mississippi in 1962, and to many freedom rallies, such as the march on Selma in 1965. Nationwide, many whites were unnerved by the rise of Malcolm X and the formation of the Nation of Islam, by the militaristic rhetoric of the Black Panther Party (1966), and by frantic race riots from Newark to Los Angeles. By the time that Martin Luther King Jr. was assassinated in Memphis in 1968, setting off riots across the nation, "white flight" from cities to all-white suburbs was well under way.

Likewise, although we now value the feminist changes of the sixties, much of Middle America was dismayed by the gender changes at the time. Many men were simply not ready to compete with women for college acceptances or jobs, to see women in positions of authority, to watch them run for office, or to marry women who would insist on domestic equality. Still, as threatened as people were by events such as Jeannette Rankin's symbolic burning of "tradition womanhood" in 1968, Americans were even more alarmed by the rise of the gay liberation movement, and many mothers and fathers no doubt blanched in front of their television sets as they watched coverage of the Stonewall riot in 1969 and the subsequent activities of the newly formed Gay Liberation Front, which commemorated the victims of Stonewall with one of several gay rights parades that took place in cites nationwide from 1969 to 1973.

Today, we remember the sixties for its emphasis on social reform, but many Americans living through the decade could see only chaos. Vietnam tore the nation apart. College campuses erupted with protests, and radical organizations, such as Students for a Democratic Society and the Weather Underground, promoted domestic terrorism as a way of stopping the war. The New Left promised radical action to promote social progress. Environmental groups did the same in the name of protecting Earth against the aggression of the capitalist, industrial machine. Violence marred politics, with one of the worst instances coming at the Democratic National Convention in 1968; hundreds were arrested as a nation watched the chaos on television. Perhaps the most devastating symbol of the trouble was the assassination of President John F. Kennedy in 1963, signaling the end of "Camelot." When Robert Kennedy was gunned down in 1968, it seemed to some like the nation was disintegrating.

Not only did the best defining narratives of the sixties carry an underside that terrified much of the nation, but even the young people who reveled in other experimental narratives weren't holding up very well. The most prominent example of this was the hippie movement. Espousing the virtues of free love and psychedelic drugs, thousands of young Americans made the journey to San Francisco for the Summer of Love in 1967. Their impact was so powerfully felt that writer Joan Didion journeyed west to cover the hippie phenomenon. What she found was a sad sight. Under the romantic myths of happy kids eschewing the bonds of middle-class conventions for drug-induced enlightenment, sensual fulfillment, and simple communal living was a sea of "children" who were living out a dangerous story. In *Slouching toward Bethlehem*, Didion described the tragic situation of several kids who had come to San Francisco with flowers in their hair, only to find that free love resulted in emotional isolation and unwanted pregnancy, that drugs led to addiction and that there were more bad trips than good, and that communal living was a mirage behind which existed massive homelessness and poverty.

The insightful Didion not only chronicled the "hemorrhaging" but saw through the carnage and to the cause—that is, why the fantasy of the hippie quest was so attractive to American youth. Disenchanted with the material conformity and spiritual deadness of the American Dream of the fifties, students came face-to-face with a modern dilemma that there seemed to be no other productive narrative by which to live. Didion wrote, "At some point between 1945 and 1967 we had somehow neglected to tell these children the rules of the game we happened to be playing. Maybe we had stopped believing in the rules ourselves. . . . They are sixteen, fifteen, fourteen years old, younger all the time, an army of children waiting to be given the words" (123). Armed with a consumerist quest for fulfillment that they allegedly did not want and surrounded by a plethora of narratives that seemed to produce as much trauma as peace, is it any wonder that many Americans felt a growing sense of estrangement as the sixties waned?

DARK HEART OF A DREAM

Thus, by the time that the 1970s rolled around, plenty of young people felt an undefined sense of alienation. Literary critic John Barth noticed a similar feeling among authors, a palpable sense of having tried so many false centers of meaning that meaning itself seemed impossible to find, a condition that he termed "exhaustion." Loosely applied to the generation coming of age in the late sixties and early seventies, this can be understood as a general feeling that the promise of the American Dream of the fifties and the progressivism of the sixties had faded into a series of sobering events.

For young people in the early 1970s, Vietnam topped the list. The war had dragged on for over a decade when, on May 4, 1970, Ohio National Guardsmen shot and killed four unarmed students at an anti-war rally at Kent State University. The event symbolized the rift between young Americans and the government that was using them to wage an incomprehensible fight that seemed to benefit only the military–industrial complex about which President Dwight Eisenhower had warned as early as 1961. While it was true that by December 1972 the fighting was winding down, it was equally true that the war had taken its toll on a generation of young men and that the United States was going to be on the losing end of things. Scenes from an unwinnable, unpopular war were a grizzly staple of the nightly news, as were countless protests that ignited the passions of angry students from Columbia to Berkeley. Almost everyone seemed to have a friend that was killed or wounded in the war. Springsteen himself had to deal with the drummer of his first band, Bart Haynes, dying in the war, and he did everything that he could to stay clear of the draft. Many young people felt a deep sense of betrayal by their government, as Springsteen confirms: "It wasn't until . . . the seventies that the awareness of the type of war it was, what it meant, the way it felt to be a subversion of all the true American ideals, twisted the country inside and out" (Marsh 307).

The distrust of the government and the generation who guided its policies was augmented by ugly political scandals. In June 1972, five men burglarized the Watergate building in Washington, DC, in hopes of finding information that would be used against the Democratic Party to ensure the reelection of President Richard Nixon. They were arrested, and Nixon tried to cover up his involvement in the crime. After repeatedly lying to the country, Nixon finally resigned in 1974. This came on the heels of the resignation of Nixon's vice president, Spiro Agnew, on charges of tax evasion and bribery. Many Americans were even more disturbed when, in September 1974, newly sworn-in President Gerald Ford pardoned Nixon, exempting him from any further prosecution. Now an angry nation—many of whose citizens already felt betrayed—would be denied the justice that it felt it deserved.

Yet, as angry as young people were at their government and as disenchanted as they may have felt regarding the waning of sixties idealism, they were even more dismayed by a worsening economy, which made the one part of their parents' American Dream that many of them actually liked—namely, upward financial mobility—seem out of reach. A number of factors caused the decline, including rising costs of production, which resulted in companies moving their manufacturing plants out of the country, a corresponding loss of jobs, and a rising unemployment rate. This played out against burgeoning international competition, especially from West Germany and Japan, whose resurgence was particularly felt in the automobile industry. Perhaps the biggest problem for the United States was OPEC (the Organization of the Petroleum Exporting Countries), whose oil embargoes caused a huge spike in gasoline prices. The rising prices increased operating costs even more for American industries, which passed on the costs to the average consumer. The resulting inflation combined with the surging unemployment rates to create a phenomenon known as "stagflation," and it left many people feeling bewildered. As Beth Bailey and David Farber confirm, "Americans during the 1970s commonly described their world and their future in a language of loss, limits and failure" (4).

It is no wonder, then, that so many of the most influential films of the seventies had dark storylines and desperate characters whose quests for fulfillment are buried under an avalanche of problems. One thinks of *Carnal Knowledge* (1971), the story of two emotionally stunted men unable to form any lasting relationships; *Deliverance* (1972), a frightening tale of American businessmen trying to reconnect with nature on a pleasant vacation only to be terrorized by in-bred locals; and *Mean Streets* (1973), a tale of young men with no prospects who try to make it in the New York mafia with devastating consequences. The year 1973 also offered *Serpico*, starring Al Pacino and featuring the problems of a working-class police officer trying to make ends meet as he struggles in an underpaid, corrupt police force, and *Badlands*, a macabre tale of two South Dakota teens who, seeing nothing profitable in their future and no ultimate meaning to life, embark on a cross-country killing spree. Al Pacino also starred in *Dog Day Afternoon* (1975), the story of an ill-fated bank robbery that sends the protagonist, Sonny, to prison, while his wife and kids are left to subsist on welfare, and Robert De Niro starred in *Taxi Driver* (1976), perhaps the darkest film of the decade, in which De Niro's character is worn down by a meaningless, poverty-laden urban environment. Many critics feel that the defining film of the decade is *Saturday Night Fever* (1977), in which desperate friends facing a grim economic landscape escape into a disco lifestyle characterized by alcohol, drugs, indiscriminate sex, and pointless and dangerous behavior. The decade ended with films such as *Over the Edge* (1979), in which teenage rebellion threatens a planned community whose organizing parents can't understand the anger and alienation of their kids. Even several of the happier, popular films and television shows of the seventies, such as *American Graffiti* (1973) and *Happy Days* (1973–1984), were productions that nostalgically celebrated life in the fifties and early sixties, a time when happiness and meaning seemed attainable.

The state of rock 'n' roll seemed just as uncertain. In 1972, Don McLean's "American Pie" surged to the top of the charts as a powerful lament of the deaths of Buddy Holly, Richie Valens, and the Big Bopper in 1959, as well as the death of the innocent, upbeat, carefree rock 'n' roll they represented. In the view of many, great rock music truly had died in the early sixties, but at least it was replaced by thoughtful, powerful music from folk artists such as the Byrds, Buffalo Springfield, and Joni Mitchell. Bob Dylan captivated an age of protest and reform with songs such as "The Times They Are a Changin'" and "Like a Rolling Stone." Yet, by the early seventies, the power of folk rock had faded as well, and record producers such as John Hammond were in search of a new Dylan, someone to reinvent the genre. The rock world lost several promising musicians, including Joplin, Jimi Hendrix, and Jim Morrison. In the meantime, punk, new wave, and glam took over the rock scene, while disco emerged as a dominant musical form in the midseventies. Flashing lights, techno music, spiked hair, gender inversion, and simple self-indulgent lyrics replaced the socially conscious music of Dylan and his contemporaries. Rock 'n' roll had lost its vision for the future and seemed as lost as America itself. As Peter Carroll confirms, the musical environment of the early seventies suggested that "the only hopeful vision of the American future seemed to exist in the past" (71).

Into this musical wasteland and this sea of alienation and discouragement, where the quest for fulfillment seemed all but lost, came Bruce Springsteen, the Dylanesque, high-energy, working-class kid from New Jersey whose music acknowledged the harshness of life but insisted on the possibility of hope, even fulfillment. From the beginning, Springsteen acknowledged that things were tough all over, but he also believed that things could get better, that there was still an essential romance to life. "Blinded by the Light," the first song from his first album, *Greetings from Asbury Park, NJ* (1973), is the perfect tune for understanding his early popularity. The song's speaker, a "teenage diplomat," is thrown from one experience to another in which he encounters all kinds of quirky characters from "madman drummers bummers" to "some silicone sister" to "some kidnapped handicap." His road is uncertain, perhaps even dangerous. He has come of age, been born into the "light," and he is blinded, bewildered at the world he has inherited— just like many kids who came of age in the early 1970s. Yet, he will not retreat. The song has a playful quality: the light is a bit disorienting, just like the song's stream-of-consciousness lyrics, but the light is also "where the fun is." The listener feels like it's alright to be off balance; one can still play, still venture forth, still "cut loose like a deuce another runner in the night." Maybe something good will come out of it.

Many of the other songs on the album carry the same tension. In "Mary, Queen of Arkansas," Mary is compared to an old "hulk," but the true subject of the song, like so many of Springsteen's works, is a young man who has been beaten down by life and who exists on the brink of economic ruin. He admits that he is a "bastard," but he maintains that his love is still "redeeming." He is in bad shape, but inspired by Mary, he vows to continue the quest in Mexico, to "get a good job and start over again clean." The same young man appears in "For You," where he is "wounded deep in battle" but stands "like some soldier undaunted." His lover has abandoned him, but he is still loyal to her. "I came for you," he says, but "you did not need my urgency." She is beaten up and suicidal. "They're waiting for you at Bellevue," he says to her just before he reminds her of "when I found you broken on the beach." He knows that like many kids in the seventies, she "left to find a better reason than the one we were living for." Yet, he wants her. In his view, there is still hope for them to make it. He invites her into "my ambulance," and he admits that he needs her to "lick my sores." The forces of life may be pulling them apart, but the quest for romance remains intact: her "cloud line urges" him, and his "electric surges free." Even the speaker in "Does This Bus Stop at 82nd Street?"—encountering down-and-out bus drivers, Christmas criers, "dock workers," "tainted women in Vista-vision," "wizard imps," "sweat sock pimps," and "interstellar mongrel nymphs"—insists on taking Mary Lou's advice that "the dope is that there's still hope." The song ends with "Spanish Rose" throwing a "rose to some lucky young matador." In an age of skepticism, Springsteen didn't deny the ugliness; he just greeted his listeners as a fellow traveler with a message of hope.

The same can be said for his second album, *The Wild, the Innocent, and the E Street Shuffle* (1973). In "Incident on 57th Street," Spanish Johnny is berated as a "cheater" and a "liar." He is poor, with few friends and fewer possibilities and with a heart "that falls apart so easy." Yet, he doesn't relent. He is "dressed just like dynamite," and he is still able to connect with the dreamy, beautiful Jane. The listener can feel that their love is tenuous, but neither is willing to quit. When Johnny hears the whispers of the street "to make a little easy money tonight," his financial desperation propels him to go. But his love for Jane is evident, and he assures her that he'll meet her "tomorrow night on Lover's Lane." They may or may not make it long-term, but they may at least "walk until the daylight maybe." The characters are, like so many in the seventies, financially and spiritually starved. Yet, like Jack Kerouac's beatific Sal Paradise, they are beautiful in their hopeful, romantic desperation. To be sure, *The Wild* features some sobering songs, such as "Kitty's Back," where the local hero, Cat, has lost his girl, Kitty, to "a city dude." However, she has returned, and though his heart has been broken, he has to take her back. The potential reunion is not happy, and as Cat "sits back and sighs," he gasps, "What else can I do?" Yet, the lonely brokenness of "Kitty's Back" is balanced by the rollicking romance of "Rosalita," in which a young singer "liberates" his girlfriend from the clutches of her parents, who don't like him because he plays "in a rock 'n' roll band." They may not like him, but he has an ace up his sleeve. "A record company just gave me a big advance," he tells her, exhorting her to come down from her room and get into his car so that they can speed away to "a pretty little place in Southern California down San Diego way." Like so many kids in the seventies, they are poor and directionless, but he assures her that they will "look back on this and it will all seem funny." Soon, they will be in the golden land, where "they play guitars all night and day." From desolation will come the flowering of hope.

In 1975, Springsteen released *Born to Run*, the album that best exemplifies why he was so popular in the seventies. The album features characters such as "Eddie" and his friend, the unnamed speaker of the song. Contemporary listeners no doubt identified with the plight of Eddie and his friend, both of whom have no connections or prospects and feel alienated from the American mainstream. The friend asks Eddie to lend him "a few bucks" and "catch us a ride." They are down to their "last chance," and they have got themselves "out on that line." The friend is so desperate that he "took the radio and hocked it," and he is willing to risk everything for only "two grand," which is "practically sitting here in my pocket." The listener is left with the haunting feeling that the gambit won't work, that the powerful circumstances in which they live will overwhelm the two men. The same is true in the next song on the album, "Jungleland," a nearly ten-minute epic in which the "Magic Rat" drives "his sleek machine over the Jersey state line" to take a "stab at romance." In the end, the Rat's dreams are crushed, "his own dream guns him down." His lonely, powerless girl can only "shut out the bedroom light," and even though outside "the street's on fire in a real death waltz," no one will remember the Rat's death or the girl's sadness: "the poets down here don't write nothing at all, they just stand back and let it all be." The Rat and his girl, like Eddie and his friend, represented the unseen youth of the seventies: lonely, poor, victimized, philosophically unmoored, and adrift in a faceless, uncaring world. While the poets in "Jungleland" may not have recognized their pain, Bruce Springsteen did. "Meeting across the River" and "Jungleland" do not end happily, but listeners responded warmly, even passionately, for the same reason that J. D. Salinger's young readers responded to the troubled Holden Caulfield. When you are down and out and feel like you are not going to make it, it's nice to know that you are not alone and that someone understands and is empathetic with your plight.

Of course, Springsteen is more than simply sympathetic. He also offers a light in the darkness, a reason to continue the quest. This is especially evident in the album's two most defining songs: "Thunder Road" and "Born to Run." The former opens as a softer tune that features a young musician who, like "Roy Orbison singing for the lonely," is wooing a young woman named Mary. The listener senses a desperation that is similar to that in "Jungleland." The suitor has been turned away before, and he doesn't want to be turned away again; he says, "I just can't face myself alone again." He acknowledges that he's "no hero," admitting that the only feeble redemption that he can offer "is beneath this dirty hood." Mary herself is "scared." She's "no beauty," and they "ain't that young anymore." The song is littered with images of tattered dreams: Mary alone in her room studying her pain, "praying in vain for a savior to rise from these streets"; the "ghosts in the eyes of all the boys" whom she "sent away," which haunt the "dusty beach road in the skeleton frames of burned out Chevrolets"; Mary's graduation gown that "lies in rags at their feet"; and a "town full of losers" whose dreams have been mowed down by life in America in the 1970s. Yet, unlike that in "Jungleland," this musical hero will not die, and he can speak for himself. He "got this guitar and learned how to make it talk," and he has a voice. His "car's out back," and he invites her to "take that long walk from your front porch to my front seat." He may not know where he is going, but "there's magic in the night," and he is ready to undertake a romantic quest for fulfillment. "The night's busting open" and "heaven's waitin' on down the tracks" for those who have the courage and faith to "make it real." By the end of the song, one believes that the singer is indeed "pulling out of here to win" and that Mary will go with him, with the wind blowing through her hair after she trades in her "wings on some wheels." This is not merely recognition of the bleakness of small town life in America in the seventies; this is a promise, which borders on the prophetic, that the bleakness can be transcended.

If "Thunder Road" advances its narrative of hope in softer tones, "Born to Run" is loud and aggressive, powered by brash guitar riffs and some of the most dynamic drumming in music history. Yet, the message is the same. The landscape of the song is populated with young people who "sweat it out on the streets of a runaway American Dream." They are trapped in an economic and philosophic nightmare, but at night they are "sprung from their cages," and they ride "through mansions of glory in suicide machines." The speaker tells his girl, Wendy, that "this town rips the bones from your back," asserting that "it's a death trap, it's a suicide rap." Indeed, the kids in the song all seem trapped; they are "huddled on the beach in a mist," and although "the boys try to look so hard," one gets the feeling that they are merely passive victims waiting to be chewed up by the society in which they live. In a few years, they will be "the broken heroes on a last chance power drive," mentioned in the final stanza. Young people in the seventies related to this feeling and these images, and they would not have been surprised when the speaker tells Wendy that "we gotta get out while we're young" because "there's no place left to hide." Just as the young man will not leave Wendy behind, Springsteen would not leave his audience behind. Just as they did with "Thunder Road," millions of young Americans recognized that Springsteen understood how confined they felt, and they loved it when he concluded the song with such a resounding message of hope. For, though the speaker and Wendy may be "tramps," they will engage the quest for fulfillment together. They are "born to run," and run they will until they find out if "love is real." If they die, they will die in "an everlasting kiss." They will never quit until they get "to that place where" they "really wanna go," when they will "walk in the sun." That place is undefined, but the romantic nature of the quest remains intact for a generation of kids who had lost faith in the possibility of fulfillment.

Some might argue that Springsteen's first three albums do not have the thematic depth and specificity of many of his later works, but they are unmatched when it comes to innocence and romance. The landscapes of the albums are bleak and reminiscent of the barrenness felt by many young people in the 1970s, and the characters are ragged, beaten, and desperate. However, they are also unvanquished, noble, and hopeful, reminiscent of Walt Whitman or Sal Paradise. The albums address the underlying zeitgeist of those coming of age in the seventies in the wake of the faded American Dream of the 1950s and the divisive narratives of the 1960s. For those who could not get past the ugliness of Vietnam, Watergate, Kent State, unemployment lines, and devastating inflation, Springsteen said that the old hope of the quest was still alive. If you were in the audience in the early seventies, you knew that while things were tough, you were not alone. Mary, Eddie, the bus driver, the Rat, and all the other colorful interstellar mongrel nymphs and those whom they represented were with you. Along with Roy Orbison, Bruce Springsteen was singing for you, and you were invited to hop in the car and take part in his quest. Millions did.

3

STREETS OF FIRE

Working-Class Heroes

In the 1970s, Bruce Springsteen had all the makings of a spokesman for the working class. Not only was he a talented musician who could write unique, powerful lyrics, but he was also an artist who drew on his blue-collar background for material. Born in Long Branch, New Jersey, and raised down the road in Freehold, Springsteen grew up with parents who labored in low-paying jobs. He saw his father's anger at working long hours in a rug mill, and he felt his father's helplessness at not being able to capture the middle-class lifestyle of the fifties and sixties that he saw others enjoying all around him. As Springsteen would remember in "Used Cars," a dismal song that he wrote in the early eighties for the *Nebraska* album, "my dad, he sweats the same job from mornin' to morn," just to buy a used car from a condescending salesman. Living on South Street in a rundown house next to Ducky Slattery's service station, Springsteen knew what it meant to feel poor. The next line of the song goes, "Me, I walk the same dirty streets where I was born." Considering Springsteen's poor performance as a student, the fact that he dropped out of college without finishing a semester, and his struggle to make it as a musician living in poverty for years on the Jersey shore, it is not surprising that Springsteen understood the problems faced by people on the underside of the American Dream.

Even after releasing his commercially successful third album, *Born to Run*, in 1975, a work that launched his music into international circles for the first time, Springsteen still had money problems. His financial issues would be complicated by a lengthy lawsuit with his first manager, Mike Appel, who owned the recording rights to Springsteen's music. Unable to record in the studio for nearly two years, Springsteen made ends meet by touring. He saw a great deal of America, and by the time he settled the lawsuit out of court in May 1977, Springsteen was ready to sing about what he had seen. As it turned out, the economic difficulties faced by many young Americans in the seventies reminded him of those faced by the people with whom he had grown up in New Jersey. "The record was of its time," he said in a 2010 interview, referring to *Darkness on the Edge of Town.* "We had the late 70s recession, punk music had just come out, times were tough for a lot of the people I knew. And so I veered away from great bar band music or great singles music and veered towards music that I felt would speak of people's life experiences" (Cameron).

STATE OF THE UNION: 1978

By the time that Springsteen produced *Darkness on the Edge of Town* in 1978, the United States was reeling. The war in Vietnam, which had torn the nation apart, ended in failure in 1975, with American troops abandoning the South Vietnamese to the communists of the north. The loss of life and national prestige were exacerbated by the fact that the defeat came at the hands of a communist enemy backed by China and the Soviet Union. The Watergate scandal that led to the impeachment and resignation of President Richard Nixon in 1974, as well as the resignation of his vice president, Spiro Agnew, on tax evasion charges, further soured a nation that had become increasingly cynical about its government and uneasy about its place as the dominant world power.

Yet, no military or political condition affected working people as much as the deterioration of the once-powerful American economy. On the strength of cheap oil and diminished competition from European countries recovering from World War II, the productivity of the American worker increased at a healthy 3 percent annual rate between 1947 and 1970. Yet, by 1973, this figure had dropped to 1 percent, where it would remain for the rest of the decade. It was an ominous sign for the United States, whose working class had grown accustomed to a robust economy, replete with jobs with good pay and benefits. Complicating the matter was the fact that so many children had been born in the postwar decades. For instance, the number of births increased from 2.6 million in 1940 to 4.3 million in 1957. Many of these "baby boomers" were coming of age in the 1970s, and they expected to inherit the same lifestyle, or better, that what their parents had enjoyed, a lifestyle that hinged on American economic might. Yet, "instead of the boundless horizons they had been promised, Americans discovered that limits were popping up everywhere" (Slocum-Schaffer 203).

By 1973, it was clear that this large group of teens and twenty somethings were feeling the rug slip out from under their feet. Increased competition from cutting-edge industries in Europe and Japan combined with a sagging U.S. dollar to send the stock market into a nosedive. By 1974, the market had lost half its 1972 value. Industry flagged, and the United States became a net importer for the first time since the nineteenth century. Then, on October 6, 1973, Arab forces attacked Israel; the United States sided with the Israelis. OPEC immediately reacted with the first of two oil embargos in the decade. This resulted in a tremendous spike in oil prices that shocked the nation. The price of a gallon of crude escalated from $3 a barrel in 1970 to $31 per barrel near the end of the decade. Industries that were already struggling had to raise prices and cut costs to cope with skyrocketing energy prices. The result was a brutal combination of inflation and layoffs. As unemployment numbers exploded, dramatically rising from 4.8 percent late in 1973 to 8.3 percent in early 1975, the value of the dollar plummeted, and the cost of basic necessities went through the roof. Housing costs rose 50% from 1972 to 1975; the same rate of inflation applied to automobiles, gasoline, televisions, food, and nearly ever other product that Americans considered integral to the American Dream. Economists referred to this new reality as "stagflation," a cruel term coined to define the malaise suffered by the growing ranks of unemployed people with little money to spend on increasingly expensive goods. Working-class Americans fell out of the middle class by the thousands. Dan Berger writes, "The early 1970s were yet another slap in the face for working class Americans, whose children had done the majority of the fighting and dying in Southeast Asia" (215). Not only did autoworkers and machinists and bank tellers and thousands of other blue-collar workers across the nation watch their children die in Vietnam under the leadership of a corrupt government, but they also had to watch the survivors stand in unemployment lines, unable to find a place in the stagnant economy.

As the decade wore on, it became clear that the effects of the recession of 1973 were not going away anytime soon. Unemployment continued to plague the nation, and by 1978, consumer prices were rising at a 12 percent rate, as the value of the dollar plunged on the international market. Many Americans turned to credit cards to help them pay for their living expenses, resulting in alarming personal debts. As more people slipped from the ranks of the middle class, bankruptcies escalated, and many lost faith in the possibility of a hopeful future. Thomas Borstelmann writes, "The performance of the U.S. economy in the 1970s dismayed most Americans. Inflation, unemployment and declining real wages pulled the prospects of American workers downward, and the gap between rich and poor began to grow quickly" (53). Many baby boomers watched this reality play out before their eyes, the pain of their economic plight sharpened by the context of their childhood hopes. "Quite simply, the history of the 1970s was a history of a rapid succession of shocks to America that ushered in a politics of austerity. Suddenly, the word on every lip was 'scarcity'" (Slocum-Schaffer 203). Lengthy gas lines became the defining symbol of the age. Edward Berkowitz writes, "The long gas lines . . . provided an instant reminder of bad times, much like the cartloads of money being wheeled down the street during the rampant inflation of Weimar Germany" (56). The morale of the American working class was as low as it had been since the 1930s. "The 1970s were America's low tide. Not since the Depression had the country been so wracked with woe. Never—not even during the Depression—had American pride and self-confidence plunged deeper" (Frum 289).

Bruce Springsteen saw this reality play out in the lives of his family and friends. Now in his late twenties, he had become "more historically aware." Springsteen admitted, "I know what it's like not to be able to do what you want to do, because when I go home, that's what I see. It's not fun. . . . I see some of my best friends. They're living the lives of my parents in a certain kind of way. They got kids; they're working hard. . . . You can see something in their eyes. . . . I asked my friend, 'What do you do for fun?' 'I don't have any fun,' she says. She wasn't kidding" (Marsh 195). What he saw in their eyes was the sense of desperation and defeat that so many working-class people felt in the 1970s, and he wanted to give them a voice. He wanted to instill in them a "determination to break out of the vicious cycle of pain and futility that robs people of the best part of their lives" (197). Springsteen explained *Darkness* to journalist Tony Parsons in October 1978, "See, it couldn't be an innocent album like 'Born To Run' because things ain't like that for me anymore. The characters on the new album ain't kids, they're older— you been beat, you been hurt—but there's still hope, there's always hope. They throw dirt on you all your life and some people get buried so deep in the dirt that they never get out. The album's about the people who'll never admit they're buried too deep to get out."

One can certainly feel the pain of the characters who populate the songs on *Darkness on the Edge of Town*. Springsteen's father is the immediate subject of "Factory," but the song is also the tale of every American worker, who "rises from bed and puts on his clothes" when the "factory whistle blows." There is no recourse for such men; they must take care of their families, and they need the very job that kills them. "The factory takes his hearing," but "the factory gives him life." The only kind of life available to many workingmen in the 1970s was "the working life." When the day ends, the whistle blows again, and, like the walking dead, "the men walk through the gates with death in their eyes." They have no hope for the future, and the deadly routine in which they are trapped has filled them with an unforgiving anger, looking for an outlet. They can be certain of only one thing: that "somebody's gonna get hurt tonight."

"Streets of Fire" seems to feature a younger version of the protagonist in "Factory." If the former gives the listener a glimpse into the brutal reality of the father, the latter depicts that foreboding reality of the son. In the first stanza, the speaker is so alienated that he can refer to himself in only the second person. "You" don't "care anymore." His "eyes are tired," and he is surrounded by "weak lies" and "cold walls" that gnaw at his "insides" until he just wants to "let go." He is alone on a quiet night, and he finally faces himself in the second stanza. He cries that he is "a loser," who is "wandering" and "dying" in the "streets of fire" in which he finds himself. No matter where he looks, there is no pleasant alternative to the life he currently lives. He hates how "they tricked" him and that the life he is living is "all lies," but he realizes that he will remain "strung out on the wire." Like the man in "Factory," he is trapped. By the end of the song, he accepts his chilling fate as one of the masses who must live "only with strangers," "talk only with strangers," and "walk with angels that have no place." This is how many baby boomers of the working class felt in the 1970s.

"Something in the Night" reveals how much they wanted to escape this condition. When we meet the speaker, he is aimlessly riding in his car, "figuring I'll get a drink." He decides to "turn the radio up loud," trying to distract himself so that he doesn't "have to think" about his life. He is desperately in "search of a moment when the world seems right," but satisfaction eludes him. Even dreaming of a better life is futile; as "soon as you got something they send someone to try and take it away." His past weighs on him with thoughts that he "just can't live down." His transgressions will not be "forgotten," and he will not be "forgiven." The song fades into a surreal closing stanza in which the speaker has a dark vision of his future. When he and his girl finally find the "things we loved," they are "crushed and dying in the dirt." There is no escape. They are "caught" and "burned" in one last fight. The final image that the listener has of the pair is of them "running burned and blind, chasing something in the night."

These three songs are not happy, but they were well received by many young Americans in the late 1970s. Why? Because when you feel broken-hearted and trapped in a terrible economic situation that you never thought that you would face and that you can't understand, it's comforting to know that someone does understand you and that he is speaking for you. In this way, the concerts of the *Darkness* tour became very therapeutic for the audiences, with a feeling of reciprocity developing between a singer and his fans, both giving each other the acknowledgment they needed.

Yet, Springsteen does more on the album than simply acknowledge and give expression to the pain that so many people were feeling at the time. He lets them know that there is still hope of finding a better life. The album's opening song, "Badlands," is testament to Springsteen's insistence that life, with all its nastiness, still carries the possibility of happiness. Like many people in the late seventies, the song's protagonist faces "trouble in the heartland." Life is "smashin' in" his "guts," and he is "caught in a crossfire that I don't understand." Like all those people "working in the fields" and "working 'neath the wheel," he has to negotiate the "badlands" "every day." Like the speaker in "Something in the Night," he can't escape. However, he can turn and stare down his troubles. He tells his girlfriend that he doesn't "give a damn for the same old played out scenes," insisting that "I want the heart, I want the soul, I want control right now." There is power in his voice, an assurance that, despite the fact that he feels a "fear so real," he will not wait around "for a moment that just don't come." He will "keep pushin'" until "these badlands start treating us good." The speaker calls on everything that Springsteen's audience needed to believe in at the time. He believes "in the love that you gave me." He invokes "the faith that can save me," and he believes in "hope" and prays that "someday it may raise" him "above these badlands."

Hope, faith, and love. These biblical overtones resonate in "The Promised Land," another portrait of a man beaten down by life who refuses to give in. Deep in "the desert," the speaker works "all day in my daddy's garage." His dreams shimmer in the desert like "some mirage." Like so many Americans in the decade, he's "done his best to live the right way." He gets up "every morning" and goes "to work each day," only to feel the world grind him down so that his "eyes go blind" and his "blood runs cold." He is "weak" and wants "to explode." But he will not quit. "Pretty soon," he tells his girlfriend, "I'm gonna take charge." Times are tough, but he defiantly says, "I'm heading straight into the storm." He commands all the lies and bad dreams that "tear you apart" to "blow away." In the refrain, he confidently tells the world, "I ain't a boy, no I'm a man. And I believe in a promised land." Interesting is the fact that the speaker says "a" promised land instead of "the" promised land. The listener is left with a powerful scene of a working man heading into a storm, not to find the land promised to him by God, but to carve out his own place with his own strength and will, an image reminiscent of the mythic American past, with its emphasis on rugged individualism and the self-made man. In a time when powerful economic and social forces seemed to be crushing the common man, the message of "The Promised Land" invoked all of the independent images that Americans needed to believe in.

"Prove It All Night" features an equally strong protagonist who has been "working real hard," trying to get his "hands clean." His circumstances may not be rosy, but he still has the courage to drive all night on a dusty road to buy his girlfriend "a gold ring and a pretty dress of blue." If "dreams came true," that would "be nice," but he doesn't believe in

fairy tales. For him, there is only the faith that he has in his love for her
and his willingness to follow a "hunger they can't resist," a hunger that
will steel his nerve in the face of difficult odds. He will "call the bluff"
and "prove it all night," doing whatever it takes to make it and buy her
the things that she wants. Nothing is off-limits. He knows what it means
"to steal, to cheat, to lie," and he will circumvent all the rules that hold
them down to "live and die" for her.

The final song on the album, "Darkness on the Edge of Town,"
captures the flavor of the entire work. Once again, we encounter a man
who is nearly broken by his circumstances. "Some folks are born into a
good life," he says, but like many of his contemporaries, he is clearly not
one of them. He confesses, "I lost my money and I lost my wife." He is
alone while "she has a house up in Fairview and a style she's trying to
maintain." She has moved on, and he is left high and dry with "a secret,"
the terrible kind of secret that "everybody's got" that "they just can't
face" but which they drag with them like an albatross "every step that
they take." Once you have lost everything but your worst secrets,
Springsteen says, you only have two choices. A person can either "let it
drag 'em down" or "cut it loose" and bravely face the hard realities of
life to see if it is possible to fashion a new dream. The speaker chooses
the latter. He will face his fears "out on that hill with everything I got."
He will put his life "on the line where dreams are found and lost." He
will drive headlong into "the darkness on the edge of town," and he will
"pay the cost for wanting things that can only be found" there. The song
is at once dark yet triumphant, dominated by sadness and loss yet
tinged with courage and hope. It is a microcosm of the entire record,
whose spirit reflected Springsteen's deep understanding of the psyche
of the working class in the 1970s and his unwillingness to let their voices
go unheard or their souls unnourished.

LIMPING TOWARD THE EIGHTIES

Things only got darker for Americans. As the seventies came to a close,
a second recession rocked the economy. Again, the setback was occasioned by an oil embargo on the part of OPEC nations, which, just as in
1973, when the United States sided with Israel in the Yom Kippur War,
were angry at American actions in the Middle East. In January 1979,

the shah of Iran, long a friend of the United States and an agent of Iranian Westernization, was forced to flee the country in the wake of a religious revolution. The Ayatollah Khomeini, who succeeded the shah, imposed strict Muslim law and called for the shah to be returned to Iran to face criminal prosecution for crimes against the Iranian people. When President Jimmy Carter decided to give the shah medical aid and grant his family political asylum, Khomeini, who disliked the West on moral principle anyway, decided to shut off the oil supply coming to the United States from Iran. Other sympathetic Arab nations followed suit, and a second oil crisis jolted the American economy. Robert Shook writes, "Khomeini turned off the spigot and created a second oil crisis. In a matter of weeks, the price of gasoline doubled. Once again, America was caught off guard" (Schmidt 170).

Indeed, history did repeat itself. As the price of oil continued to rise from 1979 to 1981, the shortages wreaked havoc on America's economy. Long gas lines, inflation, and job losses ruled the day, as "stagflation" once again dominated the news. By April 1980, inflation had surged over 10 percent, and interest rates hit 18.5 percent, making borrowing money almost impossible. With few people able to make large purchases, the housing and automotive industries went into a tailspin, taking the rest of the economy with them. By the summer, 8.2 million Americans found themselves unemployed, as the price of goods continued to soar. Still, the economy had not reached the bottom. By the summer of 1982, the poverty rate had increased to 14 percent, and the unemployment rate had risen to 10.8 percent, its highest in forty years. Businesses failed at an alarming rate, and "bankruptcies and farm foreclosures increased to levels not seen since the Great Depression of the 1930s" (Camardella 33).

If long gas lines were the defining symbol of discontent in the mid-1970s, the closing down of American businesses became the most pronounced feature of the American landscape in the late 1970s and early 1980s. The sad phenomenon seemed to touch nearly every city and town. In his study of the 1970s, *Something Happened*, Edward D. Berkowitz recounts the story of the closing of a Singer sewing machine plant in Elizabeth, New Jersey, not far from Springsteen's old stomping grounds. The tale was similar to nearly every other failing business: a long history of technological innovation, followed by an inability to keep up with cultural changes, the rising cost of doing business, and increased competition and cheap labor from Europe and Southeast Asia—all leading to a gradual cessation of hiring and decreased production until the business closed altogether. By the early eighties, the dominant employer in Elizabeth had closed its doors, sending hundreds of working-class people into the already crowded unemployment lines. "What happened in Elizabeth occurred, in one form or another, in communities across America. . . . As factories closed, people worried that new ones would not spring up to take their place" (70).

The long economic decline that hurt so many working-class Americans coincided with Springsteen's continued intellectual awareness and musical development. In the late 1970s, he started seriously listening to country music for the first time, especially the music of Hank Williams and other artists who had dedicated themselves to writing about the poor people whose lives often went unseen in a land of plenty. At the same time, he was watching such films as John Ford's cinematic rendering of *The Grapes of Wrath* and reading such books as Howard Zinn's *A People's History of the United States*, the fiction of Flannery O'Connor and Bobbi Ann Mason, and Robert Franks's photo essay *The Americans*. All these works influenced his writing on *The River* (1980), which contains several songs that speak to the plight of the working class. Springsteen was especially taken with O'Connor and novelist Walker Percy, both artists with a Catholic background like his own, who were willing to examine the effects of a cruel world on the human soul, that central part of our core being that insists on hope and possibility even in the face of economic and spiritual deprivation. This darkness is felt in stark terms on both *The River* and *Nebraska*, albums that are populated with damaged characters suffering from every manner of neglect.

Two songs on *The River* sprang directly from Springsteen's family life, though their themes spoke to audiences across the world. Critics have interpreted "Independence Day" as Springsteen's attempt to reach out to his father, attempting to heal old wounds while saying good-bye to his childhood and the part of his musical career in which many of his songs were directly about his home life. The song certainly functions on that personal level, but many listeners in 1980 recognized and were moved by the father and son in the song because they were playing out a drama that one could witness in any town in the United States. The son in the song is simply saying goodbye to his father. The young man will be "leavin' in the morning from St. Mary's gate," and he has a few departing words for his father. Things haven't been smooth between them, and the son confesses, "The darkness of this house has got the best of us." He recognizes that there is no way that "this house can hold the two of us," but he then narrows the distance between them by admitting that "they were just too much of the same kind." Perhaps the greater problem is that "there's a darkness in this town that's got us." One can't help but feel the sting of unemployment, plant closings, and inflation that bore on people in the early eighties. The son says that "there's a lot of people leaving town now." They are fleeing in the face of joblessness, as much as anything else, and their desperation is underscored by the fact they have no distinct destination; they leave "their friends, their homes," despite walking "that dark and dusty highway all alone." In the end, the son's differences with his father are eclipsed by his sympathy for his position. He tells his dad that "they ain't gonna do to me what I watched them do to you." It's Independence Day, indeed, but the song's haunting lyrics remind the listener of the powerful connections of family in the face of a rugged economic landscape.

As mentioned in chapter one, "The River" is about Springsteen's older sister, Virginia. However, it is more broadly the tale of many young couples who, full of innocence and wonder, fall in love without the slightest regard for the harsh realities of the world that can undo their youthful pleasures in the blink of an eye. The speaker and his girlfriend, Mary, have been raised, like many kids in the sixties and seventies, to believe in the American Dream, but their hopes are undone when Mary gets pregnant. Suddenly, they are married; he is stuck in a dead-end job, and she is trapped at home. They have little money; their relationship deteriorates, and they are left with nothing but regret over what happened and a deep longing for what might have been. Like "Independence Day," "The River" has a haunting melody that, combined with Springsteen's guttural moans, accurately depicts the pain that so many Americans felt at the time.

While the speakers of "Independence Day" and "The River" are young men trying to make good in the face of difficult circumstances, the usual lead characters in the early Springsteen canon, he expanded his field of vision on *The River* to include working-class women as subjects. They never get a fully developed voice of their own, and the audience knows them only through undefined male onlookers, but the female characters are the focus of both "Jackson Cage" and "I Wanna Marry You." In the former, a young woman has already been beaten down by the working life; she "has been tried and handed life, down in the Jackson cage." She lives alone in "a house where the blinds are closed." The speaker lets her know that he understands that for her "every day ends in wasted motion." He then joins his story with hers, saying that he's dreamed "of a better world," but he wakes up "so downhearted" and sees her "so tired and confused." They are two people seemingly being swept along in an ugly current, and they cannot get their bearings. They can't even "see some sun," and, in his desperation, the man reaches out to her, asking her if she can understand how "they will turn a man into a stranger to waste away." The "they," that nebulous mélange of upper-class forces that most benefited from current financial and political structures at the expense of the lower classes, would have been easily recognizable by young men and women at the time.

"I Wanna Marry You" is another song characterized by unfulfilled longing. A "working girl" walks "down the street" with a "lonely ribbon" in her hair. She is pushing a "baby carriage" and living "a lonely life" that consists of "raising two kids alone" in a "mixed up world." Working-class life is difficult, and the male speaker feels the pain as well. He is lonely, too. He remembers the words of his father that "true love was just a lie," and he knows that "an unfulfilled life makes a man hard." One can feel that these two characters are at a crucial point in their lives. They are like the man and the woman in "Jackson Cage," who are in danger of being completely swallowed by the conditions in which they are enmeshed. The anxiety of the speaker is palpable when he assures her that he doesn't want "to clip her wings." Yet there is an underlying determination in his voice as well, when he acknowledges that "true love can't be no fairytale" and that while he can't make her dreams come true, "maybe he can help them along." This is not the idealism of youth; this is the raw hope of working-class people who have taken some of life's cruel blows.

Even in the midst of the carnage, this type of hard-won happiness is available for Springsteen's characters on *The River*. For instance, in "Out in the Street," a blue-collar guy works "five days a week," breaking his back "loading crates down on the dock." His girl labors "all day" as well, "working that hard line." However, they will not be held down by the travails of working-class life. He tells her to "put on her best dress." A party awaits "beneath the neon lights," and they are "gonna have a good time." He is trapped by his dead-end job and all that goes with it, but he is not without hope. Once "the whistle blows," he is "out on the street," where he walks and talks like he wants to and where he never feels "alone." The cops "cruise by" watching them "from the corner of their eye," but it doesn't matter. He assures his girl that "we ain't gonna take what they're handing out." It is possible to feel "all right," and the song ends with the speaker entreating her to "meet me out in the street, little girl, tonight." Life is hard, Springsteen tells his audience, and I know you are hurting. But don't give up. There are, at the very least, pockets of freedom that can give you life.

The light of hope is dimmed in *Nebraska*, the darkest of all of Springteen's albums and one that deeply reflects the desperate condition of working-class people in the early eighties as stagflation reached its peak. The record is musically stark, a largely acoustic work that Springsteen recorded in his house. Its first song, "Nebraska," is essentially a retelling of Charlie Starkweather's 1950s murder spree. Springsteen pictures the young killer as a product of the same type of barren environment faced by many young people in the Reagan era. The song hits the listener in the face with the image of a boy picking up a sweet girl "twirling her baton." They go for a ride. It seems like it could be a joyous song; guy takes girl for a spin in his hot rod. Except by the end of this ride, "ten innocent people died." They ride through the "badlands of Wyoming," and he confesses that he "killed everything in my path." The song continues to jar the listener when the speaker says that he isn't "sorry for the things that we done," and he contents himself with the thought that "at least for a little while, sir, me and her had us some fun." There is no regret or remorse; there is no reason why. He simply asks that she sit on his lap when he is electrocuted, another disquieting image in a song that offers no solace. Why do people do things like this? The speaker says, "There is just a meanness in this world."

"Johnny 99" is another anthem of working-class despondency. Here, a man "went out looking for a job, but he couldn't find none." The auto plant has "closed down," and he "has debts no honest man can pay." Desperate for money, he gets drunk, buys "a gun," and shoots "a night clerk" during a robbery. The judge sentences Johnny to "98 and a year." When asked why he did it, Johnny spoke for many people who found themselves behind the financial eight ball in 1982: "The bank was holdin' my mortgage and they was takin' my house away." He knows "that don't make me an innocent man," but he wants everyone to know that it took a lot of adversity "to put that gun in my hand." He has only one final request. Admitting that he'd "be better off dead," he asks the judge to "let 'em shave off my hair and put me on that execution line." "Nebraska" and "Johnny 99" are among Springsteen's bleakest songs, but at least those who identified with their torturous spirit knew they were not alone. If you still felt isolated after hearing these two songs, you weren't truly listening.

As an album, *Nebraska* is as desperate from start to finish as the lives of many of the people who bought it. It is full of characters like Joe Roberts, the policeman in "Highway Patrolman," who wants to be a good, law-abiding officer but also loyal to his wayward brother, Franky. Roberts gets a call that Franky is in trouble. He admits that if it had been any other man, he would "put him straight away." But he loves Franky, and "nothing feels better than blood on blood." Franky has been in the army, but with the family farm having gone under, he has little to anchor him after the service. He kills a man one night in a bar, and Roberts gets the call. As he chases Franky's getaway car, he remembers all the times that he kept his brother out of trouble, and he remembers all the good times they had "dancin' with Maria." There is no perfect way out of this moral conundrum. If Roberts arrests his brother, he will likely send Franky to prison for life; if he lets him go, a murderer goes unpunished, and he betrays his badge. In the end, he chooses his brother over the law. He "pulled over the side of the highway and watched his taillights disappear." The bank could take their farm, and he may "work for the state," but the institutions that crush them do not own him. Life will beat you up, but you always have family, and a "man that turns his back on his family . . . just ain't no good." Again, there isn't much happiness for Roberts, but there is some solace in resistance and solidarity.

Perhaps the most enduring song from the album is "Atlantic City," in which a man "got a job and tried to put my money away." However, he "has debts no honest man can pay," so he decides to withdraw his money from "the Central Trust" to fund one last gambit. Like many people in the early eighties, he's "been lookin' for a job," ostensibly one that could actually pay the bills, "but it's hard to find." Finally, he meets "this guy" and finds himself desperate enough "to do a little favor for him." The prospects do not look good, but, like Joe Roberts, he will not give up. He will do whatever it takes to keep his life from collapsing, to revive his luck that "may have died" and restore a "love" that may "be cold." Even though he is at the end of his rope, he will stride with purpose into the darkness that awaits him to see if he can forge some modicum of happiness. He tells his girl "to put your hair up nice" and "meet me tonight in Atlantic City." While "everything dies," it is also possible that "everything that dies someday comes back." This is what the speaker and many in Springsteen's audience needed to believe. What looks to be dead can be revived.

Even on *Nebraska*, Springsteen allows for the possibility of some redemption. It may not be the redemption of fairy tales and myths, but that type of redemption would not have seemed realistic to Springsteen's listeners. They knew better. Instead, Springsteen gave them "Open All Night," one of the few fast-paced tunes on the record, in which the speaker makes an all-night drive so that he will be with his best girl by morning. He says that "the boss don't dig me, so he put me on the nightshift," but he vows to make "an all night run to get back to where my baby lives." This romantic attitude seems out of place on *Nebraska*, until one considers Springsteen's penchant for making sure that while he recognized the plight of the working class, he would always let them know that there is still the possibility for some joy, of being delivered "from nowhere." Likewise, "Mansion on the Hill," a slower, dreamier song that resists easy interpretation, reminded working families of the period that even though they may have felt surrounded by ugliness, beauty and peace were still possibilities. Since the speaker's childhood, there has always been a "place out on the edge of town" that rises "above the factories and fields." The children play in its shadows; he and his sister hide in the cornfields to listen to it; and his father makes a point of driving him to a silent place so that they can "look up at that mansion on the hill." Even as the cars rumble past his home on their way "from the mill," the deadly rhythms of the working life cannot block out the "beautiful full moon rising above the mansion on the hill." The working-class life can be ruthless and harsh, but Springsteen wanted his audience to know that beyond job cuts, low wages, closed plants, and rising prices, the possibility of redemption remained.

THE NINETIES AND BEYOND

Springsteen's commitment to the working class has never wavered. Even in the robust economy of the 1990s, Springsteen saw fit to make another acoustic album in the vein of *Nebraska*. In the heart of the boom, he released *The Ghost of Tom Joad* (1995), flooding an American landscape steeped in crass consumerism and peppered with dot-com millionaires with images of poor factory laborers, migrant workers, former prisoners, drifters, and beleaguered family men. In a time of plenty, Springsteen did not want Americans to forget the swelling ranks of the lower class. "I think that the American idea of equal opportunity, obviously it hasn't been realized," Springsteen said just after the album's release. "And I think what's worse, every study that's come out about the division of wealth in society over the past 10 or 15 years has shown that the middle class has been getting smaller and people have been getting farther and farther apart" (Costas). To Springsteen, the growing gap between rich and poor "leads to diminished hopes, diminished expectations, diminished possibilities." It was "that feeling of the way things feel to me right now, that colors the stories and the characters' lives on the record."

Thirteen years after *Nebraska*, some of the faces of the characters had changed, but Springsteen's defense of the common man remained the same. The album opens with Springsteen invoking the spirit of John Steinbeck, whose novel *Grapes of Wrath* inspired "The Ghost of Tom Joad." The song is a hymn to the spirit of the working class. Tom Joad, the hero of the itinerant laborers in the book, haunts the piece. All the "men walkin' long the railroad tracks," all the "families sleepin' in their cars," all those with "no home, no job, no peace, no rest" are "searchin' for the ghost of old Tom Joad." The speaker is himself a vagabond traveler who knows the score. He is part of the contemporary band of working poor. "The highway is alive tonight," says the speaker, and "nobody's kidding nobody about where it goes." The song ends with the protagonist sitting "in the campfire light with the ghost of old Tom Joad." Listeners feel like they are invited to pull up a seat around the fire and join the effort to remedy economic injustice.

Once they have accepted the invitation, the audience is hit with three powerful songs in a row that define Springsteen's loyalty to those who economic fortunes did not rise on the economic tides of the mid-

1990s. "Straight Time" is sung in the spirit of Woody Guthrie and Pete Seeger, both of whom gained influence on Springsteen's conception of the world and music as the century neared its end. The song's protagonist "got out of prison in '86" and has been trying to stay on "the clean and narrow" ever since. He gets "a job at the rendering factory," but it doesn't pay much, and he winds up just trying to "stay alive." He wants to support his family, and he loves "tossin' my little babies high," his wife smiling at him "out of the corner of her eye." The problem is that he just can't make enough money to keep his family above water. He has been laboring for "eight years," and he feels like he is "gonna die." He is trapped, doing "straight time." Like many working men, he doesn't want to cross that "thin line" into a life of crime and risk going back to jail, but he is slowly being crushed by his life. No matter what he does, he "just can't get that smell from my hands." The listener feels his pain as the song fades and he escapes into a dream, "driftin' off into foreign lands." The message is subtle, but it is clear that Springsteen finds it appalling that in the American land of plenty, a good man working as hard as he can would have to dream of foreign lands to find temporary relief.

Unlike the man in "Straight Time," the main character of "Highway 29" cannot resist the temptation to cross that "thin line." Working at a shoe store, he has little hope in the future. When he meets a woman, "a perfect size seven," he falls for her—hard. The song has a surreal quality, and it is hard to say if the couple is in love, if they are infatuated, or if they are merely caught in the fire of lust. They may not know themselves, but the man clearly knows that "it should have stopped" before things got out of hand. The man has little money, but he wants to escape with his newfound lover. Pushed along by some unholy current, they decide to rob a bank. Things go horribly wrong. He "had a gun, you know the rest." His shirt "was covered in blood." They escape, but the police pursue. The listener knows that they cannot last long, but the man is calm and philosophic. His actions were not just the result of his involvement with the woman; "it was something in me, something had been comin' for a long long time." His feeling for the woman was the final catalyst, but his desperation as a man working a dead-end job had been building for years and would end in a nightmare of "broken glass and gasoline" on the lonely pavement of Highway 29. As the windshield breaks and the "wind come silent through," the man is not sad or scared. He has finally escaped, seemingly into death. "I closed my eyes," he says, and one can feel him flying through the windshield. "I was runnin' then I was flyin'." It is another of Springsteen's songs that resists easy interpretation. However, one thing is evident. The shoe salesman finds a life of crime and even death preferable to the working life that he was enduring.

The tension that Springsteen had built through the album's first three songs is released in "Youngstown," a loud, powerful tune that Springsteen wrote to draw attention to the impoverished Ohio city that was the heart of the American steel industry until the late 1970s. When the Youngstown Sheet and Tube Company closed down in 1977, over five thousand once-proud workers lost their hopes and dreams. By the midnineties, Youngstown was in full decline, a shell of its former self, and Springsteen would not let America forget to look up from its spending spree and pay attention to the poverty of the city. The song contains the proud history of the area and its hearty people. The first blast furnaces dated to the early nineteenth century and "made the cannon balls that helped the union win the war." Over the years, generations of workers labored through conditions "hotter than hell" to build "the tanks and bombs that won this country's wars." Now, after their sons died in Korea and Vietnam, the fathers and their sons have been forgotten, and the narrator moans, "Sweet Jenny I'm sinking down here darlin' in Youngstown." In this case, Jenny is not a woman but a reference to the famous Jeannette blast furnace that powered Sheet and Tube for so many years. The man calls out in pain, but Jenny has been shut down. There is no one to answer him, and he resigns himself to death and an afterlife in "the fiery furnaces of hell." When Springsteen played Youngstown's Stambaugh Auditorium in January 1996, the mayor presented him with the key to the city.

Seventeen years later, in the face of the long recession that slowed the world economy between 2008 and 2012, Springsteen released the "angriest album" of his career, *Wrecking Ball*. Like many people, Springsteen was appalled by the nature of the first major recession of the twenty-first century, an economic disaster largely caused by individual and corporate greed that left the swelling ranks of the poor even poorer and the shrinking middle class ever more pressed while the wealthy emerged relatively unscathed. "The darker stories" of the album "lay it all bare," notes journalist Russell C. Smith. "The sadness and outrage, and the terrible truth about how we as a nation allowed incompetent, greedy human beings to lead" America "to this land of increased inequality and broken dreams." The housing bubble of 2008 that was caused by predatory lending companies peddling subprime mortgages; the fraudulent bankers of companies such as Bear Stearns making reckless investments at the expense of middle-class investors; oil companies raking in huge profits while the working class suffered at the pump; runaway inflation; and skyrocketing unemployment rates are the unholy amalgam that gave rise to *Wrecking Ball*. Smith notes, "Several of Springsteen's characters in the songs have hit an economic and emotional wall, repeatedly. They wander through burnt-out and broken urban landscapes, searching or a sliver of redemption, or maybe just a sympathetic ear. The overall feeling is one of righteous anger spilling out on the tracks, and how economic pain has impacted millions of lives."

Wrecking Ball features the darkest songs in the Springsteen canon since *Nebraska*. In "This Depression," the protagonist confesses to his lover that he's "been down, but never this down." He has "been low, but never this low." The song plods on. He has had his "faith shaken but never hopeless." He has been "without love, but never forsaken." He can barely muster enough fortitude to tell his lover how much he needs her "here in this depression." There is no hint of hope, only the grim desolation of a shell of a man trying to hold onto the one person who has not deserted him. The same bitter frustration characterizes "Shackled and Drawn," where a proud man admits that, despite all his effort and sacrifice, he "woke up this morning shackled and drawn." A lifetime of labor has left him further behind the eight ball, "trudging through the dark in a world gone wrong." As in the recession of 2008, the rich are not harmed; like the carefree bankers of Bear Stearns, a rich investor can function as a "gambling man" who haphazardly "rolls the dice." He might win, but he can't lose. If the gamble fails, "the workingman pays the bills." The common laborer has no recourse. Like the man in the song, he just has to "pick up the rock" and "carry it on," like Sisyphus pushing his stone up the hill. And then there is "Death to My Hometown," where the speaker exclaims that no cannonballs, bombs, or "rifles cut us down." Instead, "robber barons" and "greedy thieves" have "destroyed our families, factories." They "ate the flesh of everything they found" and "took our homes," leaving "our bodies on the ground." The speaker's anger builds as he contemplates the fact that the lenders, bankers, executives, and inside traders that have made fortunes at the expense of everyday Americans "walk the streets as free men." Their "crimes have gone unpunished."

The anger that builds in "Death to My Hometown" is sustained throughout the record. Yet, in true Springsteen fashion, the anger translates into redemptive action. Eventually, the man in "This Depression" gets up; he continues to fight, his gloom giving way to a frightful resistance. In "We Take Care of Our Own," the speaker knows that "the door that holds the thrown" will remain locked; those who have the power and money will not act to help those being plowed under by the recession in 2012. He knows that "the road of good intentions has gone dry." No matter what any given congressperson might say, the government will "stay home," as evidenced by the lack of committed response to the tragedy left in the wake of Hurricane Katrina in New Orleans in 2005. Yet, while "there ain't no help," the speaker remains undaunted, insisting that "we take care of our own." Government, industry, and the wealthy class may sound "the bugle" of empty rhetoric, but average working-class Americans still have "eyes with the will to see" and "hearts that run over with mercy." In the end, "wherever this flag is flown," these men and women will "take care of our own." The same power and defiance characterize "We Are Alive," in which the ghosts of workers past arise to strengthen the resolve of current Americans fighting the faceless corporations and elitist banks that brought on the present recession. The action takes place in a graveyard where "the dead come back to life" and sing. Among the spirits is a man "killed in Maryland in 1877" when "railroad workers made their stand." Another belongs to an innocent African American girl murdered in church by racists in Alabama in 1963; the last belongs to a contemporary Mexican immigrant parent killed while crossing "the southern desert" in an attempt to find a better life for "my children left behind." The listener feels Springsteen cut through the divisions of race, allowing the speaker to be uplifted by what unites the spirits. Only their bodies have died. "Our souls will rise" as one, they say with confidence, "to carry the fire and light the spark." Together, they will "fight shoulder to shoulder and heart to heart." Springsteen's message is clear. Those suffering in 2012 in the wake of a terrible recession are not alone. The fight against corporate, governmental, and class tyranny has been going on a long time, but come suffering or death, the solidarity of the working class will keep them fighting. With his last song on *Wrecking Ball*, Springsteen has the final word: "We are alive."

For Springsteen, the dream that honest working people can live a good life characterized by dignity and happiness is alive as well. This is the vision of "Land of Hope and Dreams," the song that precedes "We Are Alive." Once again, the listener understands that the man in "This Depression" has not succumbed. His voice is loud and strong, as he tells his wife to "grab your ticket and your suitcase" and embark with him on a train ride "through the fields where sunlight streams." They may not have much, but he vows, "I will provide for you and . . . stand by your side." Times are tough, but "tomorrow there'll be sunshine and all this darkness past." Springsteen takes care to make sure that his audience knows that the train carries everyone, "saint and sinners," "losers and winners," "whores and gamblers," and all the "lost souls" in need to redemption. In the end, "dreams will not be thwarted," and this sentiment sums up Springsteen's vision for the working class from the late seventies to the present. Life is brutal and unfair, but "faith will be rewarded." This is the hope of Bruce Springsteen, a hope that has been at the heart of his appeal to working-class Americans over the last forty years.

4

BOYS TRY TO LOOK SO HARD

Reinventing Masculinity

THE FIFTIES: THE RISE OF WARD CLEAVER

Bruce Springsteen grew up in the 1950s, a decade that took on a distinctly conservative flavor as the result of what happened in the tempestuous twenty years preceding it. Young men enjoying their place as privileged members of a largely white, upwardly mobile society full of prosperous fathers and well-coiffed, feminine stay-at-home mothers during the fifties might have been surprised to learn that a feminist revolution had been well under way only a quarter of a century before. In 1920, the Nineteenth Amendment guaranteed women the right to vote. Yet, even women's newfound political power was not as culturally noticeable as burgeoning female economic might. World War I had ignited the American economy while significantly reducing the total number of men available to work in the rapidly growing industrial work-force. Willing to work as telephone operators, seamstresses, assembly-line workers, and a plethora of other new, lower-level occupations, women moved into the paid workplace in record numbers. Naturally, women's increased financial power meant more visibility for them as consumers, always a conclusive litmus test for societal leverage in the United States. This political and economic influence occurred at a time of moral flexibility in the country. The Jazz Age ushered in relaxed sexual mores, and while Prohibition (1920–1933) symbolized conserva-

tive America's growing concern regarding this moral laxity, it only increased the flow of alcohol-fueled parties in the roaring twenties. The
scene was set for the ascendancy of the flapper, an independent woman
with her own money and her own life. Uninterested in marriage, she
worked hard and played hard, smoking, drinking, dancing, dressing pro-
vocatively, and enjoying sex on her own terms. Such assertions of female independence were enough to threaten many men, and all-male
activities soared in popularity. College football, for instance, was championed by none other than President Theodore Roosevelt as a necessary
training ground for men in need of being more manly. Children's book
series—such as the Frank Merriwell tales, which celebrated a virile
brand of traditional masculinity—sold like hotcakes. Perhaps the most
significant manifestation of male fear at changing gender relations was
the explosive growth of the lodge movement, in which professional men
cemented their business connections and male solidarity apart from a
growing female influence in the workplace and in society in general.

The Great Depression and World War II effectively stemmed the
tide of these gender changes for a time. If economic booms are condu-
cive to a national willingness to be experimental and to embrace progressivism, financial calamity is sometimes associated with a reluctance
or an inability to risk such changes. It is difficult to focus on enacting
social changes that would threaten the power and identity of a large
part of the populace when most of the broad population is struggling to
survive. Although the dormant economy was beginning to revive in the
early 1940s, World War II pushed the country further into a cautious
mind-set. Americans were determined to win a war that threatened the
foundations of the nation; it was a time of patriotism, tradition, and
loyalty, not a time for advancing progressive ideals.

By the time the United States had prevailed in Europe and ignited
its economy in the 1950s, the generation of Americans who had survived the depression and the war was in no psychological condition to
carry the mantle of progressivism, to wage divisive cultural battles that
would be uncomfortable, even painful. What would come to be known
as the "greatest generation" simply wanted to be happy, even if it meant
embracing a somewhat shallow version of the American Dream, rooted
largely in unbridled consumerism. As David Halberstam writes, "Shopping and buying were to become major American pastimes as the ripple
effect of the new affluence started to be felt throughout the economy"

(144). Americans bought homes and conveniences to fill them, with a near religious fervor. Televisions, wall-to-wall carpeting, fancy ovens, improved washing machines and vacuum cleaners, dishwashers, record players and stereos, easy chairs, and three-piece living room sets were only a small part of the materialist lifestyle that, of course, included an automobile in every driveway. It proved to be a satisfying tonic, at least for a while, for people who had just come through twenty years of hardship.

In particular, men found it comforting that this affluence was anchored in a nostalgic vision of gender and family. Advertisements, newspaper advice columns, women's magazines such as *McCall's* and *Redbook*, countless guides on how to be a good housewife, churches, and even fashion trends all pointed women in one direction: the home. Women had worked in industries in record numbers during World War II, but returning GIs wanted both jobs and families, and many took jobs that been occupied by women in general and by married women in particular, who would be willing to play the role of wife and mother. No medium capitalized on men's needs for the security of traditional gender roles better than television. *Donna Reed, Ozzie and Harriet*, and *Leave It to Beaver* were a few of the shows that celebrated manly fathers who tamed the corporate world by day and presided by night with gentle wisdom over happy homes infused with the pleasant spirit and beauty of temperate, satisfied housewives. *Leave It to Beaver* was the perfect example of what many men and women seemed to want in the fifties. Ward Cleaver was a solid provider, a firm but kind father, a loving husband, and a creative, benevolent patriarch who could solve nearly any problem. June Cleaver was a comely, immaculately dressed mother whose housekeeping skills were surpassed only by her nurturing, maternal qualities and eternally happy disposition. Not surprising, the Cleaver kids were well-adjusted, kind, moral boys who were just mischievous enough to be amusing. The family of four lived in a beautiful house, in a clean, quiet neighborhood full of people just like them: white, prosperous, and deservedly content. As Halberstam confirms, the Cleavers represented "the ideal . . . as articulated by *McCall's*." Like Ward, "the husband was designated leader and hero." Like June, "the wife was his mainstay on the domestic side, duly appreciative of the immense sacrifices being made for her and her children" (591).

American men and boys ate up these traditional images in the fifties, enjoying a privileged position that was soon to erode.

THE SECOND WAVE OF FEMINISM

One of the many problems with the images of gender produced in the fifties was that they encouraged young men to expect to revel in a patriarchal identity that simply proved to be incompatible with contemporary reality. For instance, while some women were, in fact, happy trying to live like June Cleaver, many were not. Betty Friedan's *The Feminine Mystique* (1963) sold millions of copies and became one of the most influential books of the twentieth century largely because there were so many women who were suffering from "the problem that has no name." They may not have thought of it quite this way, but they wanted to revive the momentum of the 1920s, giving themselves more options than simply being girlfriends in poodle skirts, wives in curlers, and mothers behind strollers. Those women had technology on their side. Not only did a revolution in domestic technology make home management much less time intensive than in the past, with such inventions as microwaves and dishwashers, but the legalization of the birth control pill in 1961 gave women unprecedented control of their reproductive rights. No longer did women have to risk pregnancy when they were sexually active. This sexual and domestic freedom combined with growing economic opportunities for women in the robust economies of the fifties and sixties. Of course, as the economy grew, so did the need for educated workers to manage the growth. That meant a tremendous rise in college graduates from 1960 to 1980, and for the first time, women led the way. By "the late 1960s and early 1970s, young women's expectations of their future labor force participation changed radically. Rather than follow in their mothers' footsteps, they aimed to have careers, not just jobs. These careers were often outside of the traditionally female occupations for women" (Francis).

The gender changes ignited in the 1960s have been so pervasive with so many permutations that it is difficult to describe all the causes that pushed them forward over the last fifty years. As Jane Sherron De Hart writes, "From the outset," the feminist revolution has been "vigorous, diffused, ideologically varied, geographically decentralized and highly controversial" (Kerber et al. 599). Though second-wave feminism is hard to fully codify, one thing is clear. Boys and men from Springsteen's generation have spent a lifetime being confronted with signs and images that have controverted all their expectations of male privilege and power. For instance, in 1963 Helen Gurley Brown released *Sex and the Single Girl*, a seminal work that became a powerful instruction manual for women on how to be professionally and sexually independent. In 1965, Brown became editor in chief of *Cosmopolitan* magazine, one of several publications that would change the way that women thought of themselves and men. The sixties featured television coverage of bra burnings, women's-rights marches, and female-led political protests. By the mid-1970s, the feminist movement was well on its way to transforming the American cultural landscape. Women organized into several potent political voting blocs, their unmistakable influence marked by consistent demonstrations that routinely altered public policy. As De Hart confirms, "It was hard to ignore 50,000 women parading down New York's Fifth Avenue, the presence of *Ms.* magazine on newsstands, feminist books on the best-seller lists, women in hard hats on construction jobs, or the government-mandated affirmative action programs that put them there. It was harder still to ignore the publicity that accompanied the appointment of women to the Carter cabinet, the enrollment of coeds in the nation's military academies, and the ordination of women to the ministry" (Kerber et al. 611).

Women's lives continued to change dramatically during the last quarter of the twentieth century. While "average real incomes for men peaked in 1973 and drifted steadily downward for the next two decades," women entered the workplace in force (Borstelmann 81). During the 1970s, the number of female lawyers, engineers, pharmacists, chemists, soldiers, and government representatives all increased by at least 100 percent. Those trends continued in the eighties and nineties. By 1990, nearly 70 percent of all mothers with school-age children held paying jobs in the workplace, and while there was still a pay gap between men and women that favored the former, the role of male breadwinner was on the wane. Women's economic gains went hand in hand with educational advances. In the early eighties, women became over half of all college students. By 2010, women composed nearly 60 percent of undergraduate enrollment in the United States and accounted for at least half the graduates in medicine, law, and other "power fields." There was no escaping the reality that many women no longer needed men to secure financial security, and that meant a loss of cultural power for men.

Even in areas of life that were completely dominated by men in the fifties, dramatic transformations were taking place. In the political arena, for example, women constituted 27 percent of state legislatures by 2010, one third of the Supreme Court, and nearly 20 percent of the U.S. Congress. Hardly full equality but a startling departure from what boys of the fifties were led to expect. The presence of women in the halls of power resulted in more stringent antidiscrimination laws in terms of hiring, sexual harassment regulations, domestic violence enforcement, and several other legal measures that loudly announced that women were watching men and had the power to correct any misbehavior, even inside the home. Likewise, women were as likely as men to appear on playing fields by 2012. Women's sports often dominate the Olympics; nearly as many girls play sports as boys in secondary schools; and women's teams outnumber men's teams at most colleges and universities. In the military, women made up 10 percent of the nation's armed forces in 1987, up from 1 percent in 1967. In 2010, women composed nearly 20 percent of the U.S. military, serving in every conceivable role, including combat. In terms of spiritual leadership, the number of female rabbis, pastors, ministers, and religious leaders grew in every decade from 1960 to 2010. In 2006, 22 percent of the ordained clergy in the United Methodist Church were women. The bottom line is that, much to the dismay of many men, women were gaining power and filling roles that men assumed would be exclusively theirs in which to fashion masculine identity (Woloch).

HURTING COWBOYS

If women were enjoying unprecedented gains, men were experiencing setbacks in nearly every facet of their lives. Economically, men were much more affected than women by the recessions of the seventies, early eighties, nineties, and early twenty-first century. This was largely due to the fact that many of the jobs lost during these lean times were positions traditionally occupied by men. Assembly-line work in the automotive industry, construction work, factory jobs, and heavy-labor jobs in fading industries such as the iron and steel trades became more and more scarce. Adding to the problem for men was the fact that many of these jobs never came back. By the mid-1970s, the country had already started its transition from the industrial economy that had dominated the decades after World War II, in which men did very well, to a corporate economy anchored less in manufacturing and more on the production and management of information. Over a short period, once plentiful construction and manufacturing jobs that required physical strength and endurance were replaced with positions in public relations, communications, and information management, which tended to be occupied by women. Of the top fifteen growing fields in 2010, thirteen were dominated by women. "Forty years ago, 30 years ago, if you were one of the fairly constant fraction of boys who wasn't ready to learn in high school, there were ways for you to enter the mainstream economy," says Henry Farber, an economist at Princeton. "When you woke up, there were jobs. There were good industrial jobs, so you could have a good industrial, blue-collar career. Now those jobs are gone" (Rosin). As men lost economic power in comparison with women, they also lost their main defining role: breadwinner. With that went some of their attractiveness to women, further lowering collective male self-esteem. Today, 42 percent of American families feature a female breadwinner, many of them single-mother households where fathers have been nearly erased.

Men gave ground in education as well. From 1980 to 2010, girls and women outperformed men at nearly every educational level. Men who once constructed an identity in nearly all-male realms, such as medicine, law, or business, found themselves outnumbered by women in their fields by the year 2000. These educational developments were so important to men because of their clear relation to another prominent but fading center of male identity: power. As blue-collar jobs slipped away, higher education emerged as the gateway to economic, personal, and, ultimately, cultural power, and women dominated higher education. By 2012, many colleges and universities were graduating classes that were 60 percent female. "Women now earn 60 percent of master's degrees, about half of all law and medical degrees, and 42 percent of all MBAs. Most important, women earn almost 60 percent of all bachelor's degrees—the minimum requirement, in most cases, for an affluent life. In a stark reversal since the 1970s, men are now more likely than women to hold only a high-school diploma" (Rosin). As Liza Mundy points out, "For young women, the returns on their educational investment are now becoming clear. In 2010, . . . in most U.S. cities, childless single women between ages 22 and 30 have a median income exceeding that of their male peers." In such cities, "single women have become prime home buyers," while many men continue to live at home (53). Men are not blind. For forty years, the men of Springsteen's generation and the following generations as well, have watched college campuses, cities, and workplaces become women-oriented environments. As they have done so, some men seem to have lost direction and will, almost as if they do not know how to construct themselves or make meaning of life apart from the patriarchal structures of the past. While women have thrived on cracking all-male bastions and felt a sense of empowerment by assuming formerly male roles, men have felt disempowered by these events and seem to feel little empowerment in competing with women.

And this is really the crux of the male dilemma since 1960. If traditional avenues of male identity that young men of the fifties thought to be their birthright—such as the breadwinner, the rational problem solver, the benevolent patriarch, or the powerful conqueror—were to be the province of women as well as men, what would men do to cultivate a sense of identity? So began an unsettling search for an answer to this question. Men reared on a steady dose of American mythology tried to fashion themselves in the image of the self-made man or the rugged individualist, only to find that corporate capitalism allows for very few of those, that there is no longer a frontier to tame, and that women can seemingly be as rugged and self-made as men. The athletic hero remained a possibility for some boys and a few younger men, but the sporting life is terribly fleeting, and women occupied this arena as well. The eighties featured the rise of the Yuppie, a self-involved, upwardly mobile professional dedicated to consumption and status. But as exposed in such novels as Jay McInerney's *Bright Lights, Big City* (1984) or films like Oliver Stone's *Wall Street* (1987), the spiritually vacuous Yuppie was hardly a fulfilling template for most of its practitioners, was available only to highly educated men, was also accessible for women, and was, to some degree, destructive because of its emphasis on a high-flying lifestyle that involved drugs, alcohol, and indiscreet sex. The sensitive man of the 1990s didn't gain much traction among men. He was perceived as wimpy, and, despite considerable hype, women did not respond to him. Even "one of the most reliable refuges for beleaguered masculinity, the soldier/protector, fell into . . . disrepute" after a failed war in Korea, an unpopular war in Vietnam, and yet another series of military boondoggles in Iraq and Afghanistan in the first decade of the twenty-first century (Kimmel 263).

The lack of masculine alternatives was particularly difficult for white men, who had always held the place of prominence in American culture. Not only did they face the aforementioned challenges, but since the 1960s, they also had to contend with the growing strength of minority men and women, the gay liberation movement, and the proliferation of feminine sensibilities, such as hippies, glams, punks, new wavers, goths, and grunge kids. This combination of failed centers and the growing empowerment of formerly marginalized subjectivities continued to panic many white men as the twentieth century drew to a close. By the early twenty-first century, traditional manhood seemed as fragile, elusive, and even unpopular as it could possibly be. "The structural foundations of manhood—economic independence, geographic mobility, domestic dominance—have all been eroding" (Kimmel 299). White men were seen as the benefactors of a colonialist, oppressive, patriarchal past. Many such men felt guilty for achieving economic success, had no idea how they should act toward women in an age of sexual harassment lawsuits and heightened gender tension, and were left completely baffled by the ascendancy of gays and lesbians, as well as the massive numbers of Spanish-speaking immigrants that were suddenly demanding a seat at the table of political power. Kimmel wrote, "American men feel themselves beleaguered and besieged, working harder for fewer and fewer personal and social rewards." Many of these men are white males who, still feeling the presence of 1950s images reminding them of their lost power, are left shrugging their shoulders and wondering, "What's a man to do?" (299).

THE LIFE AND MUSIC OF BRUCE SPRINGSTEEN

The question looms: While these new gender realities exist, what do they have to do with the reception of Bruce Springsteen and his music? The answer is rooted in the fact that Springsteen's music was being consumed, to a considerable extent, by the men who were silently enduring these new conditions, men who were often encouraged to hide their pain, to suck it up, to stifle their complaints even as they were being victimized in ways that they didn't fully understand. The signs of male suffering were popping up everywhere. High unemployment rates; low graduation rates; a bulging prison population; a growing number of divorces in which men often came out on the short end in terms of losing assets and, more important, their children; a rise in domestic violence arrests; a loss of financial, political, familial, and cultural power; a decline in social prestige; and a general loss of respect for themselves in the face of countless caricatures and satirizations have all characterized the American male experience in recent times. In the face of these adverse conditions and the antimale sentiment that has accompanied them, Springsteen and his music have served men in two ways. First, he has given expression to their pain, allowing men to see that they are not voiceless or alone. Second, he has supplied them with a healthy blueprint for a masculinity that can work in the modern world.

Even in his first three albums, all of which feature a youthful dreaminess and playfulness, there are young men, much like Springsteen himself, who long to prove themselves and find meaningful relationships but who can seem to do neither. His first album, *Greetings from Asbury Park, NJ* (1973), includes "Mary, Queen of Arkansas," a beautiful but sad lament from "a lonely acrobat" who doesn't understand how Mary "can hold me so tight, but love me so damn loose." *The Wild, the Innocent, and the E Street Shuffle* (1973) has the sometimes forgotten "Kitty's Back," in which the heartsick, beaten-down Cat takes the voluptuous Kitty back, even though she has cheated on him and it is clear that she will hurt him again. Cat's powerlessness is revisited in *Born to Run's* (1975) "Meeting across the River," where two men in dire straits plan a midnight caper, which the speaker hopes will rescue his relationship with "Cherry," who is "gonna walk" because he can't be the man she needs him to be.

By 1978, Springsteen had been through some of the grueling ups and downs of the music industry. He had toured the country and witnessed the quiet desperation that characterized the lives of so many people. Consequently, *Darkness on the Edge of Town* (1978) resonates with a more mature sound, sharpened by the disappointment of adult experience, in which Springsteen truly became a voice for the "beleaguered men" about which Kimmel writes. Three songs in particular—

"Something in the Night," "Factory," and "Darkness on the Edge of Town"—are noticeably different from the works on his first three records. "Something in the Night" is about loneliness, regret, and broken dreams. The speaker is alone in his car; it is late, and he is "riding down Kingsley, figuring I'll get a drink." The radio blares, "so I don't have to think." He is consumed by regret and has "stuff running 'round my head" that he "just can't live down." He wants to find his dream and to love, but he finds only that both are "crushed and dying in the dirt." He and his girl try to "pick up the pieces," but like so many men of the seventies, the lovers are assaulted by forces greater than themselves, forces that they don't understand, which leave them "running burned and blind," still groping for some undefined destination that they hope will bring relief.

In "Factory," the man has made it out of the car wreck; he has a family and a steady job. However, the job is brutal and takes a great deal more from him than it seems to give. Springsteen wrote the work about his own father, but it is a song whose plot encompasses the experience of many alienated men in the 1970s. The protagonist's life is guided by the factory whistle. When it blows, the tired "man rises from bed and puts on his clothes." At first light, he enters the factory, which "will take his hearing," even as it allows him to keep his family above water. It is the last he will see of the light. By day's end, when the factory whistle blows again, the men walk out into the darkness with "death in their eyes." They are caught in a pattern that grinds them down, leaving them angry and off-balance as they stagger out of the factory, ready to lash out at one another in their frustration. "Somebody's gonna get hurt tonight," but that is the natural conclusion of a "working life" that offers no meaning, identity, or joy.

The album ends with "Darkness on the Edge of Town," and Springsteen uses his last opportunity to reach his audience to unleash the story of a man who, like so many of his real life contemporaries, feels that he has lost everything. His wife has left him for a "house up in Fairview" complete with "a style she's trying to maintain." He has lost his money, as well, and he is left with nothing but secrets that he "just can't face." He can no longer stand it. He can't care anymore, because there is nothing he can do to make things right. So, he decides to "cut it loose" before his desire to live an unattainable American Dream kills him. He stops caring about "things that don't seem to matter much to me now," and he immerses himself in "the darkness on the edge of town" where no one "looks too long in your face" and the roaring engines of racing cars drown out his painful memories. He likes the anonymity, but he likes the immediacy of meaning even more. The object of the race is clear, and there are comprehensible rules and definite winners and losers. He can feel his life "on the line," and in a moment, dreams are "won and lost." Here, the dull-eyed, defeated worker from "Factory" has recognized his failure and taken the only option that seemed attractive to many men as America headed into the eighties—aggressive action that will yield some thrills and likely end in self-destruction so that, as the speaker in "Factory" says, he "won't have to think."

On a personal level, the title song of *The River* (1980) is a sympathetic lament about Springsteen's sister Virginia and her husband, who married at a young age and struggled to hold their family together in the difficult recessions of the seventies and early eighties. Of course, "The River" functioned on a larger societal level as a song that reflected the experiences of many young men who suddenly found themselves behind the economic and domestic eight ball at the time. The man in the song comes "from down in the valley," and he met Mary in high school "when we were just seventeen." They "go down to the river," two kids with dreams who are enjoying life. Then, Mary gets pregnant, and "man, that was all she wrote." They must get married, and he takes a union job "working construction." They still go down to the river, but now there is no romance and joy; it is a river of broken dreams where his "memories haunt me like a curse." He knows "the river is dry," and there is nothing they can do to recapture their hopes and desires. He will become like so many men of the time, stuck in a pattern of thankless work and domestic drudgery but with dreams of youth that never leave him alone. Soon, he will be like the speaker in "Fade Away," just hoping against hope that his wife, who has "found another man," won't leave him and that he won't "fade away" like a "ghost out on the street." This is how many men felt, like they were disappearing against a backdrop in which they were valued only for labor that was increasingly hard to find and in which they lacked intrinsic value.

For the next three decades, Springsteen would continue to feel and express the pain of men struggling against the patterns of history, men who believed in the promises of their culture that they could find meaning in various templates of masculine identity that ultimately proved to be unreliable at best and harmful at worst. For instance, the soldier as patriot has always been a powerful model for American men, and Hollywood has flooded the cultural landscape with films that glorify the military leader, such as *The Bridge on the River Kwai* (1957), *The Great Escape* (1963), *MacArthur* (1977), *Glory* (1989), *Saving Private Ryan* (1998), and *Gods and Generals* (2003). Yet, the experience of men who fought in Korea, Vietnam, Iraq, and Afghanistan has often been far different from that of the celluloid warriors they admired. All these wars were fought mostly by poor young men, for reasons that were unclear and unconvincing, and all have been perceived as less than successful by many Americans.

Vietnam in particular left many men of Springsteen's generation physically and emotionally damaged. One of these soldiers, Ron Kovic, chronicled his experiences in *Born on the Fourth of July* (1976), an autobiography that Springsteen read in the late seventies. Kovic's misguided dreams of glory left him paralyzed. He was shunned by society when he returned home, but Springsteen rescued his voice and the voices of thousands of other veterans in "Born in the USA," the booming opening track of *Born in the USA* (1984). The speaker in the song is a working-class kid who "got in a little hometown jam," which occasioned his getting shipped to Vietnam to "kill the yellow man." His brother is killed, and no one will hire him when he returns home. He is left "standing in the shadows of the penitentiary," a damaged figure who has "nowhere to go." Through his music and the many charity concerts he has played to benefit veterans since the early eighties, Springsteen has made sure that these men will not fade into the shadows. As late as 2005, Springsteen was still making Americans confront the plight of young men being sacrificed in wars that seemed more about the economic interests of a few than the preservation of freedom. The title track of *Devils & Dust* (2005) presents the listener with a young soldier who has his "finger on the trigger." He wants to believe that he has "God on my side," but he isn't sure. In fact, he doesn't "know who to trust," and he feels a "dirty wind blowing." One gets the feeling that someone has lied to him and put him in this terrible situation where he must kill "to survive." He is afraid, and he laments that the war has taken his "God-filled soul" and filled "it with devils and dust." Even if he makes it home, this soldier, like thousands of his real-life counterparts, has come to understand that the glory of the soldier as patriot can be a mirage that leaves its adherents emotionally bankrupt.

Through the decades, Springsteen has continued to write for men who find themselves on the underside of America's models of masculinity. In "Glory Days," off *Born in the USA*, and much later in "The Hitter," from *Devils & Dust*, Springsteen recognizes the limitations of the athlete. Men who base their worth on this model often have emotional and physical difficulties by the time they reach middle age because of the short-lived, taxing nature of being a sports star. In "Glory Days," the protagonist can't find a meaningful way to live after his athletic career has ended, and he drifts from bar to bar with nothing to do but to retell "boring stories of glory days." In "The Hitter," a once proud, now ravaged boxer returns to his mother's home to rest his weary body before he goes off to fight again. Like all men in his profession, he cannot outrun "the cuts, the scars, the pain" that "man, nor time can erase." The athlete is closely related to the local hero, another man for whom Springsteen has sympathy. This man may be an athlete or simply someone who has peaked early in life in some way that made him a hero in his town. In *Lucky Town*'s (1992) "Local Hero," the singer realizes this man's dilemma of never being able to live up to his heroic reputation and, ironically, being resented by many people because of his status. More people want to bring him down than raise him up. He sings, "First they made me the king then they made me the pope; then they bought the rope."

It is significant that all these men end up alone. Springsteen seems to understand that whatever template these men trusted, the worst part of their pain is the loneliness and isolation they feel. The Springsteen canon is replete with brokenhearted lovers, including many of the characters from *Tunnel of Love* (1987), the album Springsteen wrote while his first marriage, to Julianne Phillips, was disintegrating. "Brilliant Disguise," "Tunnel of Love," "Cautious Man," "One Step Up," and "Ain't Got You" are all about men who are paralyzed by their own impotence when it comes to women. Like many modern men, they are fearful, inadequate, and, like the protagonist of "Walk like a Man," left with little recourse but to pray "for the strength to walk like a man." Many of the men in Springsteen's works are husbands and fathers who, because of the uncertain economic conditions and changing gender relations of the last half century, find themselves in waters through which they do not know how to navigate. Nowhere is this more evident than on *Wrecking Ball* (2012), where the family men of "Shackled and Drawn," "Jack of All Trades," and "This Depression" struggle to make ends meet and keep their families together. The latter is perhaps the saddest song on the record, sung in the manner of an old blues number, in which a once proud man admits that he has "never felt so weak." Like many men of the day, he has never "been this lost."

It is important to note that while Springsteen allows American men the relief of seeing their desperation portrayed in his works, he does not paint them as pathetic people. They are not to be pitied. Instead, they are to be empathized with and even admired for their ability to keep fighting in the rubble of their broken dreams. His characters may be confused and shaken, but this only makes them more human. Plus, they are also hardworking, good-hearted, and well intended. They want to work, find meaning, enjoy romance, take care of their families, and be leaders in their communities. It's just that somewhere between 1950 and 2013, many of the rules for working and living changed, leaving them trying to figure out how to cope with life. Perhaps the problem is best summed up in "The Promise," which first appeared on *18 Tracks* (1999). The main character speaks for so many American men when he says, "All of my life I fought this fight," but it's a battle "no man can never win." At some point, "the promise was broken," and now all he can do is "go on living" the best he can. Many men feel kinship to Springsteen because, unlike many artists and almost all of popular culture, Springsteen understood their quiet desperation and the dignity with which they tried to bear it.

Yet, Springsteen gives men more than empathy and respect. He gives them direction. Although his songs contain a great many painful scenes, they make it clear that if a man can persevere, work hard, overcome adversity, and honestly display his vulnerability, he can find a type of rough-hewn redemption; he might even find a girl along the way, one who will stand by him through good times and bad, helping him become a good father and leader. This romantic hopefulness is undoubtedly part of the Springsteen canon. Yet, it's not an unrealistic nostalgia for a 1950s white masculinity of privilege that relied on the subordination of others; it's hard won and inclusive, and you have to take a lot of punishment to earn your stripes. What does the Springsteen version of healthy masculinity look like?

First, a man must survive unrealistic, often outdated, models of behavior that work only on the silver screen or in comic books and that continue to bombard and delude young men. Like Springsteen himself, men must persevere through romanticized, idealized versions of manhood to see life as it truly is: confusing, dirty, and hard but worth the struggle. Springsteen survived poverty, a brutal childhood, an indifferent school system, constant criticism, the fickle nature of the music industry, a lengthy lawsuit with his first manager, a hurtful divorce, clinical depression, the breakup of the E Street Band, and the trials of fatherhood. American men who know anything about his life understand this credibility. Many of Springsteen's characters are purified by the fires of demythologization, and they emerge as tougher people who are ready to live life in the real world. Consider the speaker in "Tougher Than the Rest," a song that Springsteen wrote for *Tunnel of Love*. He is no Ward Cleaver, and he doesn't build romantic fantasies around a beautiful woman, as Springsteen himself may have done with Phillips. Instead, he admits that he's no "handsome Dan," "good-lookin' Joe," or "sweet-talkin' Romeo." He's been hurt, "been around a time or two," but this has prepared him for being a good partner. He's tough and practical, ready to walk the "thin, thin line" for a like-minded woman. He's "rough and ready for love," ready to "pass the test." This is the man who appears in "Living Proof," on Springsteen's next album, *Lucky Town* (1992). Here, like Springsteen—who married Patti Scialfa in 1991 shortly after the birth of his first child—he has found a woman with whom he can make a life. He is thankful for the birth of his child, and he thinks of how far he has come. He had crawled through "the desert city," full of self-loathing, "tryin' so hard to shed my skin." He had "crawled deep into some kind of darkness" and done "some sad and hurtful things." He experienced "anger and rage," but somehow he made it through "a world so hot and dirty" to find a hard-earned love that produced a beautiful child, "living proof" that there is beauty in the world. Like Springsteen, he has weathered the storm of romance and myth, of darkness and confusion, to forge a realistic happiness.

Second, a man must find a place to use his talents. Springsteen found rock 'n' roll, and it rescued him, allowing him to make a place where he could find value and earn self-respect. As Springsteen remembers, music "gave me a sense of purpose. What I wanted to do. Who I wanted to be. The way that I wanted to do it. What I thought I

could accomplish through singing songs" (*60 Minutes*, 2008). His characters come to understand this truth as well. In true Springsteen fashion, his characters do not have to be geniuses or engage in highly paid
professions; they are often just regular men who gain value through
labor. The main character in "Galveston Bay," on *The Ghost of Tom
Joad* (1995), is an immigrant from South Vietnam who works fifteen
years as a machinist to save up enough money to become a fisherman,
an occupation that brings him pride and dignity. The hero of *Wrecking
Ball*'s "Jack of All Trades" is a handyman. He will never be rich, but he
can fix anything and build whatever you need. He can support his
family with his creativity and ingenuity. In short, he uses his talents,
and, for Springsteen, this is part of the recipe that brings a man joy.

Of course, Springsteen himself remains the symbol of this lesson for
his fans. A kid who grew up with little hope and little expectation of
success, Springsteen has become the poster boy for saving oneself by
finding a venue to use one's gifts. One of his earliest songs, "Growin'
Up," became the launching pad for his classic seventies concert rap in
which he described his troubled childhood and the romantic dreams
that his father and mother had for him to become a lawyer or a writer.
He finished the story by telling them that they would "both have to
settle for rock 'n' roll." He then launches into the song, in which he
affirms his plan to bomb "'em with the blues" and keep a "jukebox
graduate for first mate." Springsteen followed "Growin' Up" with "Rosalita," in which a young singer tells Rosie that, armed with his guitar, he
will rescue her from a life of tedium. Her parents do not like him any
more than many adults liked the young Springsteen, but he boldly assures her that "a record company, Rosie, just gave me a big advance."
Springsteen's allegiance to and increasing comfort in his place on the
stage is even more evident in *Born to Run*. "Thunder Road" features a
young musician who knows he's "no hero" and that he and Mary "ain't
that young anymore" but who nevertheless feels so confident as a musician that he compares himself to Roy Orbison. He "got this guitar," and
he "learned how to make it talk." That is, in fact, all he has, but it's
enough to allow him to entreat Mary to hit the road with him, as he
bolts "a town full of losers" and insists that he's "pulling out of here to
win." *Darkness on the Edge of Town* includes "Promised Land," in
which the speaker dreams of bigger things than "working all day in my
daddy's garage." His dream seems like "some mirage," and his "eyes go

blind" while "his blood runs cold," but he will not quit. He declares, "I'm a man," and affirms his belief that he will reach the "promised land." Using one's talents gives a man purpose and courage to face the brutality of life. Springsteen's songs reflect his desperate fight, determination, and eventual success and send a resounding message to men everywhere: keep fighting and you can earn satisfaction, a type of use value that can be experienced only when you develop your natural proclivities.

Third, a man needs to admit weakness in the face of a hard world and cultivate emotional intimacy through building close relationships based on mutual vulnerability. While some of Springsteen's early characters, like the guitar heroes in "Rosalita" and "Thunder Road," display a bravado often associated with young men, his men become increasingly sensitive and humble. *The Rising* (2002), written in the aftermath of the September 11 terrorist attacks, reveals Springsteen as a songwriter who has experienced the travails of life as a professional musician, a painful divorce, the ups and downs of fatherhood, and the burden of being an artist dedicated to writing songs that meet real people where they are, to help them through life's difficulties. In "Waitin' on a Sunny Day," for instance, the speaker's girlfriend, like many Americans in the wake of the tragedy, has been crying, and he is there to comfort her. However, he is not John Wayne riding in on a white horse to save the day or Mike Brady dispensing fatherly wisdom that solves the problem. The problem is too big for an easy answer, and the speaker is sad and shaken as well. He is "half a party in a one dog town," and he needs her "to chase the blues away." He assures her that "everything'll be okay," but he allows her to comfort him, too, telling her, "I hope you're coming to stay." *Devils & Dust* features "All the Way Home," in which the speaker confesses that he has known success and failure and that "these days I don't stand on pride." He "ain't afraid to take a fall," and, even if she isn't his first choice, he will walk her "all the way home." *Magic* (2007) includes "I'll Work for Your Love," another tune in which the male protagonist's strength lies in his maturity and desire to give and receive love. Even though "peace has crumbled" and "faith has been tossed," he insists that they can bless each other and that he is willing to "work for your love." On *Wrecking Ball*, the battered speaker of "This Depression" admits that he "had been low, but never this low." Yet, he won't give up. He just needs some help: "This is my confession, I need your heart." Such men are not pitiful; they are not wimps or losers. They are decent men, victims of life's blows, who have learned how to love and receive love, how to help others survive and accept help so that they may in turn survive.

Finally, a man needs to look beyond his own needs and desires and use his talents to better the lives of those in his community, especially those who are weak, disadvantaged, or considered outsiders. Springsteen has, from the earliest days of his career, been a spokesman for the poor. Songs such as "Jackson Cage," from *The River*, remind his listeners that the reason Springsteen writes about the poor so movingly is that he was poor for so many years. The woman in the song "just melts away" in "a house where the blinds are closed." She is invisible because she is poor, a condition in which "every day ends in wasted motion" and most people just "fade away." But, like Springsteen, the speaker is singing because "I dream of a better world," and he desperately wants to resist the poverty that "will turn a man into a stranger to waste away." Springsteen will not let them waste away if he can help it, and he is a role model for men in that the more successful he got as a musician, the more "other-focused" he became.

Springsteen has dedicated much of his career to raising consciousness, to making sure that the voiceless have a voice. As mentioned, Springsteen wrote "Born in the USA" to draw attention to the plight of former soldiers who had been used to fight unpopular wars only to be abandoned later by their government. Like the angry speaker in the song, these men were often physically or emotionally damaged, with "nowhere to run." Springsteen, who has played many benefits for veterans over the years, has never let these men conveniently slip between the cracks. In 1993, he released "Streets of Philadelphia," one of the first popular songs to humanize AIDS victims and demystify homosexuality. The track was an important tool in galvanizing the gay rights movement in the midnineties. Likewise, "Across the Border," off *The Ghost of Tom Joad*, worked to combat the demonization of immigrants. In the song, a poverty-stricken man risks his life to cross the Mexican border into the United States, not to engage in criminal activity or unfairly take advantage of American prosperity, but instead to "build a house high up on a grassy hill" with his wife, who is already on the other side. They are just desperate people who want to reunite as a family, leave "pain and sadness" behind, and "drink from God's blessed waters." Finally, there is "American Skin," a song that Springsteen released on *Live in New York City* in 2001. The song is one of several in which Springsteen speaks up for racial justice. He wrote it after Amadou Diallo, an unarmed black immigrant from Guinea, was shot forty-one times by New York police officers in a case that brought racial profiling to the country's attention. The officers were acquitted, and Springsteen spoke up for Diallo and thousands like him, writing, "It ain't no secret [that] you can get killed just for living in your American skin." The song drew protests from police officers when Springsteen sang it in New York in July 2012, but like nearly every song in Springsteen's arsenal, "American Skin" was not intended to divide but unite, another example of Springsteen's courageous, benevolent version of twenty-first-century American manhood.

In the end, then, a working-class white patriarchal masculinity that had its heyday in the fifties is renegotiated and updated by Springsteen. His characters are usually white and working class, but they are not John Waynes or Ward Cleavers. They are survivors of such unrealistic masculine templates; they are men who have found a way to absorb life's blows and find worth by using their talents; they have come to terms with their weaknesses and have committed to mutual dependence; and they have forfeited their power in favor of raising the banner of those less fortunate. Fascinatingly, all this takes place within the context of the muscular white male body and the husky voice of Springsteen. The look is the familiar, but this is not a nostalgic return to the fifties. This is masculinity renegotiated: it's tough, strong, and muscular, but it's also other focused, inclusive, and vulnerable, befitting the times. It's patriarchal yet egalitarian, professional yet domestic, macho yet soft, traditional yet progressive, white yet inclusive. No doubt this is one reason that Springsteen is so popular among men longing for dignity and women who want men they can respect and love.

5

I HAD A BROTHER AT KHE SAHN

Redefining Patriotism in an Age of War

Bruce Springsteen's life and music have unfolded against several controversial and largely unsuccessful modern wars. Born in November 1949, Springsteen entered the world in Long Branch, New Jersey, only a few months before the start of the Korean conflict.

By the time he reached high school, the United States was bogged down in Vietnam, and Springsteen experienced the anger and disillusionment that many young people felt during the sixties and early seventies. While these wars would famously shape Springsteen's view of government for much of his musical career, he would eventually be equally influenced by the Gulf War (1991) and particularly by the lengthy "war on terror" fought mostly in Iraq and Afghanistan starting in 2001. As his political consciousness has evolved, Springsteen has become a voice of protest and awareness dedicated to keeping government institutions honest and redefining American notions of patriotism.

Springsteen and his friends were too young to fight in Korea, but the specter of the Cold War and its accompanying fears of communist aggression and nuclear annihilation haunted their childhood in the 1950s. In addition, the faulty principles that informed the Korean conflict were similar to the misguided ideas that would plague Springsteen's generation in Vietnam and later damage their children in the war on terror. The common denominators in all three eras were fear, government

deceit and manipulation, war as profitable big business, and the exploi-
tation of the poor.

The fear that pushed the United States into the Korean War largely
stemmed from communism. After the defeat of the Axis powers in
World War II, the United States emerged as the lone economic and
military superpower in the world, and the 1950s saw the country soar to
unprecedented economic heights. Only the communist bloc in Eastern
Europe and Asia threatened America's global superiority, but the differences between East and West worried many Americans. While the
United States and its rebuilding allies in Western Europe featured representative, democratic governments; open markets and capitalist economies; and an emphasis on Judeo-Christian morality, individual liberty,
and personal freedom, the communist East was characterized by au-
thoritarian governments, state-sponsored economies, and the subordination of religion and individual rights to the greater good of the collective. Told by their government that communism was the greatest threat
to their way of life, Americans were conditioned to believe that the
spread of communism anywhere in the world would eventually result in
the United States being compromised. This idea, eventually known as
"the domino theory," seemed to be playing itself out in 1949 when
China became a communist country and, with the aid of the Soviet
Union, began helping communist forces in Korea. If Korea fell,
Americans were told, other countries in Southeast Asia would be next,
and the dominos would continue to fall through the Middle East and
toward Western Europe. Since each domino represented a country full
of important natural resources vital to American businesses, as well as
large tracts of land on which military bases could be installed, it seemed
imperative that the United States contain the "red menace" before the
first domino fell. While none of this was actually likely to happen, a
generation of Americans that was finally enjoying prosperity after the
Great Depression and World War II didn't want to take any chances.
After all, no one wanted to put postwar economic prosperity in jeopardy. In the end, America went to war in Korea in large part because the
government and military of the United States were able to scare its
citizens into believing in the domino theory and its alleged consequences.

The results were disastrous. While politicians who wrapped themselves in anticommunist, patriotic rhetoric got reelected, the military

continued to receive massive funding. While industries that served the military and the war effort made record profits, the working-class soldiers who largely fought the war died in large numbers. By the time that the United States withdrew its forces in 1953, it had lost over 142,000 soldiers, all in a war that, even in the most optimistic terms, ended in a strategic draw.

American citizens who had been promised security found themselves feeling more vulnerable to Cold War threats. Communists were seen behind every tree; bomb shelters appeared in backyards across the country; and the public became even more susceptible to the growing alliance among the military, politicians, and businesses that catered to the defense industry. Recognizing that such an unholy amalgamation would likely enmesh the United States in another war, outgoing President Dwight Eisenhower used his 1961 farewell address to warn the nation of the "unwarranted influence" of the "military industrial complex." Ike cautioned that "we must never let the weight of this combination endanger our liberties" and that "we should take nothing for granted," since the "potential for the disastrous rise of misplaced power exists and will persist."

Indeed, this misplaced power would rear its ugly head in the sixties, when the United States again allowed itself to be ensnared in a war against the spread of communism, this time in Vietnam. The majority of Americans opposed another war in Southeast Asia, but Cold War fears of communist aggression, exacerbated by the Cuban missile crisis (1962), made Americans vulnerable to military, governmental, and corporate interests that were favorable to war. Financially desperate media outlets, for example, became a driving force of the conflict. Media analyst Danny Schechter confirms, "War, and the threat of war, sells newspapers. Peace does not. The 'action' of war builds TV ratings" (Zezima 80). While the media made money, so did the other industries that fueled the war machine, businesses that often contributed large amounts of money to congressional representatives who needed the funds to run reelection campaigns. Of course, many of these elected officials represented states or districts whose constituents were economically dependent on military bases. And so the circle of influence turned, pushing the United States into a nearly unwinnable war that would drag on for over a decade.

As with Korea, this war was fueled by unwarranted fears and government distortions. For instance, when the United States still had the ability to pull out of Vietnam with few losses, President Lyndon Johnson "lied to secure congressional approval of the Gulf of Tonkin Resolution," which said that, due to attacks on U.S. personnel in the gulf, the president could "take all necessary steps" to quell the opposition. It was essentially "a blank check authorization for further action," which resulted in a massive invasion of Vietnam. However, it was later revealed that the dangers to the American forces were exaggerated and that Johnson, despite saying that he sought "no wider war," had been "planning to escalate military action in Vietnam six months before the Gulf of Tonkin incident" (Bella et al. 275).

These were the kind of lies that compromised the working-class soldiers who, by and large, fought the war. "In working-class neighborhoods, . . . military service after high school was as commonplace among young men as college was for the youth of the upper-middle-class suburbs—not welcomed by everyone but rarely questioned or avoided" (Appy 12). These were Springsteen's friends, people like Bart Haynes, the drummer in Springsteen's first band, the Castiles, people who didn't know anything about Vietnam but were told that they should be thankful for a chance to play the patriot and defend their country. Haynes's death would have a tremendous impact on Springsteen, who did everything possible to fail his own army physical, even going as far as to tell the draft board that he was a homosexual. The story would later make for a series of amusing concert anecdotes, but war was personal and anything but amusing for Springsteen, who saw several friends devoured by the American war machine. Poor young men like Haynes made up the lion's share of the more than 350,000 American casualties in Vietnam. Of course, many others suffered unseen emotional wounds that would haunt them long after the war was over. As his friends who survived the war came home, Springsteen could see that many of them weren't "the same anymore" (Loder). These blue-collar soldiers "not only shouldered a disproportionate share of the war's fighting, but a disproportionate share of its moral turmoil" (Appy 321).

Springsteen's anger, which would begin to show on *Darkness on the Edge of Town* (1978) and then flower full-force on *Nebraska* (1982) and *Born in the USA* (1984), is embodied in the disfigured body of Ron Kovic, a young marine who was paralyzed in Vietnam and whose book

Born on the Fourth of July (1976) Springsteen read when he was traveling across country in the late 1970s. The short memoir chronicled Kovic's story as a young working-class kid who was raised to believe in the
American Dream and the idea that, by living in the greatest country in
the world, it was an honor to defend American interests, which, according to much of midcentury popular culture, were always noble. Like
millions of young men, Kovic believed the myths and the lies that
America was somehow in danger of being taken over by predatory communists. With few financial options and his head full of romantic notions about patriotism and American glory, he enlisted in the marines
after high school. On his second tour of duty, he was wounded and
paralyzed. Upon returning home to poor medical care and general public disdain, he began to question the idealistic assumptions of his cultural education, eventually coming to the conclusion that he had been
duped, sacrificed at the alter of the military–industrial complex. When
he protested, he was called a communist and a traitor. He knew that he
had to write his book so that what happened to him might not happen
to other American kids too naive to see through the barrage of popular
images that conditioned them to fight wars that did not help them or
their country. Springsteen met Kovic in 1978 when his political consciousness was in its early stages of formation; he eventually performed
some of his first benefit concerts for Vietnam veterans in the early
1980s.

Angered by the effects of the war and the government lies and
cultural myths that trapped so many young men of his generation,
Springsteen wrote many songs that gave voice to the veterans that
America wanted to forget after the war ended so disastrously in 1975.
"Lost in the Flood," "Highway Patrolman," and "Born in the USA" all
speak to the emotional plight of returning soldiers, who gave the better
part of themselves for a country that rendered them invisible and unim-
portant once they returned home from fighting a war that, by nearly
every evaluation, was a colossal mistake. Springsteen, who for most of
his public career had remained ideologically neutral, even made a point
to criticize the hypocrisy of President Ronald Reagan, who tried to ally
himself with Springsteen and use "Born in the USA" as one of his
campaign reelection songs in 1984, misinterpreting it as a patriotic
piece. Springsteen quickly put a stop to it and addressed the president
at a concert in Pittsburgh: "It's a long walk from the government that's

supposed to represent all the people to where we [are now]. [It] seems like something's happening out there where there's a lot of stuff being taken away from a lot of people that shouldn't have it taken away from them. Sometimes it's hard to remember that this place belongs to us, that this is our hometown." Near the conclusion of the *Born in the USA* tour, Springsteen covered Edwin Starr's "War" in Los Angeles, warning his audience that "blind faith in your leaders will get you killed." The line was important enough to Springsteen that it made it onto the highly successful *Live 1975–1985* album.

Throughout the 1980s, Springsteen continued to develop his views on government and what it means to be a patriotic American; he did so in the context of his own generation's betrayal in Vietnam. Yet, much of his later music was influenced more by the post–September 11 wars in Iraq and Afghanistan. These two wars were part of a larger enterprise, awkwardly referred to as the "war on terror," a series of military campaigns that included considerable action in Pakistan, the Philippines, Somalia, the trans-Saharan region of Africa, Yemen, and Kashmir. All these engagements were part of a strategy called "Operation Enduring Freedom," with the exception of the war in Iraq, which was fought as "Operation Iraqi Freedom." While the last U.S. troops left Iraq in December 2011, American forces were still on the ground at this writing in Afghanistan, and the constant insurgency of terrorists in all the regions just mentioned has kept the American military under increasing stress for well over a decade after the Islamist militant group al-Qaeda hijacked four commercial planes and steered three of them into the Twin Towers and the Pentagon on September 11, 2001.

Perhaps no event since the Japanese bombing of Pearl Harbor in 1941 has so galvanized the American public. Overnight, American flags suddenly seemed to wave from nearly every home and business in the nation. Apathy was replaced by exigency; patriotism surged to heights not seen since World War II. Nearly everyone agreed that something had to be done to keep the country safe from terrorists. However, a problem emerged in the sharp public division regarding just what direction the government should steer its eager and nervous populace. It was President George W. Bush (2001–2009) who provided the direction by immediately authorizing Operation Enduring Freedom. On October 7, 2001, the first Allied forces set foot in Afghanistan. In his 2002 State of the Union address, President Bush stoked the already hot fires of fear by warning Americans that they were in peril because of an "Axis of Evil," made up largely of Iraq, Iran, and North Korea but also of "rogue nations" such as Afghanistan, Syria, and Pakistan, where unstable governments, Islamic law, and poverty combined to give terrorists fertile ground to plan and carry out more attacks. Many Americans were worried. Certainly al-Qaeda, with its multiple terror cells operating all over the world, would not fail to follow up on the actions of September 11, 2001. Early in 2003, Bush, flanked by Defense Secretary Donald Rumsfeld, and Secretary of State Colin Powell put the country on edge when he announced in a prime-time address that Saddam Hussein was in possession of "weapons of mass destruction" and that it would be necessary to launch a second war in Iraq to prevent him from using the weapons in terrorist strikes against the west.

By April 2003, the United States was fighting wars on two major fronts, as well as smaller engagements stretching from Pakistan to Cape Horn. While some Americans embraced the wars as a necessary sacrifice for preserving freedom, others criticized the strategy, arguing that it is impossible to fight terrorists with conventional military strategies and, therefore, these wars would not actually keep the country safe. As time passed, more people seemed to move toward the latter position. Though there were triumphs, such as the capture and executions of Saddam Hussein and al-Qaeda leader Osama bin Laden, there were many setbacks, including the fact that the conflict in Afghanistan seemed nearly as impossible to resolve as the growing tensions in the Middle East. Even though the U.S. military defeated the Iraqi army in short order, the peace proved much harder to win. The country seemed hopelessly divided along ethnic and religious lines, was structurally devastated, and was mostly populated by desperate people living in poverty. While establishing any type of lasting, stable order in such a climate proved elusive, Iran began escalating its own efforts to develop nuclear weapons. It became increasingly clear to many Americans that the United States could not wage war with every country that might be able to give aid to terrorists. Perhaps, many people began to see, the wars, like those fought in Korea and Vietnam, were simply not winnable in any sense of the word.

As the sun set on the first decade of the twenty-first century, a majority of citizens were not only tired of war but had come to the conclusion that they had once again been duped. First, it was revealed that there had not been any weapons of mass destruction in Iraq and that the nation had been pushed into war based on "a deceptive campaign that had been fueled by unsubstantiated, inaccurate, untruthful, or misleading statements" (live concert, Los Angeles Memorial Coliseum, 9 September 1985). In addition, it became clear that the "Axis of Evil," though dangerous, was hardly more dangerous than many other countries in the world and, in any event, could not be policed by the American war machine. The only reason that we had tried to do so is that we were so gripped "by a tragic sense of fear" and "an exaggerated image of the danger endemic to domestic politics and international affairs" that we were again willing to fight wars that didn't need to be fought and could not be won (Ivie 10). Then, of course, there were the costs. As the nation suffered through the recession of 2008, the price of fighting unwinnable wars became all the more upsetting. Total costs are difficult to determine, but it became clear that the price tag would be in the trillions and that a good deal of the money was being borrowed from China and other countries, a condition that, far from protecting freedom, seemed to leave the United States even more vulnerable to foreign interests. As the battle casualties surged toward fifty thousand, more and more military families felt the psychological, physical, and financial impact of years of separation. Finally, many Americans were alarmed and embarrassed by domestic legislation such as the Patriot Act (2001), which included the right of the government to wiretap its citizens and to suspend the right of habeas corpus, and by allegations of torture abroad, such as the abuse of prisoners by American soldiers at the Abu Ghraib facility in Iraq. If we were fighting to preserve freedom, why would we be stripping citizens of the rights granted to them by the U.S. Constitution? If we were fighting to stop terrorism, why were we terrorizing helpless prisoners?

To many Americans, including Springsteen, the answer to this question is that we had not been fighting to protect freedom as much as to advance the interests of the military–industrial complex. For while one might argue that the war on terror was at best only marginally successful in making the United States safer, it certainly weakened the nation's economy and made it more dependent than ever on foreign capital. While Osama bin Laden was dispatched, as well as other al-Qaeda figures, the organization remains strong, and the factors that cultivate terrorism remain in place: unstable governments in the Middle East,

South America, and Africa; Islamic fundamentalism in Afghanistan and throughout the Middle East; and widespread poverty in each of those regions. The only thing different is that anti-American sentiment is higher due to our violent intrusions into the regions.

So, in the end, who actually profited from yet another war waged on the basis of fear and fought largely by working-class, disproportionately minority soldiers? By and large, it was the same groups that profited from the wars in Korea and Vietnam: the military, whose budget increased every year of the opening decade of the twenty-first century, and the many companies working in the industries that supply the military as it wages war. For instance, Blackwater Security Consulting secured a long-term, multimillion-dollar deal to train Iraqi security personnel. Vice President Dick Cheney's former company, Halliburton, received an open-ended ten-year contract worth nearly a billion dollars to help rebuild Iraq's infrastructure. Of course, oil companies registered record profits nearly every year of the war, even as gas prices soared above $4 per gallon for everyday consumers. In other words, those who owned well-connected companies made a killing off the war. Same story, different century.

By 2003, Bruce Springsteen was so concerned about this pattern of misguided patriotism that, for the first time in his career, he publicly campaigned for a presidential candidate, in this case Democratic nominee John Kerry, whose skepticism of the war in Iraq matched Springsteen's own. Springsteen told *Rolling Stone* in September 2004, "I knew after we invaded Iraq that I was going to be involved in the election. It made me angry" (Wenner). Springsteen appeared with Kerry at campaign rallies and, with several other artists, took part in the Vote for Change concerts that preceded the election. He knew that it was time to speak out: "I felt we had been misled. I felt they had been fundamentally dishonest and had frightened and manipulated the American people into war. And as the saying goes, 'The first casualty of war is truth.' I felt that the Bush doctrine of pre-emption was dangerous foreign policy. I don't think it has made America safer." It was clear to Springsteen that "sitting on the sidelines would be a betrayal of the ideas I'd written about for a long time," especially when he felt that "we are quickly closing in on what looks an awful lot like the Vietnamization of the Iraq war. . . . How many of our best young people are going to die between now and that time, and what exactly for?" (Wenner).

With Bush's victory in 2004 and a continuation of his policies, Springsteen ramped up his political efforts, campaigning for soon-to-be-president Barack Obama because "the philosophy that was at the base of the last administration has ruined many, many people's lives." As an artist, he knew that he had to take a strong stand against governmental policies that continually led the United States down a path of perdition. "You see the country drifting further from democratic values, drifting further from any fair sense of economic justice. So you work under the assumption that you have some small thing that you can do about it" (Hagan). By 2012, Springsteen's artistry had led him beyond music that simply critiqued what he considered to be a warped view of patriotism that had characterized American government for several decades, to a full redefinition of patriotism. He told journalist Fiachra Gibbons in February 2012, "I have spent my life judging the distance between American reality and the American dream. What was done to our country was wrong and unpatriotic and un-American and nobody has been held to account. . . . There is a real patriotism underneath the best of my music but it is a critical, questioning and often angry patriotism."

THE CRITICAL EYE: EXPOSING THE PATRIOTISM OF FEAR

For much of his musical career, Springsteen has been dedicated to exposing what might be called a distorted patriotism, characterized by nostalgia, misplaced loyalty, classism, racism, and government subterfuge, among other things, which has helped fuel America's unwise conflicts for the last sixty years. "Born in the USA" is not the first song in which Springsteen examined the plight of Vietnam veterans, but it is the most famous. Originally written for the *Nebraska* (1982) album, it took the country by storm a few years later as the lead track on *Born in the USA* (1984). While the song was misinterpreted by some as a patriotic work, it is instead a picture of a man led to the brink of disaster precisely because he has been abandoned by the nation that he had served. Like many of the soldiers who fought in Vietnam, the protagonist is poor and has very little choice but to join the army. He was "born down in a dead man's town" and ends "up like a dog that's been beat too much." He spends half his "life just covering up." This is the underside of the American Dream populated by the poor who, when they get "in a little hometown jam," have little recourse but to join the army. After being banished to a "foreign land to go and kill the yellow man," he returns home to a leper's welcome. No one will hire him; no one wants to see him. He has lost his brother "at Khe Sahn," and he is utterly alone "in the shadow of the penitentiary." Abandoned, he has "nowhere to run, . . . nowhere to go." Although the song was misinterpreted as a patriotic song by Reagan and conservative columnist George Will, who "dragooned the band in general—and Bruce in particular—into a political fantasy that . . . amounted to an affirmation of patriotism and, thus, of Ronald Reagan and his administration," Bruce put the president in his place in Pittsburgh a few nights later when he mockingly asked his audience what "his favorite album of mine must've been. I don't think it was the *Nebraska* album," a brutal condemnation of Reaganomics and its effects on men like the "cool rockin' daddy" from "Born in the USA" (Carlin 318).

In "Souls of the Departed," from *Lucky Town* (1992), Springsteen juxtaposes the stories of Jimmy Bly and Raphael Rodriguez. Serving the United States in the Gulf War (1990–1991), Bly stands on the famous Highway of Death, which runs from Kuwait City "to Basra," assigned "to go through the clothes of the soldiers who died." Who are these future soldiers? They are people like Rodriguez—poor kids from working-class neighborhoods around the country who have little chance of attaining the American dream. Rodriguez is gunned down in a crossfire when he "was just seven years old," and one feels the connection between his mother helplessly crying for him and the mothers who would be crying in absentia for the soldiers at which Bly is looking on the road. The cries of the mothers stand in sharp contrast to "the self made men" in "the land of king dollar," who, safe in their beautiful homes "in the hills," simply "shake their heads." For Springsteen, something is wrong with a country that expects such young men to serve a country whose class system leaves them so vulnerable with so few opportunities. Fittingly, the song ends with Springsteen challenging himself and other Americans who "get paid" and whose "silence passes as honor" to refuse to let the "dirty little lies" be "written off the books." The song is a "prayer for the souls of the departed," as well as a challenge to Americans to rethink a system that leaves many of its younger citizens so little chance to have the life promised to them by their country's mythology.

In "Devils and Dust," the lead track from *Devils & Dust* (2005), Springsteen examines the relationship among war, faith, and patriotism. The song's narrator upsets the notion that somehow God is on America's side, an idea that harkens back to our deepest Edenic myth that casts the United States as a city on a hill, designated by God as the land in which divine principles would forge a great nation. Certainly, such a nation could consider its wars as holy, the essence of manifest destiny. Yet, while the narrator stands with his "finger on the trigger," he is hardly sure of himself or his mission. He doesn't "know who to trust." He has been brought up to believe that "we've got God on our side" and, therefore, our wars must be justified. However, his doubts have overtaken him, and he has a growing concern that his cause may not be justified. As he asks himself, "what if what you do to survive kills the thing you love?" he begins to understand that "fear is a dangerous thing," in this case so dangerous that it provoked a war that may not be righteous, that may take one's "God filled soul" and "fill it with devils and dust." Clearly, Springsteen is calling his listeners to take heed of misguided patriotism and its potentially negative effects.

If "Devils and Dust" is a sad lament, *Magic* (2007) features three songs that act as an angry challenge to governmental irresponsibility. Written during the Iraq war, "Last to Die" actually captures Springsteen's feelings about all the wars in his lifetime. The speaker, for instance, hears "a voice" that "drifted up from the radio," one that invokes "a voice from long ago." The voice was 2004 Democratic candidate John Kerry, then a young lieutenant who testified in 1971 before the U.S. Senate about the conduct of war in Vietnam (Dolan 407). Certainly, the scene that unfolds before the speaker's eyes has become all too familiar in American culture. Like Kerry years ago, he has come to the realization that "the wise men were all fools" and that the war that they provoked has resulted in nothing but dead bodies that "we stack outside the door." Some of these dead bodies are Iraqi, and some are American, but either way, "we don't measure the blood we've drawn anymore." The violence seems to have no end, "as things fall apart." The song's refrain rings eerily in the ears of the listener: "Who will be the last to die for a mistake?" When will the bloodletting end? Springsteen warns that it won't end until good people wake up and understand that they have been misled by "tyrants and kings" whose political and economic interests are served at the expense of working-class Americans. Ironically, by manipulating the country with fear and misdirected notions of patriotism, these leaders may find themselves "strung up at your city gates." Fear, it seems, eats everything, including those who disseminate it and seemingly profit from it.

"Gypsy Biker" features the homecoming of a soldier who had been serving in the war. Unfortunately, he is coming home in a pine box. His "sister Mary sits with your colors," and his "brother John is drunk and gone." His "mama's pulled the sheets" off his bed for the last time, and his friend, the song's narrator, can only pull his dead buddy's bike out the garage and wistfully shine its chrome as if they were ready to embark on another of the rides "into the foothills" that marked the beauty of their youth. Against these images of loss and waste, the town still insists on having a patriotic parade, which the speaker bitterly criticizes as "some fools parade" in which "the favored" shout "victory for the righteous." Meanwhile, the only people who profit from the war are "the speculators," who "made their money on the blood you shed." The speaker addresses his friend, acknowledging that "the profiteers on Jane Street" have even "sold your clothes and shoes." He is forgotten, "thrown away," except among his weeping family and friends, whose cries are drowned out by the parade participants who confidently "march up over the hill." The image is chilling. As one forgotten victim is brought home in a war that benefits only the military–industrial complex, the flag-waving crowd, fueled by misdirected patriotism, is poised to send another unfortunate victim into the fray.

Finally, there is "Devil's Arcade," a title that reflects the precarious situation in which the soldiers who fought in Iraq found themselves. An arcade features games of chance and skill, such as pinball or video games; in the end, however, the games are pointless. One can only imagine an arcade run by the devil. No doubt, it would feature games that seem promising and worthwhile but, in the end, result in only destruction. This is how Springsteen seems to view the soldiers who fought in the war on terror, as being caught in a game that couldn't be won. The promise, of course, is heroism and valor: "You said heroes are needed, so heroes get made." The reality is that the politicians "made a bet," and many young soldiers "paid." These aspiring heroes dream of a "tomorrow" in which they return home to inherit the American Dream, but many never do. Instead, like the subjects of the song, they wind up dead or wounded with "metal and plastic where your body caved." Each wounded survivor is just another forgotten victim in a "ward with blue walls, a sea with no name" in which the battered men "lie adrift with the heroes of the devil's arcade." Even the soldiers who make it home will be emotionally scarred, and it will take years for them to experience the "slow burning away of the bitter fires of the devil's arcade."

All these songs issue a bitter indictment of the failed policies of several generations of politicians, military leaders, and industrial giants who have gained power and made money through wars that harmed many Americans who, ironically, were easy targets precisely because they were so loyal to their country. Yet, it is important to remember that Springsteen's wrath is reserved for the policies and the perpetrators, not for America. During the *Magic* tour, for instance, Springsteen would routinely include a "things we love about America" list before launching into his nightly tirade against the policies of George W. Bush. Indeed, the genesis of his anger was not patriotism itself but the manipulative, uncritical patriotism that, in his view, had resulted in "rendition, illegal wiretapping, voter suppression, no habeas corpus, . . . an attack on the Constitution, and the loss of our best young men and women in a tragic war" (Dolan 412). The juxtaposition of hope and anger in these concert raps is typical of Springsteen. While he can deliver biting criticism, he rarely does so without shining his artistic light on some path of redemption.

THE DISCERNING VISION

For Springsteen, healthy patriotism involves uniting Americans with a common vision that we are all living together for the same things: freedom, opportunity, family, safety, and equality. We have tremendous diversity of opinion, but our fundamental vision is strong enough to accommodate that diversity. As such, there can be no demonization of "other sides," only the realization that we are on the same journey toward the same things and that we must help one another if we are to realize our goals. Perhaps this is why Springsteen identified with future presidential candidate Barack Obama when, at the Democratic National Convention in 2004, he dismissed the notion that the United States is hopelessly divided between liberal blue states and conservative red states: "We worship an awesome God in the Blue States, and we don't like federal agents poking around our libraries in the Red States. We coach Little League in the Blue States and have gay friends in the Red States. There are patriots who opposed the war in Iraq and patriots who supported it. We are one people" (416). Springsteen most powerfully trumpets this message in "Land of Hope and Dreams," a song first released on the *Live in New York City* album in 2001. We are all "saints and sinners," "losers and winners," and "whores and gamblers," who are in danger of becoming "lost souls" unless we can save one another. Springsteen is optimistic, even in the face of all of our "sorrows," that we can help one another board the train that will "roll through the fields where sunlight streams" toward "a land of hope and dreams." A truly patriotic vision is for the tide that raises all ships. As Springsteen has said many times, "no one wins unless everybody wins" (Goldberg).

The question is, how do we realize this vision? The first step seems to be to adopt a posture of vigilant questioning of the authorities over us, who often manufacture notions of patriotism that are harmful and divisive. Certainly, Springsteen has done this at least since the late 1970s when he released *Darkness on the Edge of Town* (1978), *The River* (1980), and *Nebraska* (1982) in succession, all of which contained songs that questioned whether the reigning authorities truly had the best interests of Americans at heart. As mentioned earlier in this chapter, he rebuked President Reagan's attempt to co-opt "Born in the USA" in 1984 to twist it into some patriotic song that reflected the values of a Republican party that Springsteen saw as standing for a mythic version of America that ignored and thus sanctioned class and racial discrimination. More recently, Springsteen has released songs such as "Your Own Worst Enemy," from *Magic* (2007), in which people who were once "at ease" and "slept in peace" are now coming to the realization that their government has let them down. Now, they "can't sleep at night," and you can't "dream your dreams." He wants his listeners to understand that "your own worst enemy has come to town" in the guise of a patriotic government and has compromised the values that we hold dear: "your flag it flew so high," but it has now "drifted into the sky." The point is clear. Springsteen is telling his audience to wake up and realize that this is not the country we want, nor is this a government that is looking out for us. No song typifies Springsteen's anger at this condition more than "We Take Care of Our Own," from *Wrecking Ball* (2012). The desperate speaker has been "knocking on the door that holds the throne," but there is no one there to listen. Like many Americans suffering through the recessions of the early twenty-first century, he needs help; however, "the road of good intentions has gone dry as a bone," and all he finds are "good hearts turned to stone." From Chicago to New Orleans, Americans have sought help, only to find that "the cavalry stayed home." The speaker understands that Americans only have one another and that "wherever this flag is flown," we must band together and "take care of our own." Why do we have to do so? Chiefly, because our government, despite demanding our loyalty, is not necessarily there to serve us. It has instead catered to the interests of rich, big business and the military, as chronicled earlier in this chapter.

This questioning should lead to active protest, which can lift the veil of false consciousness that keeps many Americans laboring under the idea that the government is effective and does not need to be fixed. Since the advent of the wars on terror, we have witnessed citizens doing this very thing: protesting the wars, speaking out against the abuses in military prisons and the loss of freedoms at home, calling attention to privileges enjoyed by Congress and not afforded to the people whom it represents, and, in nearly every major city, joining the ranks of the ongoing Occupy movement, which Springsteen has praised. Springsteen's work has fueled this protest and can often be heard at Occupy rallies. Springsteen's songs, of course, have always been a form of art as resistance, especially with works such as "Born in the USA," "Nebraska," and "Promised Land." However, his post–September 11 work has taken a decidedly combative turn. *Magic* (2007) features "Long Walk Home," in which the protagonist laments not only the economic downturn in his hometown but also the loss of core moral values. The "flag flying over the courthouse" has always signified that "certain things are set in stone." There are some things "we'll do" and some things "we won't." The will of the people is still good, but somehow their leaders have lost their moral compass and led them in a direction that has compromised a more grassroots, American patriotism composed of hard work, honesty, trust, respect, and fair play. A great deal of damage has been done, and it's "gonna be a long walk home."

Wrecking Ball (2012) offers "Shackled and Drawn" and "We Are Alive," both of which remind the listener of the importance of the role of protest in making sure that people can accurately see whose interests have traditionally been served by government. "Shackled and Drawn," for instance, highlights the plight of the working man who is told that he will make it, if he just works hard and is a loyal American. And he wants to work: "I always loved the feel of sweat on my shirt." However, no matter how hard he works, it becomes clear that there is no way for him to beat a system controlled by an alliance of the military, the government, and big business. The "gambling man rolls the dice," and, win or lose, he bears no risk. Instead, "the working man pays the bills," and even in the hard times, things are "still fat and easy up on banker's hill." The song's gospel rhythm invites the listener to feel the injustice of the situation and participate in resisting it. Likewise, "We Are Alive" invokes the spirit of those who have died standing against institutional abuse. In the shadow of "a cross up yonder on Calvary Hill" sits a graveyard full of people who protested political wrongs. At night, their spirits rise from the graves and demand to be recognized. There is a man "killed in 1877" when railroad workers fought for decent wages and working conditions; another is a civil rights worker killed "one Sunday morning in Birmingham" in 1963; still another is a desperate immigrant who "died last year crossing the southern desert." They died, but in Springsteen's song, they live again to remind his listeners that the journey of protest for equality and proper government never ends. All these people would have been deemed unpatriotic in their time, but their souls have endured and will always be there "to carry the fire and light the spark." The song ends with them affirming, "We are alive," and so must the spirit of protest be if a nation's citizenry is to craft a healthy definition of patriotism and make its government serve the people.

It also seems to be part of Springsteen's vision that, through vigilant questioning and protest, we can lay the groundwork from which we strive directly to improve government, reminding Americans what we are supposed to be striving for. Springsteen himself has modeled this direct action. He has played hundreds of benefit concerts to raise awareness and create policy change regarding the treatment of forgotten war veterans, the necessity of manufacturing clean energy, the importance of international justice and racial justice, the fight against hunger, the problem of homelessness, and the right of every American to a quality education and affordable health care. In addition, he risked the disapprobation of much of his fan base by supporting John Kerry in the

2004 presidential race and then by working on both of Barack Obama's campaigns, in 2008 and 2012. Springsteen traveled extensively with Obama, championing his platform and energizing rallies with emotional renditions of "Promised Land" and "Land of Hope and Dreams."

Finally, Springsteen asserts that those with wealth and power must continuously lead the way in fashioning a more inclusive American Dream in which the government is not controlled by powerful interests that serve only a few and in which it is not allowed to use warped notions of patriotism to control the rest of the population. The "rich man in a poor man's shirt," which Springsteen wrote about in "Better Days" in 1992, can't just be "pretending." He must be actively working to make life better for the middle and lower classes by using his power to make sure that we unite in a common vision that benefits all segments of the population, that we remain vigilant against abuses of power and misguided definitions of duty and patriotism, that we are always willing to protest to correct such abuses and ensure that people can make decisions based on an accurate view of reality, and that we consistently work to change ideals and policies for the benefit of those who have the least. In doing this, Springsteen is uniquely American. Far from calling for some form of top-down socialism, he embraces the freedom of capitalism operating within the constructs of representative government. He simply attaches the caveats that the government must indeed be representative and that those who benefit the most from the openness and freedom must be willing to work for the betterment of the rest. Perhaps this is why Springsteen released *The Seeger Sessions* in 2006. Upset at the economic and political peril in which regular Americans found themselves as the result of a government that seemed to wage wars and conduct business to benefit only the chosen few, Springsteen channeled the art of Pete Seeger, a man who dedicated his life and many of his personal resources to redeeming American culture. Songs such as "Bring 'em Home," "O Mary Don't You Weep," "We Shall Overcome," "John Henry," and "How Can a Poor Man Stand Such Times and Live" all remind listeners of the powerful legacy of men such as Seeger, Woody Guthrie, and Springsteen, who earned a good deal of money but never stopped campaigning for the rights and interests of those with less.

It is not surprising that Springsteen included a song like "Death to My Hometown" on *Wrecking Ball* (2012). In it, the speaker laments the fact that so many forces of greed and power have "brought death to my hometown." He has bowed his back and, with gritty determination, will fight these forces; he tells his son "to be ready when they come." Specifically, he tells him, "Get yourself a song to sing." He should "sing it hard and sing it well," with the hopes that it will "send the robber barons straight to hell." Indeed, this song within the song is a reminder of how consistent Springsteen's message has been. So much of his early material came straight out of Freehold and Asbury Park, New Jersey, towns where he grew up and watched regular Americans struggle and sometimes fail to achieve an American Dream that seemed to be so elusive. He watched friends fight and die in wars that seemed unnecessary, and he watched powerful interests misdefine ideologies such as patriotism and duty to use them against the majority of citizens. In response, Springsteen has performed many benefits over the years for schools, churches, and several other organizations in towns along the Jersey shore. He has never been just a rich man in a poor man's shirt, and his musical career is a reminder of what we should expect of our government and how we can hold our representatives accountable for working toward a society in which the American Dream approximates the American reality.

6

IT AIN'T NO SIN TO BE
GLAD YOU'RE ALIVE

Social Justice

In an America where so many suffer from various forms of injustice, how do we proceed to act when we live in an age of self-indulgent consumerism, escapist entertainment, and a broken government that causes people to become jaded about the possibility of ameliorating serious social problems? While Bruce Springsteen does not offer nuanced answers to this pressing question, he does champion the cause of social justice, reminding us that a basic vision of equality is what makes the American experiment noble. It is that fundamental commitment, not crass materialism or individualistic political agendas, that gives the American Dream its soul. This is a theme that runs through much of his career but most powerfully resonates in his works of the last two decades, many of which draw attention to those on the margins of American life and advocate for empathy as well as financial and political help for those most in need.

AMERICANS AT RISK

It is a cruel irony that a country whose founding document boldly declares that "all men are created equal" is characterized by embarrassing inequalities. Growing up on the edge of poverty in working-class Freehold, New Jersey, Springsteen learned some hard early lessons about economic injustice. However, it was not until the late 1970s that he would begin to cultivate a view of the United States as a country that was not living up to its ideals. Touring the country, going overseas and looking back at America through foreign eyes, and reading books such as Henry Steele Commager and Allan Nevins's *History of the United States*, Springsteen gradually "opened his eyes" (Marsh 281). What Springsteen saw and what he continues in many respects to see is a country rife with discrimination based on race, ethnicity, and sexual orientation, whose health care system neglects a significant portion of its citizens; it is a nation in which millions of children are at risk, which spawns and then neglects a large homeless population, and which largely ignores its high poverty rate and a growing financial gap between its classes.

Although Springsteen's audience is mostly white, his music has a decidedly pluralistic feel, and he continues to uphold the ideals spawned by the civil rights movement of the 1960s that informed his development as a teenager. He told journalist Fiachra Gibbons in February 2012, "I have spent my life judging the distance between American reality and the American dream." In terms of discrimination based on race, ethnicity, and sexual orientation, that distance seems still to be quite dramatic. For instance, African Americans and Latinos continue to suffer disproportionately in terms of educational investment, health care, political representation, financial benefits, and career advancement. Conversely, they are wildly overrepresented as prisoners, on the unemployment line, and in hospitals as victims of nearly every disease. Economic statistics are the most glaring. For instance, while only 9 percent of white families live in poverty, roughly 30 percent of African American and Latino families (not including those who are undocumented) live beneath the poverty line (Smedley and Smedley 343). In addition, the unemployment rate for African Americans and Latinos continues to be double that of whites.

While the United States has a long way to go to realize racial equality, it is also playing catch-up with the rest of the Western world regarding health care. According to *The 2000 World Health Report*, the U.S. health care system ranks thirty-seventh in the world, despite spending more than any other country. Such waste has resulted in ranks of "39th for infant mortality, 43rd for adult female mortality, 42nd for adult male mortality, and 36th for life expectancy" (Murray). In terms of obesity and the many diseases informed by poor diets and exercise routines, the United States ranks number one in the world. Nearly 70 percent of American adults are overweight or obese, and many of the record number of cases of heart disease, kidney failure, strokes, cancer, and diabetes are in part caused by a combination of unhealthy lifestyles and the fact that many Americans have little or limited health care. Nearly fifty million Americans had no medical coverage in 2010 (Chou and Kane). A disproportionate number of the 16 percent of the American public with no access to health care are poor members of minority groups.

Even more vulnerable are children. It is hard to believe that the richest country in the world has so many children whose welfare is precarious. Yet, over sixteen million children live in poverty. Millions are malnourished, undereducated, neglected, abused sexually or emotionally, or forced to live in fear of unfit parents. High divorce rates, single parents living near the poverty line, a media consumed with making money by exploiting teenage sexuality, a snack industry dedicated to making money by selling poor children cheap sugary treats, and an educational system ill-equipped to handle "at risk" students all make America a dangerous place to live for many kids. Scariest of all is that the United States, with its liberal laws regarding pornography and relatively light punishments for sex offenders, is one of the prime destinations for the trafficking of children for illicit sexual purposes. No group of children feels the sting of these degradations more than that of undocumented immigrants, whose questionable legal status makes them even more vulnerable to those willing to go outside the law in the name of exploiting them.

One of the factors that leaves these children even more vulnerable is the growing epidemic of homelessness in the United States. It is difficult to determine the exact numbers of homeless in America, but scholars estimate that at any given time there are nearly one million people without shelter of any kind, including up to a hundred thousand in some major cities (Levinson and Ross). Approximately three million people are at least temporarily homeless over the course of a year. Some are victims of downturns in the economy, but perhaps as many as 40 percent of people on the streets suffer from an untreated mental illness. Nearly a quarter of the homeless are families with children.

Again, the homeless are disproportionately racial minorities or members of the LGBT (lesbian, gay, bisexual, and transgender) community. All of this indicates that all the major social issues affecting the country intersect with the problem of homelessness.

Yet, undergirding all the social hemorrhaging is poverty and a growing gap between a small group of wealthy Americans that control the majority of the resources in the country and the swelling lower classes, which find themselves with less and less. Approximately 20 percent of the people control 85 percent of the country's wealth, while the other 80 percent are left to split the remaining 15 percent (Domhoff). Nearly 150 million Americans are considered poor or as living in poverty, and 57 percent of children live in a home that is poor or "low income." Such homes suffer in disproportionate numbers from health problems, including mental illness, minimal education, unemployment, poor health care, and a deep sense of helplessness—the same kind of helplessness that Springsteen felt as a kid.

All these problems continue to grow despite the fact that many Americans would like to remedy them. Why? Perhaps two of the reasons involve government inefficiency and an entertainment culture that functions to "drug" Americans into a kind of distracted amnesia. The former seems to be a product of our inability to manage diversity. Power in Washington and other centers of governance throughout the country is not only split between Republicans and Democrats, who do not see eye to eye on many issues, but also divided among various interest groups who would rather sacrifice national health to advance their agendas. The gridlock on Capitol Hill has become legendary, even reaching the point in January 2013 where Congress allowed the nation to roll off a "fiscal cliff" that threatened to send the economy into yet another recession. Infighting among diverse parties has stalled meaningful legislation on gun control, immigration, health care, poverty, homelessness, tax reform, and small business relief, among other things. According to the Pew Research Center, only about 30 percent of Americans have even a minimal degree of trust in their government. Quite simply, many people have given up on making any progress in the area of social injustice.

At the same time that Americans feel that addressing such ills is all but pointless, the entertainment industry, strapped with debt and in desperate need to make money, continues to produce new ways of distracting disgruntled consumers from the serious problems they can't remedy. Video games, online games, television, film, radio, e-readers, fantasy leagues, cell phones, new musical gadgets, and millions of interactive Internet sites designed to cater to a million different fetishes greet the average American every day. Critic Neil Postman saw this sea of distraction coming years ago when he penned *Amusing Ourselves to Death* in 1985, a prescient work that warned any Americans who would listen that the culture industry was not only dedicated to making us stupid but also guilty of lulling us into a pleasant state of amnesia whereby we eschewed social responsibility in favor of enjoyable diversion. In the end, Postman proved to be prophetic. This unfortunate combination partly explains public apathy to the Occupy movement of 2011 and 2012 in which a handful of concerned citizens occupied public space in cities across America to campaign for the amelioration of social injustice. Perhaps they were met with so much hostility, not because they threatened current class structures, but because they annoyingly reminded us that we had collectively abdicated our duty to the less fortunate. Perhaps Americans did not want to be distracted from their distractions?

SPRINGSTEEN AND THE GOSPEL OF SOCIAL JUSTICE

Bruce Springsteen recognizes this condition and has dedicated a significant portion of his career to peeling off the layers of our culturally generated amnesia. In doing so, he encourages us to recognize our common humanity, and he challenges us to take care of one another. His vision of social justice emphasizes unity and inclusion in the face of what sometimes appears to be hopeless divisiveness, as well as a feeling of hope in the face of despair. For instance, Springsteen spoke well of the Occupy movement, and his music could regularly be heard at its rallies. More than likely, this happened because, while Springsteen is not a social technician who can offer specific solutions for social ills, he is a populist artist dedicated to waking people up from their diversions so that they might focus on the people who need their help. This, more than anything else, seems to be Springsteen's strategy to help America live up to its lofty goals.

For example, in an age where so many suffer from discrimination, many of Springsteen's songs celebrate diversity as an American strength, inspiring his fans to embrace multiculturalism and cultivate an empathy toward those different from themselves. As early as 1984, Springsteen released "My Hometown," a song replete with images of "troubled times," especially racial discord. The "tension was running high" at his "high school." The halls and school yard were full of "fights between black and white." At the time, "there was nothing you could do." But the speaker, synonymous with Springsteen, is reflecting back on this time with the benefit of two decades of experience, and there is still a sense that he and his wife will not give up on the place. Listeners are left with the definite impression that one should not run from or ignore the tensions produced by pluralism. You will always be tempted to head "south," but in the end, "this is your hometown," and you must help it adjust to new realities.

Everyone is welcome in Springsteen's hometown. For instance, in 1993 he released "Streets of Philadelphia," one of the first popular songs to humanize AIDS victims and demystify homosexuality. The song's narrator is "bruised and battered." He is in the latter stages of the AIDS virus and is "unrecognizable to myself" when he looks in the mirror. Wandering the streets friendless and alone, he wonders if we are "gonna leave" him "wastin' away on the streets of Philadelphia." With his "friends vanished and gone," the nameless narrator also feels the sting of spiritual desolation. There will be "no angel" to "greet" him. It is up to us to give him some relief as he feels himself "fading away." He begs the listener to "receive me brother." It is either that or "leave each other alone like this on the streets." The song ends with the speaker alone and desolate. It seems that he will not be received, even with a "faithless kiss"—except, of course, by Springsteen, whose song rescues those suffering from AIDS and the stigma of being gay from anonymity. It is difficult to listen to the mournful sound of the narrator's words without feeling his humanity. This is the kind of empathy that Springsteen tries to create. The track was, not surprising, an important tool in galvanizing the gay rights movement in the midnineties.

Brown-skinned people recently immigrated from around the world are also welcome in Springsteen's hometown. The main character in "Galveston Bay," on *The Ghost of Tom Joad* (1995), is an immigrant from South Vietnam who works fifteen years as a machinist to save up enough money to become a fisherman, an occupation that brings him pride and dignity. Yet, Le Bing Son has an enemy. Billy Sutter grew up in Texas, fought in Vietnam, and came home to the same ignominious reception that other veterans received. In addition, he watched helplessly "as the refugees came," settling "on the same streets" where he grew up. Billy is not alone. Others are angry enough to try to "burn the Vietnamese boats." Le Bing shoots two such intruders, and Billy is angry when he is acquitted of murder charges. He contemplates revenge, even warning Le Bing, "My friend, you're a dead man." He waits in the dark for Le Bing to pass, ready to stick a knife into his belly and end his life. However, in the moment of truth, Billy's better self prevails. He "stuck his knife into his pocket" and "let him pass." Billy goes home and kisses "his sleeping wife." The next morning, he heads "into the channel" to cast "his nets into the water," alongside Le Bing. Typical of Springsteen is his lack of blame for Billy's feelings. He understands his resentment, but he also believes in Billy's goodness, which allows him to recognize himself in Le Bing and do the right thing in the end.

In similar fashion, Springsteen takes up the cause of Mexican immigrants in "Across the Border," a seemingly unobtrusive song near the end of *The Ghost of Tom Joad* (1995). The song is slow and quiet, highlighting the pain and desperation of a good-hearted husband and father who risks his life crossing into the United States in hopes of providing a better life for his family. The song is designed to make Americans stand in the shoes of a man whose family is fragmented and who will do anything to save it. He is no different from the millions of people from Europe who preceded him a century or two earlier. He is not an enemy invader; he is a brother.

Those with black skin will also be welcomed with open arms into Springsteen's spiritual community. *Devils & Dust* (2005) features "Black Cowboys," the story of Rainey Williams, a young black kid trying to grow up on tough city streets. As he moves "past melted candles and flower wreaths" that mark the graves of other young men who have died before their time, he understands that all he has to keep him safe is his mother's home and her love. She tells him to "come home from school and stay inside" where he can watch Westerns featuring "black cowboys of the Oklahoma range." However, the violence and degradation of the street finds its way into the house. Rainey's mom takes "up with a man whose business is the boulevard." Soon, her smile "dusted away," and all Rainey can feel when he hugs her is the "ghost in her bones." To save himself from the violent fate of so many black males, he runs away, taking the train west toward the "rutted hills of Oklahoma." One can sense that Springsteen hopes that Rainey will thrive. He does not deny the brutality of urban life that swallows the hopes of black youth, but for Springsteen the fault is in an environment characterized by poverty and desperation. He is sympathetic to Rainey and his mother. They are good people, worthy of decent living conditions that would match their inner decency. Perhaps this is why Rainey winds up in the west, in the open spaces of the "frontier" where he has the space to define himself through his own character. Most of Springsteen's later work features other songs which, like "Black Cowboys," work to promote racial equality and social justice. As discussed in earlier chapters, two of the best are *Live in New York City*'s "American Skin" (2001) and *Wrecking Ball*'s "We Are Alive" (2012).

Part of the reason that Springsteen is so passionate about social justice is that every type of inequality hurts children. Many of his songs, even early in his career, highlight the vulnerability of young people. In "The Angel" (1973), a young exile "rides with hunch-backed children," while "the interstate's choked with nomadic hordes" searching for a home. Released only a few months later, "4th of July, Asbury Park" features two lovers "left stranded" among "stoned-out faces" and "switchblade lovers." The "tramps" in "Born to Run" (1975) are left to "sweat it out on the streets of a runaway American dream."

Most of these songs have a biographical feel. They are about Springsteen and the people he knew—kids who were poor and felt displaced. Of course, Springsteen grew up and became a wealthy superstar, but when he became a father, he once again turned his attention to children at risk. For the last twenty years, he has consistently performed benefit concerts on behalf of various schools and charities that serve children while writing songs like "Balboa Park" (1995), which laments the condition of immigrant children who, having come across the border from Mexico without documentation, find themselves fair game for drug dealers and pimps. The listener feels for the young protagonist who sleeps in "his blanket underneath the freeway," runs from "the border patrol," and does what he has "to do for the money." One would also have to be hard-hearted not to be convicted by recent works such as "Silver Palomino" (2005) and "Rocky Ground" (2012), both of which are haunted by children who have been left unprotected in a harsh world.

Springsteen has also written several songs populated by adult characters who are emotionally hobbled. While he does not explicitly write about health care, many of Springsteen's protagonists are clearly suffering from depression or some form of mental illness. Most obvious is "This Depression" (2012), in which the protagonist confesses to his wife that he has "been down, but never this down." The song is his "confession," his admission that he has "never felt so weak," and that his prayers have "gone for nothing." He is "forsaken." Not long after the song was released, Springsteen himself confessed to battling depression for most of his adult life. In a lengthy article in *The New Yorker*, Springsteen revealed his soul, partly to raise awareness about the devastating power of mental illness that often goes unchecked because so many people do not have health care that covers such problems. Springsteen talks candidly about how he was "deeply affected by his father's paralyzing depressions, and worried that he would not escape the thread of mental instability that ran through his family." That fear, Springsteen told David Remnick, was the reason that he never succumbed to the lure of drugs: "My issues weren't as obvious as drugs," Springsteen says. "Mine were different, they were quieter—just as problematic, but quieter" (38).

Springsteen's transparency has allowed millions of people suffering from mental illnesses to have a voice and feel like they, too, have a right not to be ashamed, that they even have a right to feel valued. Many of Springsteen's songs feature characters battling what seems to be depression. As early as 1978, Springsteen was releasing songs such as "Darkness on the Edge of Town" and "Adam Raised a Cain," which expressed his fear that the powerful legacy of his father's depression might be revisited in his own life. In "Adam Raised a Cain," the speaker and his father are "prisoners of love, a love in chains." Just as Springsteen feared that he, too, would suffer from the malady that isolated his father, so the speaker fears that he will forever be "paying for the sins of somebody else's past." Two years later, Springsteen included "Point Blank" on *The River* (1980), a song in which the protagonist laments that "you wake up and you're dying" and "you don't even know from what." Springsteen recorded *Nebraska* in 1982, the same year that his own suicidal thoughts drove him to enter therapy. The album itself is dark; nearly every song features a troubled character driven by internal demons. The record's final cut, "Reason to Believe," relates the stories of several beleaguered characters who, despite the fact that they have been dealt cruel blows in life, "find some reason to believe." Yet, the speaker finds this belief unwarranted, perhaps even ridiculous. As he says, "It seemed kinda funny sir to me" how people could possibly make meaning out of a demeaning existence.

Still, Springsteen usually does not let his characters stay in this state of dismay. Just as important as giving these hurting people a voice is that fact that the characters, like Springsteen himself, never stop fighting and insist on the possibility of living a productive, worthwhile life. For instance, "Trapped," originally written by Jimmy Cliff about a man trapped in a bad relationship, was reinterpreted by Springsteen in the 1980s and eventually released on *The Essential Bruce Springsteen* (2003). The song's speaker is, indeed, confined. His chains may be a relationship gone sour, drugs, or mental illness. It depends on your point of view. However, one thing is for sure. He is "caught up in your trap again," and he's "wearing the same old chains." He has been pushed to the brink, but he will not give in. He affirms that "good will conquer evil" and repeats that "someday I'll walk out of here again." The troubled protagonist of "Adam Raised a Cain" will press on, and the victims in "Reason to Believe" continue to fight for each "hard-earned day." Even the desperate man in "Depression" continues to tell his wife, "I need your heart," indicating his willingness to seek help in his quest to find hope and purpose. He is similar to the speaker in "Rocky Ground" (2012), a man who acknowledges a long history of defeats but still insists that it's time to "rise up" because the "sun's in the heavens and a new day is rising." In many ways, then, the Springsteen canon is a soothing balm for tormented souls, all of whom are given dignity and hope in Springsteen's vision of inclusion and social justice.

Springsteen has also dedicated his career to giving a voice to the homeless and the hungry. Over the last twenty years, he has performed several concerts to benefit organizations that help those without homes, and he has, for many years, collected special donations at his concerts to help fund soup kitchens and food pantries in the cities in which his shows take place. As early as 1985, Springsteen released "Seeds," an angry song that relates the sad tale of a man who experiences the underside of capitalism. He is not lazy or drug addicted, nor does he embody any other ugly stereotype of the homeless. He is simply a man who made a bad investment. He "headed down south with a spit and a song," only to find himself out of work and out of money, living in his car with his wife and kids. They are not alone. There are more unfortunates "hunkered down by the railroad tracks," and others have "tents pitched on the highway in the dirty moonlight."

Perhaps no other album in American history has sympathetically exposed the problem of homelessness more than *The Ghost of Tom Joad* (1995). "Balboa Park," "The New Timer," and "Across the Border" all reveal different faces of the problem. However, the centerpiece of the record is "The Ghost of Tom Joad." which invokes the spirit of John Steinbeck's hero from *The Grapes of Wrath* (1939) to draw attention to the plight of those who sleep "in their cars in the southwest," with "no home no job no peace no rest." These are the people who have fallen through the cracks, who populate shelters and heat "soup on a campfire under the bridge." Yet, like Steinbeck, Springsteen gives these lost souls dignity and a fighting spirit. The song's chief protagonist may have "a hole in" his "belly," and he may be "bathin' in the city aqueduct," but he is stalwartly "waitin' on the ghost of old Tom Joad." He lives on the hope of Tom's words. "Wherever there's somebody fightin' for a place to stand," he whispers in the dark, "look in their eyes" and "you'll see me." The song and, indeed, the entire album shine a light on people that many would rather not see. They, too, are part of Springsteen's community and vision of equality.

If there is one condition that informs all the other social maladies under which Springsteen's characters and millions of Americans suffer, it is poverty. From his first album, Springsteen has populated his songs with tired people so poor that they can barely afford to die. *Greetings from Asbury Park, NJ* (1973), for instance, includes "The Angel," a short ballad about a ragged motorcyclist who "rides" with other "hunchbacked children" through a dingy landscape "choked with nomadic hordes." They are all "following dead-end signs into the sores" of beaten-down lives. They have no destination in mind; they ride only to escape a dreary existence. But there is no way out. The angel is destined for an early death, and the listener's final glimpse of him is lying in a metal heap by the side of the road. He is nothing but "bones" strung among "polished chrome." The angel's desperation is similar to that of the poor kids who inhabit "4th of July, Asbury Park," released only a few months later on *The Wild, the Innocent, and the E Street Shuffle* (1973). Set against a tawdry amusement park, the song is full of "stoned-out faces," "switchblade lovers," aimless "boys from the casino," and "silly New York girls." They drift down the boardwalk and encounter "greasers" who "tramp the streets," "angels" in "cheap little seashore bars" who "have lost their desire for us," and predatory cops who "finally busted" a popular fortune-teller named "Madame Marie." There seems to be no future for those who grow up poor in Asbury Park, people like Springsteen and his youthful compatriots. The speaker tells his girlfriend, Sandy, that for him "this boardwalk life" is "through" and that she "ought to quit this scene too." Like Springsteen himself, the speaker knows that it will take bold, dramatic action to escape the effects of poverty.

Yet, Springsteen has no illusions. He knows that economic circumstances can sometimes crush the heartiest soul. Some of the characters opt for desperate action, only to find that no amount of courage and risk can help them outrun poverty. In "Meeting across the River" (1975), an unnamed man petitions his friend Eddie to "lend me a few bucks" and "catch us a ride." He has one last chance to make a big score and show his girl, Cherry, that life is "gonna be everything that I said." To that end, he has arranged "a meeting with a man on the other side." All they have to do in this criminal enterprise is "hold up our end," and "two grand" will be "sitting here in my pocket." Then, surely, Cherry will stay, and they can be happy. However, the song's sad melody and ominous warning—that "if we blow this one they ain't gonna be looking for just me this time"—leave the listener feeling that Eddie and his friend are riding into disaster. This is what poverty compels people to do. Even those characters who do not turn to crime are compelled to take risks that, if they are lucky, will keep them from falling off the edge of civilized society.

"Racing in the Street" (1978), for instance, is the story of an unnamed street racer and his girl trying to survive life in a dimly lit American landscape. He rides "from town to town," racing with "no strings attached" until he meets a girl "on the strip." His love for her is what prevents him from slipping through the cracks and becoming like the men he knows on the circuit who "just give up living and start dying little by little, piece by piece." But things are getting worse. There "are wrinkles around" his "baby's eyes," and "she cries herself to sleep at night." He is doing his best, but no matter how much he risks his life on the strip, he seems to keep falling further behind. Now, "all her pretty dreams are torn," and "she stares" with "the eyes of one who hates for just being born." Together, they would like to get clean and "wash these sins off our hands," but one wonders if they will be able to outrun their condition. Then, there is "Johnny 99" (1982), in which a young man who has "debts no honest man can pay" decides to rob a store after he loses his job in an auto plant. He "shot a night clerk" in the process and now must face "98 and a year" in prison. The song is dark and offers little hope. In the end, we find Ralph in the depths of despair. He tells the judge he'd "be better off dead" and implores him to "shave off my hair and put me on that execution line."

Yet, for every song that depicts the unrelenting and often destructive power of poverty, Springsteen offers another that reveals that there is at least some hope. Take, for instance, two of the songs that he wrote about his father in the late 1970s. "Factory" (1978) depicts the dark hopelessness his father felt as he went from one dead-end job to another throughout Springsteen's youth, a condition that worsened his depression. The man in the song "rises from bed" when "the factory whistle blows." Through the "fear" and "pain," he makes his way to the factory in "the rain." Inside, the "factory takes his hearing" in exchange for giving "him life." But it is the "working life," a dull, pointless existence in which he merely earns enough money for his family to survive. At the "end of the day," the men leave the factory with "death in their eyes." Their bitterness and anger often erupt into violence, but there is nothing that they can do to alter the deadly pattern of their lives on the bottom of the capitalist food chain. Yet, the futility of "Factory" is not Springsteen's final message about his father.

"Independence Day" (1980) features the strained relationship between Springsteen and his father, who have watched their feud play out against the background of a deteriorating factory town. While the son acknowledges "a darkness of this house" that has gotten "the best of us," it is clear that it is partly the result of "a darkness in this town that's got us too." There are "a lot of people leaving town," and the listener is left with a feeling that the town is similar to Freehold, New Jersey, where Springsteen grew up, a once prosperous place that became part of an industrial wasteland in the lean economic years of the seventies and eighties. It is a town whose lack of opportunity has ground down the speaker's father and left him with nothing to do but to affirm that "they ain't gonna do to me what I watched them do to you." In the end, the narrator leaves town and tries to make peace with his father, his parting gesture of filial love providing an emotional challenge to the narrative of poverty that has placed them in jeopardy. Many of his fans listening to the song know that Springsteen did, in fact, make it out of his dire financial situation and that he did eventually make peace with his father. They also know that he experienced poverty, understood its degrading effects, and knew that it could be transcended—that one can even heal some of its deepest wounds. This makes the rays of hope that Springsteen gives in subsequent songs as believable and comforting as his stark depictions of poverty are convicting.

Indeed, poor people, while not romanticized, are given dignity in most of the Springsteen songs in which they are featured. In fact, their well-being is integral to his American vision. Even sober albums such as *Nebraska* (1982) and *The Ghost of Tom Joad* (1995) have songs that rescue the poverty-stricken characters that inhabit the records from despair. The former includes "Mansion on the Hill." Rising above the misery of "the factories" and the toil of "the fields" is a mansion surrounded by "steel gates." Amid the images of crime, violence, depression, and faded hopes that dominate the record, the mansion stands as a symbol of hope for better things. Children play "on the road that leads to those gates of hardened steel." The speaker's father takes him there at night when everyone is asleep, just so they can look and listen to the grand house where "all the lights would shine" and where "there'd be music playing all the time." The song ends with the soothing image of a "beautiful moon rising above the mansion on the hill." The listener also senses the hope embedded in "Across the Border" from *The Ghost of Tom Joad*, a song about immigrants fleeing the "pain and sadness" of Mexico for America, where there are "pastures of green and gold." The male protagonist promises his lover that he will build her "a house high up on a grassy hill" amid "sweet blossoms" and "cool waters." Once "across the border," the couple will "drink from God's blessed waters." Life is deadly for those in poverty, but even on the darkest Springsteen albums, there is always a narrative of hope that trumps the social ills of the world.

Over the last decade, Springsteen has continued to produce music that forces us out of our comfort zones, composed of apathy or consumerist distraction, to pay attention to the evils of poverty. Of special note is *We Shall Overcome: The Seeger Sessions* (2006), composed of Springsteen's interpretation of several American classics made famous by social activist Pete Seeger. Springsteen released the album in April 2006 as the country was slipping into a deep recession. All the songs are dedicated to making sure that an affluent nation would not forget those who might be struggling unseen in the shadows. "How Can a Poor Man Stand Such Times and Live," with its stories of predatory doctors, crooked politicians, and a privileged, uncaring elite, sounded as relevant to contemporary American audiences as it did during the Great Depression. However, as with all the works on the album, there is an undercurrent of hope that fortifies the mistreated characters. The song's narrator recognizes that he "ain't got no home in this world no more," but he also affirms that there is "gonna be judgment" and that his hopes are in "a righteous train rolling down this track." The song is thematically similar to "My Oklahoma Home," in which a man labors all his life to build his homestead. He and his wife work hard, build a house, plant crops, and try to live morally, only to have everything "blowed away." He loses everything, but his will is not broken. He carries on, and wherever he goes, he can feel that his "Oklahoma farm is overhead." It is "wherever dust is whirled" and "in that dust cloud rolling by." Most of all, it is "in the sky." Like many Springsteen protagonists, he will not give up. Wherever he is, his "home is all around." Then, there is "Eyes on the Prize," the story of two rag-tag characters who, being named "Paul and Silas," bear strong resemblance to the biblical characters of the same names who, though beaten and reviled, nonetheless sang hymns to God while in prison. They kept their "eyes on the prize" and were eventually released. Yet, even when they were pardoned, they would not go away quietly. Instead, they protested the injustices done to them, forcing those who had abused them to face their sins in the light of day. As Springsteen sang the song from stages across the world, one could see him shining a harsh light on those who victimize the Pauls and Silases of the twenty-first century.

In 2012, Springsteen released *Wrecking Ball*, an album whose songs became staples at Occupy rallies and proved that, at age sixty-two, he was as dedicated as ever to providing a voice for those in poverty. The album is dark, filled with the pain and ill-will harbored by so many Americans in the wake of the economic and political corruption that resulted in the 2008 financial meltdown that saw millions of hard-working citizens lose their jobs, benefits, and pensions while CEOs and other high ranking executives escaped the crisis via golden parachutes that allowed them to waft safely over the carnage. The terrible mix of heartbreak and anger felt by so many comes through in songs such as "Swallowed Up (In the Belly of the Whale)," in which Springsteen laments that "though we trusted our skills and our good sails," it wasn't enough. Though so many put their faith in the notion that, "with God the righteous in this world prevail," many innocent people were "swallowed up" and "disappeared from this world." "The bones" of these victims "lay high in a pyre in the belly of the beast," a clear symbol of the corporate and political alliance whose collective greed chewed up its workers and then tried to hide their remains far from view so as to exonerate the powerful forces that were culpable.

The anger foments in "Jack of All Trades," where the speaker is caught in a familiar story in which the "banker man grows fat," while the "working man grows thin." It is a tale that has "happened before and it'll happen again." The speaker wants vengeance; if he had "a gun" he'd "find the bastards and shoot 'em on sight." However, like most Americans, he knows that he can never really get revenge on the wealthy people who cause and even benefit from recessions and depressions. They have made their money and cut their ties. All he can do is use his wits and determination to carry on: "You use what you've got and you try to survive." Still, as revealed in "Wrecking Ball," the anger never fades. No matter how much punishment people absorb in the throes of class warfare, most never lose their spirit. Such is the case with the fiery protagonist of the album's title song, who stares the bankers and politicians in the face and dares them, "if you've got the balls" to "take your best shot" and "bring on your wrecking ball."

This defiance is typical of Springsteen's tone in *Wrecking Ball*, an album in which the voices of the downtrodden express their pain, but also insist on the possibility of resistance and even triumph. The speaker in "Jack of All Trades," for example, can and will do many things to survive. He can "mow your lawn," "mend your roof," and "harvest your crops," among other things, and he assures his loved ones that "we'll be alright." In "You've Got It," the speaker and his wife have been pummeled by hard times but he knows they will survive, for there is something in her that inspires the speaker, a force of will that cannot be broken by the worst injustices. "Ain't no one can break it" or "steal it" or "fake it," and you "just know it when you see it." Like many Americans, his wife has it, and it will sustain them. Even in "Wrecking Ball," the feeling is palpable that, though the corporate greed that knocks down hopes and dreams will have its day, the people will rise again. There are no hard times that cannot be overcome.

In the end, Springsteen delivers an amalgam of hope composed of one part religious fervor and one part social activism. St. Peter meets John Steinbeck. In "Rocky Ground," he invokes the story of Christ wandering in the desert to inspire those who are suffering. Just as Jesus was tempted and tested in every possible way for "forty days and nights," so the hard-working people of America are being tested by another unfair set of circumstances. Just as Satan tested Christ, so hard times brought on by the greed and criminality of wayward leaders will test the resolve of good people. Springsteen reminds these folks that they have to keep the faith, that if they keep fighting the good fight they will find that the sun is still "in the heavens and a new day is rising." Springsteen repeats that, "a new day is coming," and in "American Land" he makes it clear that God will smile on those who have been mistreated and give them the strength to forge a better life. "American Land" assures us that, despite our setbacks, the American Dream that has inspired and sustained so many still exists, and that we can achieve it if we work together. Springsteen reminds us that this country was built by immigrants and exiles who started out with very little money but a great deal of hope and courage. And these people represented several races and religions: "the Blacks, the Irish, Italians, the Germans, and the Jews," among many others. Such is the humanist vision of the song. We are down now, but our diversity and our resolve will see us through. There is still "treasure for the taking, for any hard working man," and everyone who has the character to reform corrupt and unfair political and economic systems is welcome to "make his home in the American Land." This is the quasi secular-religious hope of Bruce Springsteen that has been, over the last half-century, at the heart of his appeal to Americans feeling the effect of poverty and other social ills.

Perhaps one of the reasons why Springsteen's vision of America is so compelling is that it is so inclusive. While he has unquestionably aligned himself with the Democratic party, his vision is still populist. He doesn't blame or proscribe as much as he exposes and entreats his listeners to empathize. He trusts his audience. It's as if he is saying, "Look at what is happening. I know that once you see it, you will do something about it. We all know that we are better than this." Inspiration and faith go a long way in a day and age of political scapegoating and mindless distraction.

7

DELIVER ME FROM NOWHERE
Redemptive Myth

A significant part of Bruce Springsteen's appeal to many Americans is that he addresses their pain in comforting ways. And there is a lot of pain. Economic downturns, joblessness, classism, gender woes, racial and ethnic conflict, homelessness, inadequate health care, controversial wars, government distrust, terrorism, tattered relationships, alienation, and personal failures are all consistent fodder in Springsteen's writing. Yet, all this trauma is undergirded by a gnawing philosophic uncertainty that makes these burdens even more difficult to bear. For instance, well into the twentieth century, the daily lives of many Americans were fortified by a Christian faith whose pillars had not yet borne the full brunt of the challenges of new ideas in evolutionary biology, physics, astronomy, anthropology, psychology, linguistics, literature, and history, as well as a host of technological and cultural changes that would gradually erode the primacy of religion on the American landscape. During the latter half of the twentieth century, many Americans became less certain of the spiritual foundations, Christian or otherwise, that formerly allowed them to cope with hardship and answer our most fundamental questions regarding meaning and purpose. The rise of postmodern relativism and rationalist skepticism in the last fifty years, in particular, has left many Americans in a state of spiritual resignation, wondering if any ultimate redemption from the ills of this world is possible. Indeed, the entire Springsteen canon plays out against a postmodern milieu in which many Americans have lost faith in several traditional narratives. Even in his first albums, *Greetings from Asbury Park, NJ* (1973) and *The Wild, the Innocent, and the E Street Shuffle* (1974), Springsteen's characters are searching for a deeper redemption. Loss of faith in religion, government, marriage, and the American Dream only intensifies their search over the next two decades. *The Rising* (2002), *Devils & Dust* (2005), *Working on a Dream* (2009), and *Wrecking Ball* (2012) reveal his most complete vision of spiritual belief, the culmination of his lifelong attempt to rescue his audience with a larger narrative that can be trusted to nurture and redeem. When considered against the landscape of discarded philosophies of the late twentieth and early twenty-first century, is it any wonder that Springsteen stands as a nearly prophetic figure for so many people?

POSTMODERN AMERICA

Postmodernism was defined by philosopher Jean-Francois Lyotard as "an incredulity toward metanarratives." In essence, this simply means that the grand stories that we tell ourselves to make meaning of the world are not accurate—including Christianity, Islam, Judaism, and other religions; Manifest Destiny, Marxism, socialism, and other political frameworks; or secular philosophies such as humanism or the American Dream. The primary reason is that they are not rooted in any reliable, absolute truth that exists beyond human space and time. In fact, according to postmodern thinking, there is no absolute realm, no fundamental order to the universe, no God or transcendent being who makes unalterable rules on which we can rely. There is only an ever-complex array of power structures in which we must forge ever-changing views and identities. We cannot have the thing that we desire most: the certainty that allows us to know exactly who we are and that enables us to cope with the major problems that life presents, including death.

To illustrate postmodernism and its rise to prominence in the United States in the late twentieth century, it is useful to consider what life was like for the average American farming family in the mid- to late nineteenth century. Despite the growth of cities during the industrial revolution, most people still lived in the country and made their livelihood as farmers or in small businesses that served agricultural communities. The center of life was, in fact, the traditional nuclear family, whose patriarchal structure went largely unquestioned. The father functioned as the head of the family, gleaning his authority from established traditions deeply rooted in the Christian faith. He governed his family with the help of his wife, who dutifully served him and their children in a manner consistent with Judeo-Christian dictates. Each member of the family had to perform duties so that the farm or business could run effectively. Everyone worked long days from Monday to Saturday to do these chores. At night, many families would eat dinner together, perhaps listen to someone play a musical instrument if one was available, and read from the family Bible. It was not an easy life, but the family also often reaped the fruits of their labor by producing enough food to sustain their farm. They also enjoyed a sense of stability that they believed was cosmically sanctioned. God had given them this country to be a "city on a hill," a new Eden in which the institutional abuses of European churches and governments could be corrected. To them, the United States was a divine gift, and it was their Manifest Destiny to bring the land under their dominion for his divine service. All they had to do was work hard and follow God's rules, and He would bestow his blessing upon them. Certainly, there would be trials, but they could all be accounted for within this larger Christian, American metanarrative by which they lived. It must have been very comforting, indeed. And for generations, this foundation sustained many Americans whose relative geographic isolation and austere habits shielded them from many of the educational, technological, or cultural changes that might have upset the balance.

However, modern life would eventually challenge this uniquely American sense of stability. It can be argued that developments in higher education provided the most powerful part of this challenge. In 1859, Charles Darwin published *The Origin of Species*, signaling the development of evolutionary biology, a field that would come to dominate Western science with ideas that included the distinct possibility that there was no God; that life had evolved amorally over millions of years, with its only guiding principle being that the strongest of any given species survives by killing off its competition; and that humans had evolved directly from apes. The Darwinian revolution occurred alongside a movement among theologians and philosophers rooted in the Enlightenment to expose the Bible to rigorous criticism. Scholars who practiced this "higher criticism of the Bible" concluded that the holy text was not divinely inspired but was instead created by fallible humans writing with specific power agendas. The Bible, then, was not to be taken literally and could not be relied on as a divine guide by which to live.

By the early twentieth century, scholars in new fields such as psychology and anthropology were complicating matters even more. Sigmund Freud published *The Interpretation of Dreams* in 1899, a seminal work in which Freud contended that human action was, to a great extent, explainable by our subconscious mind, over which we have little control. Instead of being fully rational creatures created by God, we were evolving animals whose actions were often dictated by primordial impulses. At the same time, early anthropologists, taking advantage of advances in transportation, were beginning to study cultures from around the world. Of special interest were the many religions that existed, most of which had similar structures to Christianity. Most of them had creation myths, gods, systems of judgment with an afterlife, and end-of-the-world stories. The questions loomed: With so many religions, which one was correct? Were they all just human creations, and, if so, what true value did they have as ordering mechanisms for life?

Modern philosophers took cues from Darwin. Friedrich Nietzsche, for instance, contended that God was dead, that there was no underlying order to the world, and that humans were relatively dull brutes waiting to be led by a strong *Übermensch*. Political and economic philosopher Karl Marx advanced the notion that not only was there no God, but religion, particularly Christianity, was responsible for keeping the suffering masses in poverty. Educator Herbert Spencer brought Darwin and Nietzsche to the classroom, ushering in a new pedagogy based on scientific rationalism and social evolution. Humans were in charge of their own destiny, not God, and an important goal of secular education would be to undo the damage of a capitalist system supported by Christianity.

Of course, these ideas were not enough, in and of themselves, to ignite a century-plus-long breakdown of traditional narratives. It took several cultural and technological changes to augment their influence, spreading them across the country and rooting them in local communities whose foundations had heretofore remained relatively undisturbed. For instance, between 1880 and 1930, the numbers of young people attending and graduating from the universities where modern educational ideas were being discussed and taught increased dramatically. This meant that thousands of the future gatekeepers of American business, law, medicine, education, journalism, and, indeed, religion were being weaned on the ideas of Darwin, Freud, and Spencer, among others. Not only that, but advances in transportation and communication ensured that modern secular ideas would be carried not just to the university elite but to the masses as well. The first transcontinental railroad was completed in 1869, and by the 1920s, the entire country was connected by rail. The invention of the automobile in the late nineteenth century spurred a flurry of road building, as well as the introduction of paved roads. At the same time, advances in printing, higher literacy rates, and the rise of print journalism made for a more literate public with an appetite for the increasing numbers of newspapers, journals, magazines, and books that were being produced. It was a marriage made in capitalist heaven. There were new and exciting ideas coming from every discipline and field, a public hungry for such ideas, new and inexpensive mediums for conveying the ideas, and trains, automobiles, and (soon) airplanes to carry the ideas into small town America. Pandora's box was open.

The industrial revolution fueled the entire process. The communication and transportation revolutions were due in part to the demands of industries that wanted to market and sell their products across the country. As machine/tool technology evolved and early mass production techniques developed, industries grew. As industry flourished, cities expanded. By the roaring twenties, America was no longer primarily an agrarian nation. Millions of people poured into swelling urban areas. The spiritual effects were predictable. First, the throngs were more readily exposed to the multiplicity of modern thought emanating from the universities and newspapers located in cities, something that would make it difficult for people to hold on to conventional values. Second, the unseemly nature of the burgeoning urban environments made traditional faith seem quaint at best and a terrible joke at worst. Industrial progress and its accompanying population growth far exceeded the ability of city governments to handle the changes. The results were disastrous. The masses worked in horrible conditions, often laboring twelve to fourteen hours a day in loud, dark, malodorous factories with little ventilation. They lived in cheap company housing or squalid tenements that were boiling hot in the summer, freezing in the winter, and dark most of the time. With no indoor plumbing, people often dumped their waste in alleys or the street. Disease was rampant, as was poverty. For many people, the long hours of labor resulted only in heavy debt and a feeling that they were hopelessly falling behind. Crime flourished, as did sexual promiscuity with its usual by-products of social diseases and unwanted pregnancies. These brutal conditions produced a staggering level of alcoholism, which in turn spawned an epidemic of domestic violence.

For Americans raised on farms or in small towns, where they enjoyed fresh air, their own land, the fruits of their labor, and control of their destiny, the terrible conditions wrought by urban living and an industrial workplace where their labor advanced only the interests of wealthy absentee owners were hard to square with the traditions and faith with which they had been raised. It was easier to believe that God had blessed you as part of a favored nation, a new Eden, when you owned your land and your labor was your own. It was much harder to believe in a benevolent God with a divine plan for you, your family, and your country when your life was miserable and surrounded by brutality and ugliness. What good was life, liberty, and the pursuit of happiness if you were held captive in a wretched working life for which your children also seemed destined? What good was the Protestant work ethic if it resulted in your degradation, instead of God's blessing? For many Americans in this situation, life seemed to jibe much more with social Darwinism and Nietzschean fatalism than romantic, American-style Christianity.

As the twentieth century progressed, the conditions that spawned modernist doubt would grow exponentially. The number of college graduates has grown every year and now annually numbers in the millions, and the curriculums from which they learn have become only more diverse and, to a great degree, more philosophically confusing. Not only are students confronted with advances in the hard sciences that cast doubt on religious doctrine and our chances of ever truly figuring out a vast universe, but astronomers tell them about an open universe with no originating creator; physicists affirm a general uncertainty of knowledge regarding molecular positioning; theological historians convincingly document the horrifying abuses committed in the name of religion (the Crusades, various inquisitions) since the beginning of recorded history; military and political historians relay the geno-cidal tragedies caused by secular absolutism (the Holocaust and the Stalinist purges); feminist, African American, and post-Colonial schol-ars point out that all dominant Western narratives and traditions, relig-ious and secular, have been built on malicious inequalities endemic to totalizing narratives; and linguists have insisted that language itself has no ultimate source or meaning and is therefore always destined to be a site where powerful forces manipulate words to support their nefarious agendas.

The watchwords, then, are *uncertainty* and *suspicion*. There is no overarching order or meaning in life, so if someone comes along telling you that there is, be careful; there is a dangerous agenda at work. This feeling of distrust has been magnified by technology—particularly the television, the personal computer, and the Internet. By the 1960s, tele-vision had accelerated the process of exposing seemingly stable features of American life. Coverage of the Vietnam War, the women's move-ment, civil rights protests, the hippies, the New Left, Woodstock, and Stonewall in the sixties gave way to multiple traumas of the seventies, when millions of Americans huddled around their televisions to watch President Nixon resign in disgrace over Watergate, long gas lines due to oil shortages caused by the newfound power of OPEC, the Boston bus riots, two brutal recessions, and the humiliating Iran hostage crisis. As if this exposure of the instability of religion and American traditions were not enough, the advent of the personal computer in the eighties and the World Wide Web in the nineties muddied the waters even more. Sud-denly, the average citizen could sit in his or her home and access a sea of information over the net. The problem, of course, is that so much of the information is inaccurate and contradictory. The result is the fur-ther destabilization of knowledge and the deepening suspicion of any story, which will almost immediately be met with several opposing sto-ries that attempt to debunk it. Want information to support the resur-rection of Christ as an historical event. No problem. Need information to cast doubt on the resurrection? Also, no problem. All this has left many people feeling uneasy, adrift in a conflicting mélange of ideas and a hopelessly complex array of social, political, economic, and religious problems. As theorist Terry Eagleton writes, "In the pragmatist, street-wise climate of advanced postmodern capitalism, with its skepticism of big pictures and grand narratives, its hard-nosed disenchantment with

the metaphysical, 'life' is one among a whole series of discredited total-
ities." At the very time when people most need answers, contemporary
postmodern life has left them "philosophically disarmed" (16).

RUNNING INTO THE DARKNESS

Springsteen's characters exist in the midst of this confusion. They en-
dure economic hardship, dehumanizing wars, perplexing social conditions, broken families, fragmented identities, the numbing effects of
mindless entertainment, uncaring institutions, corrupt governments,
and debilitating loneliness, all while standing on shifting philosophic
ground that seems to offer little in the way of spiritual comfort. It is not
surprising, then, that contemporary listeners would feel the pain of the
"ragamuffin gunner" from *Greetings from Asbury Park*'s "Lost in the
Flood" (1973). He resembles "a hungry runaway" as he "walks through
town all alone." He is isolated, "dull-eyed," and "empty-faced." Why?
Part of the reason is that any foundational faith has disappeared or been
rendered comical. The song is littered with tattered, empty religious
symbols, which are just part of the "junk" strewn "all across the horizon." Meanwhile, "nuns run bald through Vatican halls, pleadin' immaculate conception." There is nothing to believe in here, and the
"pure American brother" is reduced to being "lost in the flood." In the
end, he is shot down in a gunfight that is as confusing as his life has
been. His "body hit the street with such a beautiful thud," but there is
no resolution. Everyone is still "messed up" from "drinking unholy
blood."

But what is holy? So many of Springsteen's characters, like many
Americans, don't seem to be sure. This is certainly true of the young
couple from "4th of July, Asbury Park," the second cut off *The Wild, the
Innocent, and the E Street Shuffle* (1973). The speaker tells his girlfriend Sandy that the "carnival life" they are living has no merit. Whatever the prevailing zeitgeist is, it is empty. The boardwalk is populated
by "stoned-out faces" who have been "left stranded." There are "switchblade runners," pinball "wizards," "boys from the casino" who chase
"silly New York girls," and aimless "greasers" who "tramp the streets."
The speaker, too, is struggling to keep the faith, telling Sandy that "the
angels have lost their desire for us" and that "they won't set themselves

on fire for us anymore." Even the fortune-teller "Madame Marie" has been "busted" by the cops. There is no authority, no clear way to go. The speaker affirms that "this boardwalk life for me is through," and he tells Sandy that she "ought to quit this scene, too." However, as is the case with many of their contemporaries, there does not seem to be any clear-cut alternative as to where to go.

Darkness on the Edge of Town (1978) features "Streets of Fire" and "Racing in the Street," both of which feature charged settings in which desperate characters search for meaning. In the former, the protagonist is "tired," doesn't "care anymore," and just wants "to let go." He is sick of "weak lies," angry at being "tricked," but he has no truth to posit against those lies. He is "wandering" in self-loathing, even calling himself a "loser." He has no idea where to go. He walks "only with strangers," among "angels that have no place." Likewise, the main character in "Racing in the Street" is caught in a pointless life in which he rides "from town to town" to take part in races that he hopes will allow him to support his best girl. However, he is failing. She "cries herself to sleep at night," and he realizes that "all her pretty dreams been torn." She "stares off alone into the night," as if she is in search for answers, but she has "the eyes of one who hates for just being born." One feels the sincerity of the speaker. He wants to provide the answers for her, to save her, but he just can't do it. He wants to whisk her away on a "ride to the sea," where they will "wash these sins off our hands," but the listener knows that they have no true sense of how to get clean.

The River (1980) is full of characters who, like so many Americans, feel beaten down by life's circumstances with little spiritual recourse. In "Jackson Cage," for instance, the main character just "melts away" sadly "into a house where the blinds are closed." She feels that she "has been judged and handed life." For her, "every day ends in wasted motion." He male admirer "dreams of a better world," but he wakes "up downhearted," "tired," and "confused." He is "alone" and, like her, feels like "a stranger" doomed to "waste away." When such characters turn to prayer, as is the case in "Point Blank," there is little solace. Here, a young woman's suitor asks her whether she still "says her prayers at night?" She used to pray in the hopes that "everything" would "be alright." However, it is clear that the prayers, which could be interpreted as the true subject of the song, were impotent. Both characters have been hurt to the point where they realize that they are "dying," but sadly they are so confused that they "don't even know what from." They look for a stable road but find only "pretty lies" and empty "promises." When one first listens to the song, one keeps waiting for them to get shot "point blank" with a gun. Finally, however, we understand that they have already been emotionally shot and philosophically left for dead. As the singer concludes about his girlfriend, "you forgot how to love" and "forgot how to fight." Certainly, "they must have shot you in the head."

Several characters actually do get shot with guns on *Nebraska* (1982), Springsteen's darkest album, which he recorded as he began to get treatment for his own depression in the early eighties. No song sums up the record quite like "Reason to Believe," which is composed of a sad collection of tragic scenes that, in the end, cast a darkly comic light on the power of faith to sustain us. The listener is immediately confronted with the macabre scene of a man "standin' over a dead dog," poking him with a stick, as if he might "get up and run." The image throws the listener off balance, just as the characters in the song are off kilter in wonderment at a world that seems to make so little sense. The remaining stanzas feature a forlorn wife whose husband has left her, even though she did everything for him; the unsettling juxtaposition of a baby being baptized with the lonely death of an old man; and a forlorn groom waiting for a bride who will never arrive. Each stanza ends with the speaker asking, "What does it mean?" But no one knows how to explain the pain and the loneliness and the death. All the speaker can do is "wonder how at the end of every hard-earned day people find some reason to believe."

Many of Springsteen's characters ask this question, in one way or another. *Tunnel of Love* (1987) includes "Spare Parts," a song that takes one of the most hopeful events in the human experience, the birth of a child, and turns it into a melancholy tale of abandonment in which the father leaves the family, the mother retreats to prayers that seem to land on deaf ears, and the innocent child is reduced to a spare part. In *Human Touch*'s (1992) "Soul Driver," the spare parts are confronted with a hard world in which they are at the mercy of some fate that no one understands. People have no idea "which way love's wheel turns" or whether "the angels are unkind." Like the protagonist in "Youngstown," recorded a few years later for *The Ghost of Tom Joad* (1995), they know only that life is hell and that, if there is a heaven, they would want "no part of" it, the implication being that the ruler of such a place, if he exists, must not like them very much. This is the theme of some of the songs on *Tracks*, many of which were written much earlier than the 1998 release date. For example, the message of "Roulette" is that life is, at best, a game of Russian roulette in which we are waiting until we hit the fatal chamber with the bullet, while the speaker in "Gave It a Name" contends that, if there is a God, he seems to have cursed humanity. Like many Americans, the speaker certainly feels cursed, telling anyone who will listen that "I can feel that poison runnin' 'round my veins."

These songs are not uplifting, but, ironically, there is a certain comfort in knowing that someone out there recognizes the same terrible existential uncertainty that you feel. Part of the spiritual power of Springsteen's music is that he makes people feel less alone. However, another part of his power is that he does not leave his listeners in the darkness to which he exposes them. Indeed, for every song in which a character seems to border on despair, there is one in which another character refuses to capitulate, insisting on the possibility of some sort of redemption. *Darkness on the Edge of Town* (1978) includes "Streets of Fire," but it also boasts "Badlands," in which a man facing a bleak existence maintains that he will "spit in the face of these badlands." He is "caught in a crossfire that I don't understand," but he vows "to keep pushin' till it's understood, and these badlands start treating us good." He tells his girl, "I believe in the love that you gave me" and "in the faith that can save me." One is not exactly sure what this faith looks like, but it is there in many of Springsteen's songs, and it builds steadily and is increasingly defined as his career moves along.

One gets the same dichotomy of faithlessness and faith in *The River* (1980). While some of the songs are bleak, others, such as "The Price You Pay," employ biblical symbolism as a way of establishing cosmic hope. The speaker of the song takes comfort in story of Moses, for whom life's brutality was rewarded with his ultimate entrance into "the chosen land." The speaker, like Moses, believes in a promised land. Like the speakers in "Mary Queen of Arkansas" (1973), "Born to Run" (1975), "The Promised Land" (1978), "Dancing in the Dark" (1984), "Walk like a Man" (1987), "Leaf of Faith," (1992) and "Galveston Bay" (1995), he will keep fighting for a sense of meaning and stability that he believes is rightfully his. This spirit is best captured in the song "Ice-man," from *Tracks* (1998), where the speaker rejects the "mechanical" faith of his girlfriend's father, a preacher, but never stops believing that he will find something authentic in which to ground his actions. Life in contemporary America may have tried to "steal" his "heart," but he affirms that their "emptiness has already been judged." As a son of this society, he "was born dead," but that has not stopped him from searching for meaning with his "arms wide open." He is "fighting for the right to live," and instead of settling for tired narratives or postmodern ennui, he has embraced "the search." This is the same kind of search that Springsteen and his listeners have been on. The question is, would it yield anything productive beyond the simple exhilaration of the search?

THERE IS MAGIC IN THE NIGHT

The answer to that question is an unequivocal yes. Springsteen does indeed organically craft a vision a half century in the making, which provides his audience with a narrative of hope rooted in spiritual belief. It is hardly the Catholic faith of his youth, though his songs are ripe with Catholic imagery. It is also not the pseudofaith of postmodern prophets who, accepting the notion that there can be no stable self or ultimate meaning, advise us to enjoy playing in the rich fabric of life, enjoying its diversity and fashioning an ever-changing, ever-fluid identity based on our current needs and desires. No, Springsteen's driving narrative, which seems to have sustained such a wide, jaded audience for so long, is a tenuous but beautiful mix of liberal versions of traditional theological concepts with postmodernity's emphases on community and solidarity. Anyone who has been to a Springsteen concert has felt this vibe. Springsteen himself recently described this phenomenon:

> You are isolated, yet you desire to talk to somebody. You are very disempowered, so you seek impact, recognition that you are alive and that you exist. We hope to send people out of the building we play in with a slightly more enhanced sense of what their options might be, emotionally, maybe communally. You empower them a little bit, they empower you. It's all a battle against the futility and the existential loneliness! It may be that we are all huddled together around the fire and trying to fight off that sense of the inevitable. That's what we do for one another. (Remnick)

How does Springsteen accomplish this? The first step seems to be to take control of one's life. Springsteen wants his listeners to understand that life will punish them, but they do not have to be passive victims. They will face the inevitable challenge of trying to outrun the sins of others, just as he had to find a way to cope with the legacy that his father bequeathed him. This is clear in "Adam Raised a Cain," in which Springsteen admits that "you're born into this life paying for the sins of somebody else's past." You "inherit the sins," and you have to face them. They will punish you, but you can overcome them. Springsteen did. Through years of therapy and hard work, he made peace with his father and himself. He even successfully raised a family with the idea in mind that he had to be intentional about not letting his sins become a burden for his children. This is evident in songs such as "Long Time Comin'," released on *Devils & Dust* (2005), in which a man buries his "old soul" so that his "kids" can be released from his "mistakes" and their "sins" will be their "own." The song, like Springsteen's life, sends the message that this is possible. This man is determined to take authority over his destiny and to give his kids a fighting chance to do the same. It is not a distant hope, either. It is a hope that has been hard won, "but now it's here," and he is determined "not to fuck it up this time."

A huge part of assuming control of one's life is being determined to sift through all of life's ugliness and postmodern uncertainty to remain open to the possibility of the transcendent. This does not take a specifically Christian form for Springsteen, though his landscapes are full of biblical allusions, and he claims that Catholic literary greats Flannery O'Connor and Walker Percy are two of his greatest artistic influences. Instead, Springsteen's characters, like the singer himself, develop a less codified, less historically situated faith in a higher power. Sometimes, this power seems distant, but in the end, it is always there if we are open and willing to work hard enough to receive it. This message is evident in some early songs, such as "Promised Land" (1978), in which the protagonist tells the world, "I'm a man" who, despite life's difficulties, is determined to "believe in the promised land." Many of Springsteen's later songs are clear that this hope is both of this world and the next one. In "Countin' on a Miracle" (2002), for instance, the speaker taps into his faith in a higher power to affirm his belief that miracles can rescue people in despair. "Jesus Was an Only Son" (2005) carries the same message. Faith is warranted, and it can transform your life if you will let it. By the time that he writes "This Life" in 2009, Springsteen's "universe" seems to be "at rest." The speaker tells his wife that "this lonely planet never looked so good" and that he looks forward to "this life and then the next." This kind of faith that features present joy and the possibility of eternal reward is important to Springsteen.

Equally important is that this faith is open to everyone, regardless of class, gender, race, ethnicity, or, indeed, religion. In "Land of Hope and Dreams," (2001) for example, Springsteen acknowledges that, no matter our background, we will all face "sorrows." However, it is also true that everyone can access a "land of hope and dreams" where "there'll be sunshine and all this darkness past." The train of faith that can provide both worldly joy and eternal security is for "saints and sinners," "losers and winners," "whores and gamblers," and all "lost souls." In the end, no matter where you come from, how dirty you are, or how insignificant your story may seem to you or others, your "faith will be rewarded." Such lines make those who have followed Springsteen's spiritual growth over the years recall his famous declaration that "no one wins unless everyone wins" (Goldberg). No one need be left behind, a sentiment that jibes well with the diversity of thought and the spirit of inclusion that guides the present age.

The main task for a person of faith therefore becomes how to nurture and protect this faith. For Springsteen, there seems to be several facets to this process. First, we all need to find and contribute to community, an idea that plays well among postmodern secularists and people espousing traditional religious beliefs. Nowhere is this idea more vibrant than in *The Rising* (2002), a record that Springsteen made to help create a community for his fans who were trying to cope with the terrorist attacks of September 11, 2001. People needed answers, and Springsteen provided "The Rising," a song in which the protagonist, despite the fact that he "can't see nothing . . . through the darkness," put on the "cross of my calling" and faced the tragedy head on. Not only that, but he exhorts others to join him, to "come on up for the rising," a celebration of life and faith. Death will not sway them; they are bound together by the "precious blood" of the victims of the attacks, and together they will "stand before" the Lord's "fiery light." "Lay your hands in mine," Springsteen writes. There is strength in a community of faith. Somehow, the faith and love that resonate there make everyone believe a little more. Such is the case with "Into the Fire," where a loved one has died trying to save others. "I need your kiss," the speaker sings, "but love and duty called you someplace higher." That place is "somewhere higher, into the fire" of faith, which burns much brighter when fueled with self-sacrifice. The song is a prayer and an elegy. This beautiful soul will not be forgotten. Instead, he or she will be remembered as the proof of the power of "faith," "hope," and "love." For the speaker, these things are "the light," and he repeats the line "may your strength give us strength," reminding all who listen that the faith we need so much burns brightest when we all give sacrificially in a community that celebrates acts of love.

This kind of action makes for a solidarity that also has the function of strengthening the bonds of faith. This can be seen in "We Take Care of Our Own," the opening cut from *Wrecking Ball* (2012). Larger institutions and narratives may have failed, and the "cavalry" may have "stayed home," but in a community guided by faith, hope, and love, there will always be "eyes with the will to see," "hearts that run over with mercy," and a "love" that will inspire "the work that will set my hands, my soul free." For Springsteen, one can get trapped in a cycle of depression that breeds despair, but one can also participate in a community whose faith sets in motion a self-fulfilling prophecy in which love begets love, hope produces hope, and faith makes for more faith. That is the power of solidarity, a concept championed by existential philosophers such as Jean Paul Sartre and Albert Camus but which is given an eternal, supernatural flavor in many of Springsteen's songs where characters are determined not to let one another fail.

This type of faith is also nurtured by maintaining strong family ties, another concept that cuts across all religions and most secular camps. Just as Springsteen began to achieve peace and a sense of stability when he married Patti Scialfa in 1991 and embarked on a difficult but successful journey of raising three children with her, so many of his characters are able to cultivate faith when they can contribute to and experience the closeness of a loving family. We get a glimpse of this feeling in such songs as "What Love Can Do" (2009), in which the speaker tells his wife not to worry about the fact that they "bear the mark of Cain," for he will show her "what love can do." The same spirit is evident in "Leah" (2005), where the narrator vows to build a "house on higher ground," beyond "this road, filled with shadow and doubt." He will "figure it all out with Leah," and the song ends with him saying a prayer and climbing the stairs to their bedroom. Still, the strongest endorsement for family as a stay against confusion comes on *Lucky Town*, released in 1992 as Springsteen was starting his family. The album contains "Living Proof" and "Beautiful Reward," both of which celebrate the power of family to instill and renew faith. In the former, the speaker has been "searching for a little bit of God's mercy" to rescue him from a "world so hot and dirty." He finds it in the birth of his son, "living proof" that life is not "just a house of cards." In the latter work, the protagonist has been beaten down by life and even "came crashing down like a drunk on a barroom floor." He sees a house in which "a sacred light shines," but there is no place for him there. In the end, however, the listener feels that he will find that place with the woman whose "hair shone in the sun." The song ends with the singer transformed into a bird "flying over gray fields" with the "wind at his back." Like Springsteen himself, the speaker seems to be on the cusp of finding his reward in the context of his wife and family.

There are, according to Springsteen, at least three other elements that are necessary for a person to cultivate the kind of faith that one needs to flourish in the modern world. First, playing off the biblical parable of the talents, a person needs to find his or her "calling," a word often used by Springsteen and his wife. The idea is simple: Everyone has some gift, some skill, that, if used properly, will not only result in a great deal of personal satisfaction but also likely yield a glimpse of the supernatural source from which that gift emanates. This is the sentiment that drives "Working on a Dream" (2009), in which the narrator acknowledges that "the cards I've drawn's a rough hand" and that "trouble can feel like it's here to stay." However, he draws strength from his talent and his mission. He vows to "straighten my back" and keep "working on a dream." One can imagine the song being about Springsteen as a young man who struggled to make a meager living as a singer but felt such hope and satisfaction in his calling that he stayed with it until he gained commercial success and spiritual comfort.

Second, just as Springsteen emotionally survived for years by telling stories with his guitar, so our faith must be nourished by stories that affirm its authenticity. Several of Springsteen's songs serve this function; one of the best is "We Are Alive," released on *Wrecking Ball* in 2012. In the song, the dead rise from their graves to sing to those who have ears to listen. Their "spirits rise to carry the fire and light the spark" of faith. One was murdered in 1877 when "the railroad workers made their stand." One died fighting for civil rights "in 1963 one Sunday morning in Birmingham." Another, an immigrant coming to the United States to seek a better life for his children, was killed "last year crossing the southern desert." They end their stories with the plea "Oh please let them know." What we all need to know is that "it's only our bodies that betray us in the end." Our souls remain, and if we have lived well, our souls "will rise" to sustain those who come after us. Our stories remind us that there is an ultimate right and wrong and that we will be rewarded if we strive toward righteousness through actions based on using our talents sacrificially in the service of others.

Finally, Springsteen wants us to know that this faith is hard won. We have to work at it with tenacity and determination, enduring the many pitfalls of modern life that make spiritual health so difficult to foster and maintain. This is the kind of vigilance displayed by the protagonist in "I'll Work for Your Love," from *Magic* (2007). Like many in America, the speaker is jaded. He refers to corruption and "deals going down" and to failed narratives and "the dust of civilizations." He is not afraid to look into the darkness and admit that he is surrounded by shaky ground. Yet, he still insists on the power of faith and love, and he tells Teresa that he is willing to work for them. "I'll work for your love," he repeats over and over. Doubt surrounds us, and "our book of faith's been tossed," but we can still find our "own piece of the cross" if we are steadfast. *Working on a Dream*'s (2009) "Kingdom of Days" has a similar feel, but the narrator's focus is on working hard to enjoy the present. "This is our kingdom of days," he tells his lover. He promises to dedicate himself to loving her and to "prove it" every minute if he can. Hard work sustains faith, hope, and love, but for Springsteen the greatest of these is love. This is what makes the days bearable and life redeemable.

Anyone who has attended multiple Springsteen shows over the years knows that they function as spiritual events as much as rock concerts. The music is great, and you can dance to it, but there is also a feeling that you are participating in the celebration of a larger narrative of shared belief. Unlike traditional religious narratives, Springsteen's vision has no history of institutional abuse, coercion, or violence. In addition, fans perceive it to be inclusive, approachable, and relatively flexible, in the sense that it is not rule driven and is seemingly free of the dogmatic assertions that make traditional religions and current secular philosophies seem divisive to many people. Yet, it also has clear attach-ments to the certainty of the past and thus flies in the face of postmod-ern disbelief and confusion. God, country, family, community, faith, hope, and love are still the cornerstones of the narrative; Springsteen has simply reframed them in a way that meets the psychological and spiritual needs of his audience. As Jake Clemons, nephew of the late Clarence Clemons and the newest sax man for the E Street Band, suggested, "Maybe he comes from the line of David, a shepherd boy who could play beautiful music, so that the crazy become less crazy and Saul the king finally chills out. Religion is a system of rules and order and expectations, and it unites people in a purpose. There really is a component of Bruce that is supernatural" (Remnick).

8

THE MINISTRY OF ROCK 'N' ROLL

MUSICAL DESCENDANTS

In May 2011, Lady Gaga, one of the top-selling artists in the world, talked about the importance of Bruce Springsteen to her career. "Springsteen had such an influence on our home," she affirmed.

> My father gave me, I believe it was for Christmas, a Bruce Springsteen songbook for the piano and on it was "Thunder Road," which is my favorite Bruce Springsteen song. My dad said, "If you learn how to play this song we will take out a loan for a grand piano, a baby grand." So I remember it was the hardest thing for me. I was playing these huge [classical] pieces, like 15 pages long, . . . and then there was this Bruce Springsteen song. I opened up the book and there was like chords, guitar chords. I was so confused. I didn't understand it, so I just started to read it and eventually, eventually I got it down. (Gallo)

She got the piano, as well as an early lesson from Springsteen on the possibility of the underdog transcending difficult circumstances to find both personal identity and professional success. In some ways, songs such as "Born to Run" (1975) launched songs such as "Born This Way," in which Lady Gaga declared her independence from restrictive societal gender norms only a few days after she spoke about The Boss's influence on her work.

It is nearly impossible to explain the musical legacy of a man whose legendary career spans almost fifty years, but it is clear that Lady Gaga's brief anecdote is representative of thousands of similar stories told by artists who have been weaned on Springsteen's music. One cannot list them all, but a short list would range from such diverse acts as Catman Cohen, Charles Tanton, Colie Brice, Craig Wilson, Daniel Pearson, Darrell Evans, Dave Garner, Jackie Barnett, Janine Wilson, Jim Dyck and Richard Franklin, Jimmy Philip Pillar, Joe Tunon, John Riccio, Johnny Only, Jon Brooks, Jude Spears, Kidbrother, Lee Rogers, Mywallflower, Ray Younkin, Ron Kemp, Sarah Dashew, Sean Walsh, Shane Papatolicas, the Steve Palmer Band, the Free Press, the Hesh Inc., and the Other Christopher. And that is just to name a few.

While Springsteen has certainly had an effect on high-profile artists such as U2, Bob Seger, and fellow New Jersey rockers Bon Jovi, his influence has been most profound on up-and-coming indie bands such as Arcade Fire, a group whose affinity Springsteen acknowledged in 2007 when he invited them onstage in Ottawa to sing his "State Trooper" and their "Keep the Car Running." As critic Ed Masley notes, "There's a reason Springsteen brought these indie kids onstage to join him on a raucous cover" of the songs. With its wistful mix of images of captivity and freedom, "Keep the Car Running" (2007) thematically feels like "Thunder Road" (1975), "Born to Run," and some of Springsteen's other songs from the 1970s that featured young men trying to break free of cultural constraints to fulfill their dreams. One can almost feel Springsteen's pain from his personal quest to break free from poverty and obscurity in the seventies when Arcade Fire's lead singer Win Butler laments, "While every night my dream's the same," he is stuck in "the same old city" and knows he "can't stay." The river he needs to cross is "so deep" and the "mountain" that he must climb "so high" that he fears he will be stuck "living with the fear I keep so deep." However, like Springsteen's protagonists, he will not give up. He is determined to "keep the car running" until that moment comes when, like the poets in "Jungleland" (1975), he can "reach for" his "moment and try to make an honest stand."

Arcade Fire's *Neon Bible* (2007) bears some resemblance to *Darkness on the Edge of Town* (1978) in terms of the themes and the instrumental work. Yet, while the accordion swells and guitar riffs recall those of the E Street Band of the seventies, it is the emphasis on escaping the claustrophobic effects of family and society that most remind the listener of Springsteen. In "Windowsill," for instance, the narrator declares, "I don't want to live in my father's house no more," and "I don't want to live with my father's debt." One can almost hear Springsteen's "Adam Raised a Cain" (1978) or "Independence Day" (1980), as Butler cries that "the tide" of his past "is high" and that he does not want to "see it at my windowsill." Many critics have compared the band's album *The Suburbs* (2010) to *The River* (1980). When one listens to songs such as "The Suburbs," one can see why. The protagonist longs to outrun his past. Like the boys in "Born to Run" (1975), he and his friends want to "look so hard," but in his "dreams" he is "still screamin' and runnin'." As with Springsteen's work, there is not only a longing to forget, or at least be able to deal with, the past but also a desire to construct meaning against a seemingly indifferent universe. This is evident when the speaker pleads with a distant God to send "[me] a daughter while I am still young" so that "I can show her some beauty before" the "damage is done."

Another band profoundly influenced by Springsteen is New Jersey's The Gaslight Anthem, whose lead singer, Brian Fallon, credits Springsteen as the man who made him feel like he could become a musician: "That there was somebody from the same place I was from, who walked the same streets, whose mother drove him around the same towns, and went to the same parks and schools as I did—it was something I could relate to. It made me feel like if he came up the same way I did, and he got out, maybe I can get out too" (Schlansky). The band has covered several Springsteen songs, and the Boss has joined Fallon and his mates onstage on more than one occasion. One can hear Springsteen's impact on several tracks from the highly acclaimed *The '59 Sound* (2008). "Meet Me by the River's Edge" is a song that borrows many lines from different Springsteen numbers and whose ambiguous nature has evoked several interpretations from fans. It is difficult to fully define the band's intent, but its debt to Springsteen is unmistakable. When the protagonist vows to "Bobby Jean" in the first stanza that there will be "no surrender," one cannot help but think of Springsteen's songs by the same names. The fact that they have been burned by "our father's factories" recalls the desperation of "Factory" (1978), while the "Eden" burning "against the stars" is reminiscent of "4th of July, Asbury Park" (1973), where "Little Eden" must be abandoned because the angels "won't set themselves on fire for us anymore." As with "The River" (1980), the beleaguered couple heads to "the river's edge." They want to "wash these sins away," much like the characters in "Racing in the Street" (1980), who will "ride to the sea" to "wash these sins off our hands." As with many Springsteen songs, the plot resolves with the main character riding in a car late at night trying to figure out where to go.

More than one of the Gaslight Anthem's songs is about the Mary of "Thunder Road" (1975). The band's latest effort, *Handwritten* (2012), contains a moving number entitled "Howl," in which the musicians speculate that Mary did not go with the young troubadour when he came calling in "Thunder Road." She "waited on his call and made . . . plans for great escapes," but she did not have the courage to go. Now, years later, she "still" listens to "the sound of the thunder," while she lies up by herself. She is still waiting, much as she did in 1975. The speaker remembers how her "dress would wave," and he wonders if she will go with him after so many years. "You can find me on the hood under the moonlight," he says, much as her suitor did so many years ago. He even tells her, "There's still some magic left," recalling the line from "Thunder Road" in which the hero tells Mary to "show a little faith, there's magic in the night." He is still there to rescue her "in this city by the sea that has always haunted me." Asbury Park is still there. Mary is still there, scared and waiting. The speaker forgives her "doubts" and blesses her "waters."

Like the Gaslight Anthem, the Hold Steady, from Minneapolis via Brooklyn, New York, are indebted to Springsteen's albums from the 1970s. The band covered the rollicking and romantic "Rosalita" in a 2006 tribute to Springsteen, in which the Boss joined them onstage, and its *Boys and Girls in America* (2006) approximates the same wall-of-sound quality that one finds on *Born to Run* (1975). Still, if there is one album that informs many of the Hold Steady's songs, it is *Greetings from Asbury Park, NJ* (1973). Pieces such as "Stuck between Stations" and "Crucifixion Cruise" feature the riotous wordplay of many of the songs on *Greetings*, and their themes are rooted in the tense, surreal search for place and meaning that characterize many of the characters on Springsteen's debut album. "Crucifixion Cruise" explodes in a short, desperate burst in which "a real sweet girl who's made some not so sweet friends" seeks divine guidance. Her name is "halleluiah," and she "came to in a confession booth, infested with infections, smiling on an abscessed tooth." Like many Springsteen characters, she is young, poor, and emotionally hurt, but she is also beautiful and hopeful. The listener can't help but smile when she asks, "Lord, what do you recommend [for] a real soft girl who's having real hard times?" By contrast "Stuck between Stations" is over twice as long, with an extemporaneous feel reminiscent of Springsteen's "Blinded by the Light." We meet "boys," "girls," "John Berryman," "the devil," "doctors," and "deep thinkers." Everyone seems to be looking for meaning and joy, but no one can find it. The "boys and girls in America, they have such a sad time together," and people are either "stuck between stations" or "tired of all the dehydration." The narrator laments that for all of their efforts, they end up in the same pattern. "We drink and we dry up" he concludes, "and now we crumble into dust."

The Hold Steady clearly features the desperate characters and landscapes that Springsteen fans are used to, but missing is some of the hope that often lingers in Springsteen's songs. The Killers, however, are more optimistic than the Hold Steady. As lead singer Brandon Flowers says about his first encounter with Springsteen, "I couldn't believe how happy his music made me and how good it was. He's a gift, and I didn't know. I mean, I knew 'Born in the USA' and 'Glory Days,' but I didn't know that he covered so much ground, and there was something in his music that touched what I was going through, the process of falling back in love with my America" (Montgomery). One can hear this on "Read My Mind," off of *Sam's Town* (2006), which is replete with Springsteen-like images of "the honest man" with a "restless heart" who remembers "the good old days" and is relentless in his search for "the Promised Land." It will not be easy, but he never "gave up on breakin' out of this two star town," and he tells his lover that he's "gonna turn this thing around." He sounds like the determined hero of Springsteen's "Badlands," as he vows not to leave his girl behind. "Put your back on me," he says. "The stars are blazing like rebel diamonds cut out of the sun," and, like the hero of "Badlands," he is ready to face the worst that life can hand him.

The narrator of "Heart of a Girl" is equally optimistic, despite his circumstances. He is trapped "in this transient town" amid other lonely people, mostly "waiters and dealers trying to get their foot in the door." Then, he meets "an angel," a beautiful girl who, like him, has "been

trying to find" her "place in the world." Together, they begin to manufacture hope. He soon tells her, "I believe that we never have to be
alone." Their love makes them feel connected to "a presence of something that was long ago," some unseen "hand guiding the river." They
help each other have faith in some higher good, and he tells her, "I am
not afraid" as long as "you stand beside me." As Flowers comments,
"Springsteen touches on the American dream, and that's everybody's
dream. And it's such a great idea—whether or not it's still happening
today. Most of the songs are about getting to that place, of making it to
the promised land. I don't think it's about getting rich; it's the idea of
working hard and having your castle in the sky" (Montgomery).

Inspired by Springsteen's underlying optimism, the National, a
Brooklyn-based indie band that has developed a strong fan base over
the last decade, covered Springsteen's magical "Mansion on the Hill" on
its *Virginia EP* (2008). The band members credit Springsteen with giving them sage advice over the years, and several of their songs are
musically and thematically informed by The Boss. "Heavenfaced," from
Trouble Will Find Me (2013), for instance, is reminiscent of several of
Springsteen's love songs where the lovers swear loyalty in the face of
seemingly insurmountable difficulties. The narrator says, "I could walk
out, but I won't," even though "things are tougher than we are." He tells
her that he only wants to be "in your arms," and he affirms that, in the
end, they will "arrive in heaven alive." There is a similar hopefulness to
"Brainy," from *Boxer* (2007), where the ragtag protagonist tells his intellectual lover that she is the "tall kingdom that I surround," reminding
her that "you might need me more than you think."

Other punk bands that cite Springsteen as an influence include
Crooked Fingers, Titus Andronicus, and Social Distortion, the last being a Springsteen favorite whose "99 to Life" feels like it could be part
of the *Nebraska* (1982) lineup. Like Springsteen's Johnny 99, the speaker is a "brokenhearted man," having been sentenced to "ninety-nine to
life" for killing his lover. He has nothing but regret, and he's "in a living
hell." Unlike Johnny 99, he does not ask for the death penalty. Instead,
he begs the "good lord" for "mercy," but the effect is the same. Both
characters' lives are over, and they are looking for a way to cope with
having lost everything. By contrast, Crooked Fingers' "Call to Love," off
its *Dignity and Shame* (2005) album, feels more like one of Springsteen's tributes to Roy Orbison, with the narrator sending out an inno-

cent love call to his girlfriend. As he asks her in return, "Won't you send me your call to love?" Meanwhile, Titus Andronicus's *The Airing of Grievances* (2007) channels Springsteen's existential angst with songs such as "No Future, Part II: The Days after No Future," which includes a reading of a section of Albert Camus's *The Stranger*.

Solo artists with a debt to Springsteen include such artists as Badly Drawn Boy, Josh Ritter, Steve Earle, and Jesse Malin, the last having covered "Hungry Heart." Malin has also performed with Springsteen on several occasions and has written many songs that remind one of The Boss. One such number is "Broken Radio," from *Glitter in the Gutter* (2007), on which Springsteen actually sings with Malin. The piece is about the beauty of lost love, and the young couple is romantically described as "raised on robbery and rock 'n' roll." Circumstances may pull them apart, but he reminds her that the angels will always "love her more than [she] will know." Like Malin, Ritter has covered songs from *The River* (1980), but he is better known for producing several sobering works that are comparable to those on *Nebraska* (1982). "The Remnant," for instance, ends with the forlorn speaker accepting that "nothing that is hidden will be revealed." Earle is another artist whose music reflects the same kind of battle with inner demons that plagued Springsteen for much of his career. Earle—who says that the inspiration for his first album, *Guitar Town*, came from a Springsteen concert during the *Born in the USA* tour—has several songs featuring a tortured protagonist trying to hang on to the possibility of finding meaning. "My Old Friend the Blues" is a perfect example, with the sad narrator wryly admitting that "lovers leave and friends will let you down" but he can always rely on "the blues." In fact, he tells his "old friend" that his only solace is when he can "hide my weary heart in you." Badly Drawn Boy, an Englishman whose actual name is Damon Michael Gough, released *The Hour of Bewilderbeast* in 2000, a record whose songs of strained relationships and heartbreak are much like those on *Tunnel of Love* (1987). One of the best examples is "Disillusion," in which the speaker tells his girl that it "seems you created your own illusion fueled by an image of me." This is the same type of misconnection that characterizes "Cautious Man" and "One Step Back" on *Tunnel of Love*.

While Springsteen's work in the seventies and early eighties has been especially influential with punk bands and indie artists, his entire body of work has made a surprising impact on the country music world.

Drive-By Truckers, for example, is a Georgia band that blends alternative country with Southern rock to relate tales about everyday men and women trying to make it through the trials of life. The group routinely covers "Adam Raised a Cain" and "State Trooper," and *The Big To-Do* (2010) is one of its most Springsteen-esque albums, in that the band deals with larger societal problems, including drug abuse, suicide, domestic failures, broken marriages, and the personal devastation brought on by war. "This Fucking Job," for example, bears similarities to many songs, from "Factory" (1978) to "Jack of All Trades" (2012). Like so many of Springsteen's characters who find themselves behind the economic eight ball, the hero of "This Fucking Job" bitterly states that "this job" isn't "gettin' me farther . . . for all my starvin'." He hates "the dead end" that is his life, but he knows that to support his family, he just has to keep moving "until I'm dead and there is nothing to show for my uses."

Philadelphia-based Marah fuses country and punk in a way that interested Springsteen enough to play guitar and sing background vocals on "Float Away," from *Float Away with the Friday Night Gods* (2002). "He's my hero," says Dave Bielanko, the band's singer and guitar player. "I've always been a huge fan of him as a guitar player. He's a very expressive, high-end-y, dramatic guitar player and that's what we wanted—and ultimately he wound up singing on it a bit as well" (Devenish). "Float Away" has all the elements of a Springsteen love song: the alienating world where "all the streets are lonely"; the brokenhearted people who are "drifting from the arms of somebody"; and the romantic hope of "lovers today" who have "faded away" only "to wake up tomorrow" and try it all again. Hope never dies. It just floats away to be reborn and live again.

In truth, Springsteen has long been influential on the country music scene. Johnny Cash covered "Johnny 99," among other songs. Emmylou Harris covered "Mansion on the Hill," while Mel McDaniel's version of "Stand on It" reached number twelve on the country charts in 1986. Kenny Rogers's single "Morning Desire," which reached the top of the charts in 1985, was born from his desire to make a song that captured the feel and intensity of "I'm on Fire." Kenny Chesney is perhaps the biggest of several contemporary country stars to cover Springsteen classics on recent albums, including "I'm on Fire" and "One Step Up." However, Springsteen has recently shown up in the songs of several other popular country artists. Rodney Atkins's "It's America" (2009) celebrates the United States by insisting that "a picture perfect post-card" of America would include "one nation under God," "a ride in a Chevrolet," and "a Springsteen song." In his 2006 hit song "Feels Just Like It Should," Pat Green describes the perfect afternoon activity as riding in his car with his girlfriend "with The Boss on the radio," the two of them ready to "take whatever comes" as he steps on the gas and they go "flying down the highway with my arms around you singing 'Born to Run.'" Then there is Eric Church's "Springsteen" (2011), a song that no doubt captures a moment of lost youth for millions of Americans. Church says of Springsteen,

> It's blue-collared working-man music. He sings about the plight of the people working in the factories, the people who are downtrod-den. "Thunder Road," the whole premise is picking up the girl and letting the wind blow through your hair. It's about that escape, and I think that relates so much to what goes on everyday with country music. People have their issues, they are working more than they should, getting paid less—Bruce takes up the plight with his pen and puts it to paper, and it's as good as anybody in country ever has. (Roland)

"Springsteen" captures the magic that Springsteen's music has had for many Americans. A man hears a Springsteen song on the radio and immediately thinks of his first love, when he was seventeen. "To this day when I hear that song, I see you standing there on that lawn," he sings to his lost lover. "Somewhere between that setting sun, 'I'm on Fire' and 'Born to Run,'" he remembers, "You looked at me and I was done." He remembers them singing to each other, sitting in "his jeep," looking at "the stars in the sky" on a "July Saturday night." "When you hear 'Born in the USA,'" he wonders, "do you relive those glory days from so long ago?" He certainly does. Like many of his listeners, he revels in the thought, saying that it's "funny how a melody sounds like a memory," how "a soundtrack" leads "to a July Saturday night." Indeed, the song captures the feeling that many Americans have when they hear certain Springsteen songs. Such is the fate of a singer who has so keenly tapped into the collective American psyche for nearly fifty years.

In many ways, the large number of Americans who feel that the beauty and pain of their individual pasts are inextricably tied to Springsteen explains the popularity of Springsteen tribute bands that exist in nearly every major U.S. city. They, too, are indicative of his musical and cultural influence. There are too many to mention in this volume, but a few notable lineups include Bruce in the USA, the Bstreetband, Tramps like Us, Jersey, the E Street Shuffle, the Rising, Glory Days, My Own Boss, Springsteen, the River Street Band, Asbury Fever, and Cover Me. The number of popular artists who have covered Springsteen songs in tribute to The Boss is also indicative of his influence. Some examples include David Bowie singing "It's Hard to Be a Saint in the City" and "Growin' Up," Manfred Mann playing "Blinded by the Light," and Natalie Cole performing "Pink Cadillac." Of course, there is also Patti Smith's "Because the Night," a track originally written by Springsteen for the *Darkness on the Edge of Town* album but later given to Smith. Finally, there is the ultimate cover album, *Badlands: A Tribute to Bruce Springsteen* (2000), in which many indie artists re-created *Nebraska* to celebrate the album's important legacy as a piece of art that changed the direction of rock 'n' roll.

CULTURAL INFLUENCE

When Springsteen became the first artist of any medium to appear simultaneously on the covers of *Time* and *Newsweek* on October 27, 1975, anyone paying attention knew that he was bound for musical glory and cultural significance. However, even his biggest supporters would not have been able to predict just how far-reaching his influence would be. For instance, many movie producers and directors have cited Springsteen's importance to their personal and professional lives, and Springsteen's music has been featured in several films. One of the first directors to make use of Springsteen's talents is Yaky Yosha, whose *Dead End Street* (1982) incorporates "Jungleland," "Hungry Heart," and "Point Blank" to tell the heartbreaking story of a young prostitute whose unsuccessful effort to abandon the streets ends in a disturbing suicide. Paul Brickman also used "Hungry Heart" in his 1983 blockbuster *Risky Business*, starring Tom Cruise. John Sayles made Springsteen the musical focus of his 1983 romance *Baby It's You*, which includes "It's Hard to Be a Saint in the City," "The E Street Shuffle," "Jungleland," "She's the One," and "Adam Raised a Cain." Springsteen's

"Streets of Fire" inspired Walter Hill to make a film by the same name in 1984. Hill's *Streets of Fire* is the story of a soldier who returns home to find that he must rescue his girlfriend from a deadly kidnapper. Three years later, Paul Schrader enlisted Michael J. Fox to make *Light of Day*. Springsteen's title track was eventually revised and released on *In Concert: MTV Plugged* in 1993.

Springsteen's presence in the world of film increased in the nineties and early twenty-first century, as several actors, writers, and directors raised on his music came into their own professionally. Though it is not within the scope of this project to discuss all these works, it is interesting to see how many notable films have used Springsteen's music to bring different messages to a wide range of audiences. Springsteen's influence on Sean Penn was so great that the famous actor based *Indian Runner* (1991), one of his first films as a director, on "Highway Patrolman." The entire film is Penn's version of the backstory of the *Nebraska* classic, which ends with patrolman Joe Roberts opting for family loyalty over legal justice when he allows his murderous brother to escape across the state line. Penn utilized Springsteen again in 1995 when he directed *The Crossing Guard*, on which Springsteen's "Missing" helped Penn advance a tense plot in which a devastated father ponders whether he will murder a drunk driver who killed his daughter. As powerful as *Indian Runner* and *The Crossing Guard* are, they would be overshadowed by Jonathan Demme's *Philadelphia* (1993), a movie whose gripping story of Andrew Beckett's battle with AIDS and homophobia brought new energy to the gay rights movement. Demme tabbed Springsteen to write the film's lead song, and "Streets of Philadelphia" made Springsteen a hero in the LGTBQ (lesbian, gay, transgender, bisexual, queer) community and furthered his reputation as an artist with the ability to move Americans toward social justice. Springsteen won an Academy Award for his efforts.

Other significant cinematic efforts in the nineties to which Springsteen contributed range from the dramatic to the comedic. Tim Robbins's *Dead Man Walking* (1995), on which Springsteen composed the lead song, is a film that brought the death penalty into the public consciousness, as well as questions regarding religious faith and moral virtue. Springsteen's "Secret Garden" provided the musical background to one of the most memorable scenes of Cameron Crowe's *Jerry Maguire* (1996), a romantic film in which a sports agent finds professional and personal redemption after overcoming a nervous breakdown. Then there is Frank Coraci's *The Wedding Singer* (1998), a lighthearted comedy that, among other things, celebrated the music that defined the 1980s. Naturally, such a movie would have to include "Hungry Heart."

Springsteen continues to figure prominently in Hollywood in the twenty-first century. Stephen Frears and John Cusack scored a tremendous coup when they actually got Springsteen to make a cameo appearance in *High Fidelity* (2000), a successful film about music and the difficulties of modern relationships, which also made use of "The River." A few months later, Warner Brothers released Wolfgang Petersen's *The Perfect Storm*, yet another film to feature "Hungry Heart." Kevin Smith employed Springsteen's "My City of Ruins" to deepen the plot of *Jersey Girl* (2004), a film about the transformative power of fatherhood. One might point to 2007 as the most Springsteen-oriented year for films. Mike Binder's *Reign over Me* featured "Out in the Street" and "Drive All Night"; Peter and Bobby Farrelly effectively used "Rosalita" in their remake of *The Heartbreak Kid*; and Curtis Hanson included "Lucky Town" and "The Fever" in *Lucky You*. Most recently, Derek Cianfrance picked Springsteen's "Dancing in the Dark" to help dramatize *The Place Beyond the Pines* (2012), the story of a man so desperate to support his family that he turns to a life of crime. It would be difficult to find a better artist than Springsteen to help raise consciousness regarding the effects of recessions on the poor.

Perhaps the most telling sign of Springsteen's influence on American culture is the number of accolades that he has received over the years. From 1984 to 2009, he earned twenty Grammys and two Golden Globes to go along with his Academy Award. In 1996, he received the John Steinbeck Award for his commitment to humanitarian values and the dignity of the common man. He was awarded the Polar Music Prize, often referred to as the "Nobel Prize of Music," in 1997, and he was feted with a Kennedy Center Honor for his outstanding contribution to American culture in 2009. His song "Born to Run" is, by legislative decree, the official anthem of New Jersey. He is among a handful of artists to be selected to perform at halftime of the Super Bowl (2009), the ultimate American sporting event, and he even performed at President Barack Obama's 2009 inauguration. He has been inducted into the Rock and Roll Hall of Fame (1999), the Songwriters Hall of Fame (1999), the New Jersey Hall of Fame (2007), and the American Academy of Arts and Sciences (2013). He has now been the subject of three major academic conferences, including the recent "Glory Days: A Bruce Springsteen Symposium," held in September 2012 in his birthplace of Long Branch, New Jersey. Now in his sixties, Springsteen shows little signs of slowing down. In 2013, he was named the MusiCares Foundation Person of the Year for his lifetime dedication to philanthropic endeavors.

INTERNATIONAL ACCLAIM

One of the most interesting developments in Springsteen's career is his surging popularity in Europe, where he routinely draws larger audiences than he now does in the United States. In 2012, at age sixty-three, Springsteen sold out stadiums all over Europe. He sold out ten straight shows in Australia, selling over 150,000 tickets. He attracted 38,000 people to the Parken Arena in Copenhagen, Denmark, 39,000 fans to the RDS Arena in Dublin, Ireland, and 39,984 at Valle Hovin Stadion in Oslo, Norway. A total of 40,417 patrons packed Rhein Energie Stadion in Cologne, Germany, while Finland's Olympic Stadium in Helsinki saw 42,000 move through the turnstiles. Springsteen broke the 50,000 barrier several times during the *Wrecking Ball* tour, including audiences of 50,293 in Austria at the Ernst Happel Stadion and 54,639 at the Estadio Santiago Bernabeu in Madrid, Spain. In London, Springsteen drew 76,656 at Hyde Park on July 14, 2012. The European crowds are not only large; they are passionate and dedicated. Why?

The answer lies in the fact that Springsteen's ultimate influence is not just his music; it is the political and social vision that it conveys, a vision that appeals to any country where people, particularly young people, are economically and spiritually deprived. And many people in Europe have felt this kind of deprivation in the twenty-first century. In truth, conditions across Europe have left many countries in circumstances even more difficult than those faced by people in the United States.

On one hand, Europeans face most of the problems confronted by Americans over the last half century: gender changes that have resulted in confusing notions of masculinity and femininity, as well as high divorce rates; fatherlessness and single-parent families, which are often

financially vulnerable and in which children often fall behind in education; a staggering and fairly sudden increase in immigration, which has
led to racial and ethnic diversity that has been unsettling to some and
sometimes hard to manage because of its pace and intensity; social
problems, such as homelessness, child welfare issues, and the dramatic
rise of various mental illnesses; political corruption and government
distrust; budget deficits and forced financial cuts that damage social
safety nets, such as welfare or other types of public assistance; divisive
moral issues, such as abortion, the death penalty, gay marriage, and
drone warfare; and, of course, the growing tension between classes as
the divide between rich and poor not only grows but is continually
exposed through media outlets in ways that inflame the passions of
those on the lesser end of things. Finally, as in the United States, all this
trauma plays out against an unsettled spiritual landscape characterized
by postmodern uncertainty and a sharp decline in traditional religious
faith in many European countries.

On the other hand, all these problems are exacerbated by economic
challenges in Europe that, in many ways, surpass those faced in the
United States. In its current form, the European Union was established
in 1993, and membership has now grown to twenty-seven countries. It
was created to remedy the long-standing political conflicts and financial
disturbances that had plagued Europe for generations. However, in the
last twenty years, many European countries have experienced recessions, complete with high rates of unemployment, low wages, and higher taxes. In 2012, for instance, Spain's unemployment rate reached a
staggering 27 percent. Sadly, that is not the highest unemployment rate
in the union, with Greece's being 27.2 percent. France's overall jobless
rate was a shade under 11 percent, but the rate for people under thirty
was 25.5 percent. Italy was not far behind. When one country, such as
Greece, suffers a setback, it affects all the other nations, usually resulting in the healthier states having to make sacrifices to rescue the falter-
ing country, a situation that has caused financial hardships in countries
that were previously economically stable. In fact, the resulting inflation
has had such an impact on all of the European Union that the few
relatively healthy countries recently had to bail out Greece, Ireland, and
Portugal and may soon have to rescue France and Italy. European
countries have not seen such travails since the Great Depression. Naturally, this has created a great deal of resentment within the union,

especially among the rising numbers of people who already resent the union's watering down of traditional nationalist identities.

While punk, new wave, hard rock, acid rock, metal, rap, hip-hop, and techno-music have dominated the European music scene over the last several decades, many young Europeans are in need of a type of understanding and faith that artists in those genres do not offer. Springsteen, by contrast, is one of America's best exporters of that kind of hope. His songs let people under siege know that they are not alone and that there is light at the end of the tunnel. Is it any wonder that European audiences, which are much younger than those in the United States, would be attracted to the romantic Springsteen of "Rosalita," a song in which a poor but hopeful singer assures his girlfriend that "someday we'll look back on this and it will all seem funny"? This confidence and hopeful sentiment are exactly what young Europeans, afraid that they will not make it, need to hear. The same is true of "Born to Run," "Thunder Road," and other songs from the seventies' Springsteen canon that recognize the brutality of life but insist on the possibility of joy. Yet, even later works, such as *Magic* (2007), *Working on a Dream* (2009), and *Wrecking Ball* (2012), have proven to be as or more popular among younger audiences in Europe than older, more established fans in America. Again, maybe this should not be a surprise. Songs such as "Shackled and Drawn," "Wrecking Ball," and "We Take Care of Our Own" seem to speak directly to the financially vulnerable and politically jaded young listeners of Europe: They, too, are out of work. They feel betrayed by their governments. They feel at the mercy of a class system in which the rich get richer and the poor get poorer. When they sing along with Springsteen in stadiums filled with 40,000 voices crooning in unison, they are not just having fun; they are talking back to the conditions that bind them and the people holding those conditions in place. Of course, they are also singing songs such as "Working on a Dream," "Kingdom of Days," and "I'll Work for Your Love," representative of the hope that Springsteen gives his audience that love, success, intimacy, and meaning are all still within reach. That is the magic of Springsteen in Europe. Just as he did in the seventies and early eighties in America, he meets young people where they are, to help them through the darkness. Perhaps that is why, as social critic David Brooks writes, "Springsteen crowds in the U.S. are hitting their AARP years, or deep into them. In Europe, the fans are much younger.

The passion among the American devotees is frenzied, bordering on cultish. The intensity of the European audiences is two standard deviations higher. The Europeans produce an outpouring of noise and movement that sometimes overshadows what's happening onstage."

In the end, it is hard to fully quantify Springsteen's musical and cultural legacies. He has influenced so many artists, politicians, businesspeople, judges, athletes, actors, and all manner of everyday people in many different ways. Some are public and explainable, such as his musical influence on Arcade Fire or Jesse Malin or his growing popularity in Europe. Most are private and go undetected, although they operate in important ways in millions of lives that go unexamined by the media or by scholars. Either way, his ultimate legacy is beautiful, powerful music that sustains faith, hope, and love—the promise that we can all look "for a little bit of God's mercy" and find "living proof." John S. W. MacDonald writes,

> Today, while Rome burns and the economy withers, Springsteen signifies a simpler, happier, more authentic time before the Internet split music fans into tribes and made record-buying an act of decadent bourgeois nostalgia. Whether he's actually there or not, we hear Bruce in today's "important rock records" because we want to, and because The Boss very nearly invented the whole idea of the "important rock record" in the first place. Now at 60, he's become its most prized protector.

FURTHER READING

60 Minutes. CBS. New York. 25 July 2008. A powerful interview in which Springsteen explains his support of presidential candidate Barack Obama and how he uses his music to move his fans toward a more inclusive version of the American dream.

60 Minutes. CBS. New York. 11 February 2009. An in-depth interview in which Springsteen details his political and social vision for the United States.

Alterman, Eric. *It Ain't No Sin to Be Glad You're Alive: The Promise of Bruce Springsteen.* Boston: Little, Brown, 1999. Alterman is a columnist for *The Nation* and a frequent contributor to *Rolling Stone.* His biography is beautifully written from the perspective of an informed fan.

Appy, Christian G. *Working Class War: American Combat Soldiers and Vietnam.* Chapel Hill: University of North Carolina Press, 1993.

Bailey, Beth, and David Farber. *America in the Seventies.* Lawrence: University of Kansas Press, 2004.

Bauerlein, Chuck. "The Day Bruce Springsteen Capped a Softball Game with a Hat Trick." *Sports Illustrated* 14 October 1985.

Behr, Edward. *Prohibition: Thirteen Years That Changed America.* New York: Arcade, 2011.

Bella, David A., Gregg B. Walker, and Steven J. Sprecher, *The Military–Industrial Complex: Eisenhower's Warning Three Decades Later.* New York: Lang, 1992.

Berger, Dan. *The Hidden Seventies.* Piscataway, NJ: Rutgers University Press, 2010.

Berkowitz, Edward. *Something Happened: A Political and Cultural Overview of the Seventies.* New York: Columbia University Press, 2006.

Blumenthal, Sidney. *How Bush Rules.* Princeton, NJ: Princeton University Press, 2006.

Borstelmann, Thomas. *The 1970s: A New Global History from Civil Rights to Economic Inequality.* Princeton, NJ: Princeton University Press, 2012.

Brooks, David. "The Power of the Particular." *New York Times* 25 June 2012.

Brown, Helen Gurley. *Sex and the Single Girl.* New York: Pocket Books, 1963.

Camardella, Michelle L. *America in the 1980s.* New York: Stonesong Press, 2006.

Cameron, Keith. "Bruce Springsteen." *Guardian* 23 September 2010.

Cannon, Charles A. *The Military–Industrial Complex in American Society, 1953–1979.* Ann Arbor, MI: Xerox University Microfilms, 1976.

Carlin, Peter Ames. *Bruce.* New York: Touchstone, 2012. One of the most complete biographies on Springsteen, largely because Carlin is the only scholar to whom The Boss has ever granted full access.

Carnes, Mark C. *Secret Ritual and Manhood in Victorian America.* New Haven, CT: Yale University Press, 1989.

Carroll, Peter. *It Seemed Like Nothing Happened: America in the 1970s*. New Brunswick, NJ: Rutgers University Press, 1990.

Charlie Rose Show. PBS. New York. 20 November 1998.

Child Welfare Information Gateway. https://www.childwelfare.gov.

Chou, Joey, and Jason Kane. "Obesity in America: By the Numbers." *PBS.org* 8 May 2012.

Corn, David. *The Lies of George W. Bush*. New York: Crown, 2003.

Costas, Bob. "Bruce Springsteen: The Ghost of Tom Joad." *Columbia Radio Hour Interview* November 1995. Compelling interview in which Springsteen and Costas discuss the plight of the poor in America and the role that art can play in social and political reform.

Crouse, Janice Shaw. *Children at Risk: The Precarious State of Children's Well-Being in America*. London: Transaction, 2010.

Deardorff, Donald L., II. *Hero and Anti-hero in the American Football Novel: Changing Conceptions of Masculinity from the Nineteenth Century to the Twenty-first Century*. Lewiston, NY: Edwin-Mellen Press, 2006.

DeCurtis, Anthony. "What Springsteen Kept to Himself." *New York Times* 4 November 2010.

Devenish, Colin. "Springsteen Singing with Marah." *Rolling Stone* 21 March 2002.

Didion, Joan. *Slouching toward Bethlehem*. New York: Farrar, Straus and Giroux, 1968.

Dolan, Mark. *Bruce Springsteen and the Promise of Rock 'n' Roll*. New York: W. W. Norton, 2012. Dolan is a gifted scholar whose book is one of the most insightful and exhaustive appraisals of Springsteen's life and work. Beautifully written and painstakingly researched.

Domhoff, William G. "Wealth, Income, and Power." *Who Rules America* 1 February 2013.

Dunar, Andrew J. *America in the Fifties*. Syracuse, NY: Syracuse University Press, 2006.

Duncan, Robert. "Lawdamercy, Springsteen Saves!" *Creem* October 1978.

Eagleton, Terry. *The Meaning of Life: A Very Short Introduction*. Oxford: Oxford University Press, 2008.

Ed Sullivan Show. CBS. New York. 28 October 1956.

Eisenhower, Dwight D. *Exit Speech* Washington, DC, 17 January 1961.

Feuerbach, Ludwig. *The Essence of Christianity*. Minneola, NY: Dover, 2008.

Fischer, Claude, and Michael Hout. *Century of Difference: How America Changed in the Last One Hundred Years*. New York: Russell Sage Foundation, 2006.

Fletcher, Michael A. "Black Jobless Rate Is Twice That of Whites." *Washington Post* 14 December 2012.

Foucault, Michel. *Discipline and Punish: The Birth of the Prison*. New York: Vintage Books, 1995.

Francis, David R. "Why Do Women Outnumber Men in College?" *National Bureau of Economic Research* 7 January 2012.

Friedan, Betty. *The Feminine Mystique*. New York: Norton, 1983.

Friedman, Myra. *Buried Alive: The Biography of Janis Joplin*. New York: Morrow, 1973.

Frum, David. *How We Got Here: The 70's*. New York: Basic Books, 2000.

Gallo, Phil. "Lady Gaga Reflects on Springsteen Influence for 'Inside the Outside' Doc." *Billboard* 18 May 2011.

Garman, Bryan K. "The Ghost of History: Bruce Springsteen, Woody Guthrie and the Hurt Song." *Popular Music and Society* July 1996. Garman does an excellent job of showing how Springsteen's legacy will hinge as much on his role as a folk singer as it will on his powerful rock songs.

Gibbons, Fiachra. "Bruce Springsteen: 'What Was Done to My Country Was Un-American.'" *The Guardian* 17 February 2012.

Goldberg, Jeffrey. "Jersey Boys." *The Atlantic* July 2012. Goldberg discusses the influence of Springsteen on current politicians, including New Jersey governor Chris Christie.

Grusky, David, Bruce Western, and Christopher Wimer, eds. *The Great Recession*. New York: Russell Sage Foundation, 2011.

Hagan, Mark. "Meet the New Boss." *The Observer* 17 January 2009.

Halberstam, David. *The Fifties*. New York: Ballantine Books, 1993.

Ivie, Robert L. *Democracy and America's War on Terror*. Tuscaloosa: The University of Alabama Press, 2005.

Kaledin, Eugenia. *The United States, 1940–1959: Shifting Worlds*. New York: Greenwood Press, 2000.

Kerber, Linda K., Jane Sherron De Hart, and Cornelia H. Dayton. *Women's America: Refocusing the Past*. New York: Oxford University Press, 2004.

Killen, Andreas. *1973 Nervous Breakdown: Watergate, Warhol, and the Birth of Post-sixties America*. London: Bloomsbury, 2006.

Kimmel, Michael S. *Manhood in America: A Cultural History*. New York: Oxford University Press, 2006.

Kirsch, Lawrence. *For You: Original Stories and Photographs by Bruce Springsteen's Legendary Fans*. Montreal, Quebec: Lawrence Kirsch Communications, 2007.

Lasch, Christopher. *The Culture of Narcissism: American Life in an Age of Diminishing Expectations*. New York: Norton, 1978.

Leftfield Media. *Bruce Springsteen: Under the Influence*. New York. 18 May 2010. This is one of the best sources available for those who want to understand the musicians and writers who most influenced Springsteen as he was crafting his own identity as an artist.

Levinson, David, and Marcy Ross, eds. *Homelessness Handbook*. Great Barrington, MA: Berkshire, 2007.

Loder, Kurt. "Bruce Springsteen on 'Born in the USA.'" *Rolling Stone* 6 December 1984. The legendary MTV host gave Springsteen a forum to discuss, among other things, what the song "Born in the USA" means. This is especially important considering President Ronald Reagan's misuse of the song during the 1984 presidential campaign.

Lyotard, Jean-Francois. *The Postmodern Condition: A Report on Knowledge*. Minneapolis: University of Minnesota Press, 1979.

MacDonald, John S. W. "Springsteen, Arcade Fire and Ecstasy of Influence." *The Faster Times* 8 August 2010. This is one of the best articles to discuss how Springsteen is influencing the contemporary music scene, from punk to folk to country.

Marsh, Dave. *Bruce Springsteen: Two Hearts, the Definitive Biography, 1972–2003*. New York: Routledge, 2003. The first biography of Springsteen reads more like a hagiography but is indispensible reading for anyone who wants to understand the relationship between Springsteen and his fans in the early part of his career.

Marx, Karl, and Friedrich Engels. *The Communist Manifesto*. New York: Bantam, 1992.

Masley, Ed. "Ten Young Albums Inspired by Bruce Springsteen." *Arizona Republic* 11 September 2009.

Miller, John J. *The Big Scrum: How Teddy Roosevelt Saved Football*. New York: HarperCollins, 2011.

Montgomery, James. "Killers' Next LP Will Show Strong Influence of . . . Bruce Springsteen!?" *MTV.com* 2 May 2006.

Mundy, Liza. *The Richer Sex: How the New Majority of Female Breadwinners Is Transforming Sex, Love and Family*. New York: Simon & Schuster, 2012.

Murray, Christopher, and Julio Frenk. "Perspective." *New England Journal of Medicine* 14 January 2010.

National Public Radio. New York. 10 November 2010.

National Public Radio. Toronto. 15 November 2010. Edward Norton interviews Springsteen at the Toronto International Film Festival in anticipation of Springsteen's film release *The Promise: The Making of Darkness on the Edge of Town*. Springsteen relates several revealing anecdotes about the album, his life, and the E Street Band.

Niall, Lucy. *Postmodern Literary Theory: An Anthology*. Malden, MA: Blackwell, 1999.

Nietzsche, Friedrich. *Thus Spoke Zarathustra*. New York: Barnes & Noble, 2007.

Parsons, Tony. "Bruce: The Myth Just Keeps On Coming." *New Musical Express* 14 October 1978. Parsons reveals the mythology that grew around Springsteen as he rose from obscurity to rock 'n' roll stardom.

Pavelec, Sterling M., ed. *The Military Industrial Complex and American Society*. Denver, CO: ABC-CLIO, 2010.

Pemberton, Miriam, and William Hartung. *Lessons from Iraq*. Boulder, CO: Paradigm, 2008.

Percy, Will. "Rock and Read: Will Percy Interviews Bruce Springsteen." *DoubleTake Magazine* 28 January 1996. One of the best articles detailing the growing influence of authors Walker Percy and Flannery O'Connor on Springsteen. Anyone interested in Springsteen's Catholic imagination should consult this piece.

Pew Research Center. http://www.people-press.org 31 January 2013.

Piereson, James. *Camelot and the Cultural Revolution.* New York: Encounter Books, 2007.

Postman, Neil. *Amusing Ourselves to Death: Public Discourse in the Age of Show Business.* New York: Penguin Books, 1986.

Remnick, David. "We Are Alive: Bruce Springsteen at Sixty-Two." *New Yorker* 30 July 2012. A fantastic article in which Springsteen discusses, for the first time, his long battle with depression, as well as his view of his role as an artist.

Rielly, Edward J. *American Popular Culture through History.* Westport, CT: Greenwood Press, 2003.

Roland, Tom. "Bruce Springsteen's Enduring Effect on the Country Charts Influences Two Top Ten Singles." *Billboard* 8 May 2012.

Romano, Renee, and Leigh Raiford, eds. *The Civil Rights Movement in American History.* Athens: University of Georgia Press, 2006.

Rosin, Hanna. "The End of Men." *Atlantic* 6 July 2010.

Rowbotham, Sheila. *A Century of Women.* New York: Viking Press, 1997.

Sagert, Kelly Boyer. *The 1970s.* London: Greenwood Press, 2007.

Salamone, Frank A. *Popular Culture in the Fifties.* Oxford: University Press of America, 2001.

Schlansky, Evan. "The Many Influences of Brian Fallon." *American Songwriter* 5 January 2012.

Schmidt, Mark Ray. *The 1970s.* Farmington Hills, MI: Greenhaven Press, 2000.

Schulman, Bruce. *The Seventies: The Great Shift in American Culture, Society, and Politics.* New York: Free Press, 2001.

Slocum-Schaffer, Stephanie A. *America in the Seventies.* Syracuse, NY: Syracuse University Press, 2003.

Smedley, Audrey, and Brian D. Smedley. *Race in North America: Origin and Evolution of a Worldview.* Boulder, CO: Westview Press, 2012.

Smith, Russell C. "Wrecking Ball: Springsteen's Populist Vision of America." *Huffington Post* 1 May 2012.

Spencer, Herbert. *Essays on Education and Kindred Subjects.* New York: Dutton, 1963.

Springsteen, Bruce. "Keynote Speech." *Southwest Music Festival* 15 March 2012. A revealing speech in which Springsteen explains his view of the music industry and offers advice to young artists.

Strauss, Neil. "Human Touch." *Guitar World* September 1995.

Sweeting, Adam. "Bruce Springsteen: Talking to the Boss." *Vox* September 2002. A short but revealing article in which Springsteen discusses his reunion with the E Street Band.

Tucker, Ken. "Springsteen: The Interview." *Entertainment Weekly* 28 February 2003. Excellent in-depth article in which Springsteen discusses *The Rising*, his family, and his role as an artist concerned about social justice.

U.S. Census Bureau. "Income, Poverty, and Health Insurance Coverage in the United States: 2009." 9 September 2010, 22.

Wenner, Jann S. "We've Been Misled." *Rolling Stone* 9 September 2004. If you want to understand Springsteen's anger at the administration of President George W. Bush, as well as many of his songs from *Devils and Dust*, this is the article for you.

Wieder, Judy. "Bruce Springsteen: *The Advocate* Interview." *The Advocate* 2 April 1996. An important article in which Springsteen discusses the importance of social justice, especially in regard to the LGBT (lesbian, gay, bisexual, transgender) community.

Wilson, Sloane. *The Man in the Grey Flannel Suit.* New York: Simon & Schuster, 1955.

Woloch, Nancy. *Women and the American Experience.* New York: McGraw-Hill, 2011.

Young, William H. *The 1950s.* Westport, CT: Greenwood Press, 2004.

Zezima, Mockey. *The Seven Deadly Spins.* Monroe, ME: Common Courage Press, 2004.

FURTHER LISTENING

Greetings from Asbury Park, NJ (January 5, 1973), album, Columbia Records.

Springsteen's first studio album is met with critical praise but modest sales. A rollicking, romantic record full of desperate characters and lovable would-be heroes, many of the songs, such as "Spirit of the Night," became concert fixtures for years. Yet, the only hit song was "Blinded by the Light," and it rose to the top of the charts only after Manfred Mann covered it in 1976.

The Wild, the Innocent, and the E Street Shuffle (September 11, 1973), album, Columbia Records.

The album is again met with critical success and lagging sales. Critics and die-hard fans loved the determination of the record's iconic characters, as well as the fact that Springsteen had the courage to release an album with only seven songs. Still, the songs hardly hit the radio, even though "Rosalita" was destined to become a fan favorite with which Springsteen ended most of his concerts until the late 1970s.

Born to Run (August 25, 1975), album, Columbia Records.

The record that made Springsteen a popular success, allowing him to launch his first overseas performances. The furor surrounding the album resulted in Springsteen making the cover of *Time* and *Newsweek* during the same week in October. "Born to Run" and "Thunder Road" are consistently rated as being among the top songs in the history of rock 'n' roll.

Darkness on the Edge of Town (June 2, 1978), album, Columbia Records.

The release of this long-awaited album was delayed for nearly two years because of Springsteen's lawsuit with his first manager, Mike Appel. Eager fans devoured the album, which Springsteen described as "relentless." It is a record that reflects a move away from the dreamy, romantic songs of Springsteen's early career to harsher songs that reflected the difficulties of Americans living through the recessions of the 1970s. "Adam Raised a Cain" and "Factory" are biographical songs about the financial trials that Springsteen's father faced during the sixties and seventies.

The River (October 17, 1980), album, Columbia Records.

Springsteen's first double album includes his first top-ten hit, "Hungry Heart," a song that Springsteen originally wrote for the Ramones. The record is also the first Springsteen effort to hit number one on the U.S. pop charts, and several of the songs, including "Hungry Heart," "Drive All Night, "Stolen Car," and "Out in the Street," are among the first Springsteen works to be featured in Hollywood films. "The River" is about the economic struggles of his sister, Virginia, and her husband in the 1970s.

Nebraska (September 30, 1982), album, Columbia Records.

Springsteen's darkest album reflects his depression as well as the economic deprivation faced by so many in the United States at the time. It was recorded in Springsteen's New Jersey home on a simple four-track cassette, and although its bleak tone and sparse folk sound surprised some fans, the record was a critical success, a work that redefined the way that many artists thought of a rock 'n' roll album. Many of the songs were later covered by other prominent singers, some of which are featured on the cover album *Badlands: A Tribute to Bruce Springsteen's "Nebraska"* (2000).

Born in the USA (June 4, 1984), album, Columbia Records.

The record that launched Brucemania and made Springsteen a premier international superstar sold over thirty million copies worldwide. It included no less than seven top-ten singles, including "Born in the

USA," "Cover Me," "Dancing in the Dark," "Glory Days," "I'm Goin'
Down," "I'm on Fire," and "My Hometown." The video for "Dancing in
the Dark" launched the career of actress Courteney Cox.

Bruce Springsteen & the E Street Band: Live 1975–1985 (November
10, 1986), album, Columbia Records.
    The first live album released by Springsteen and the E Street Band,
the record is composed of forty songs, including yet-to-be-released concert favorites "Fire" and "Because the Night." The work debuted at the
top of the Billboard charts and continues to be the second-best-selling
live album in U.S. history.

Tunnel of Love (October 9, 1987), album, Columbia Records.
    His last full album with the E Street Band for several years, this
work is the culmination of Springsteen's failing marriage to Julianne
Phillips and his fading relationship with his legendary band. The album
is largely composed of heart-wrenching songs about the fragility and
painful nature of love. "Brilliant Disguise" reached number five on the
charts.

Chimes of Freedom (August 1, 1988), album, Columbia Records.
    A four-song effort released to benefit Amnesty International's "Hu-
man Rights Now!" tour, this is Springsteen's second live album. It features Springsteen's "Tougher Than the Rest," "Born to Run," and the
initial release of "Be True," as well as a rousing cover of Bob Dylan's
"Chimes of Freedom."

Human Touch (March 31, 1992), album, Columbia Records.
    Released in conjunction with *Lucky Town*, this record is Spring-
steen's first effort without the E Street Band. New band members
include Randy Jackson on bass, Jeff Porcaro on drums, and former E
Streeter David Sancious on the Hammond organ. Keyboardist Ray Bittan is the only holdover from the longtime starting E Street lineup.

Lucky Town (March 31, 1992), album, Columbia Records.
    Thought by most critics to be superior to *Human Touch*, Spring-
steen, inspired by his marriage to Patti Scialfa and the birth of his first
child, Evan, included several happy songs on the album. These include

"My Beautiful Reward," "Book of Dreams," "Living Proof," and the popular single "Better Days." The album features future E Street regular Soozie Tyrell as a background vocalist.

Bruce Springsteen in Concert: MTV Plugged (December 15, 1992), film, Columbia Records.

Released six months before the CD by the same name, the film contains three extra songs not included in the audio version. The record features the first appearances of "Light of Day" and "Red Headed Woman," a fun, raunchy song that Springsteen seemed to enjoy performing with his own redhead, wife Patti Scialfa. The album was actually part of MTV's *Unplugged* series, but Springsteen played all but one song with his trademark electric guitar.

Greatest Hits (February 27, 1995), album, Columbia Records.

Springsteen brought back several members of the E Street Band to record this album of fan favorites. There are also some new releases, including "Philadelphia," "Secret Garden," "Blood Brothers," and "This Hard Land."

The Ghost of Tom Joad (November 21, 1995), album, Columbia Records.

Musically and thematically similar to *Nebraska*, this sober album is a tribute to John Steinbeck and his insistence that we are all obligated to defend human rights. Like *The Grapes of Wrath*, the album has a decidedly Western flavor, with songs such as "Galveston Bay," "Sinaloa Cowboys," and "Across the Boarder," which deal with the plight of immigrants.

Blood Brothers (November 19, 1996), album, Columbia Records.

Springsteen reunited with the full cast of the E Street Band to produce this five-song effort, which included new releases "High Hopes" and "Without You." The album was released in conjunction with the VHS documentary *Blood Brothers*, which detailed the brief reuniting of Springsteen and the E Street Band to work on the *Greatest Hits* album.

Tracks (November 10, 1998), album (box set), Columbia Records.

This is the treasure trove of unreleased songs for which fans had been waiting for years. The four-disc box set contains sixty-six songs in all, most of which had never been released to the general public. The songs range from the early seventies to the midnineties and feature an amazing breadth of material and musical styles.

18 Tracks (April 13, 1999), album, Columbia Records.

A scaled-down version of *Tracks*, this record is full of up-tempo songs meant for the casual fan. New releases include "The Promise," "The Fever," and "Trouble River."

Bruce Springsteen & the E Street Band: Live in New York City (March 27, 2001), album, Columbia Records.

Recorded at Madison Square Garden during the final two shows of the E Street Band's reunion tour in 1999–2000, this two-disc live concert was also captured in DVD form as part of an HBO documentary. Fans were treated to the first-ever live releases of "Prove It All Night" and "Jungleland," as well as two powerful new songs: "American Skin (41 Shots)" and "Land of Hope and Dreams."

The Rising (July 30, 2002), album, Columbia Records.

Springsteen's first studio album since *The Ghost of Tom Joad* and his first full studio album with the E Street Band since the 1980s, the record is a response to the terrorist attacks of September 11, 2001, but is also a universal testament to human endurance and hope.

The Essential Bruce Springsteen (November 11, 2003), album, Columbia Records.

A compilation consisting of songs from every Springsteen studio album through 2003, this record was intended to introduce a new group of young fans attracted by *The Rising* tour to the songs that made Springsteen a living legend.

Devils & Dust (April 26, 2005), album, Columbia Records.

Reminiscent in style to *Nebraska* and *The Ghost of Tom Joad*, this folk album features several songs that were written around the time Springsteen recorded *Joad* in 1995. The title track foreshadows some of the antiwar songs that Springsteen would write later in the decade. "Reno" remains one of his most overtly sexual and controversial songs.

Hammersmith Odeon London '75 (February 28, 2006), album and DVD, Columbia Records.
     A full-length recording of Springsteen and the E Street Band playing one of their first overseas concerts, the legendary November 18, 1975, show at the Hammersmith Odeon in London.

We Shall Overcome: The Seeger Sessions (April 25, 2006), album, Columbia Records.
     A celebration of folk songs popularized by Pete Seeger, who, though he did not write any of the songs on the record, dedicated his entire career to promoting uniquely American music. This record is a sign that Springsteen has now taken on the role of protecting American musical traditions.

Live in Dublin: Bruce Springsteen with the Sessions Band (June 5, 2007), album and DVD, Columbia Records.
     Springsteen assembled an eighteen-piece band to remake some of his own music as well as the classic American folk songs featured on *We Shall Overcome: The Seeger Sessions*. This live performance, captured on audio and film, is from the band's last stand in Dublin and includes a rousing rendition of "American Land."

Magic (October 2, 2007), album, Columbia Records.
     Springsteen brought the E Street Band together for this eleven-song effort, which includes one uplifting number, "Girls in Their Summer Clothes," and one piece of commentary on contemporary music, "Radio Nowhere." Most of the songs, however, are dedicated to voicing Springsteen's disgust at governmental lies and misguided policies that result in unwise wars and American deaths. "Gypsy Biker" is particularly haunting.

Working on a Dream (January 27, 2009), album, Columbia Records.
     A decidedly upbeat record, Springsteen's sixteenth studio album contrasts with the angry songs of *Magic*. "Working on a Dream," "This Life," and "Kingdom of Days" reveal an optimistic Springsteen. Howev-

er, the release also includes "The Last Carnival," an emotional ode to founding E Street member Danny Federici, who died of melanoma in 2008. His son Jason plays accordion on the album.

The Promise: The "Darkness on the Edge of Town" Story (November 16, 2010), album and DVD, Columbia Records.

Another highly anticipated release, this album features the "lost album" that would have appeared between *Born to Run* and *Darkness on the Edge of Town* if Springsteen had not been embroiled in a lawsuit with his first manager, Mike Appel. The record provides insight into the songs that Springsteen was writing but never released, just after his rise to stardom in the midseventies. It also features a gripping documentary story of the band's activities from 1976 to 1978, including the grueling sessions that resulted in *Darkness*.

Wrecking Ball (March 6, 2012), album, Columbia Records.

Eleven new songs grace Springsteen's seventeenth studio album, an angry condemnation of economic and social injustice in America. "Wrecking Ball," "We Take Care of Our Own," and "Shackled and Drawn" bear testament to the fact that, at age sixty-two, Springsteen had lost none of his lyrical abilities, musical power, or dedication to equality.

INDEX

ABOUT THE AUTHOR

Donald L. Deardorff II joined the Cedarville University faculty in 1996 and was granted tenure in 2002 and promotion to full professor in 2006. He teaches courses in American literature, writing, and criticism. He has published several articles on literature and men's studies and is a frequent presenter at meetings of the American Literature Association, the American Culture Association, and the Conference on Christianity and Literature. His books include *Sports: A Reference Guide and Critical Commentary* (2000), *The Hero and Anti-hero in the American Football Novel: Changing Conceptions of Masculinity from the Nineteenth Century to the Twenty-First Century* (2006), and *The Image of God in the Human Body: Essays on Christianity and Sports* (2009). He is an avid ice hockey player, loves to read and write, and has attended over thirty Bruce Springsteen concerts. He lives with his wife, Julie, a librarian, and their shih tzu, Calvin, in Xenia, Ohio.

CPSIA information can be obtained at www.ICGtesting.com
Printed in the USA
BVOW07*2002171113

336442BV00002B/5/P